Grab That Moment

Other titles:
Memoirs:
Fragments from a Life
Fragments that Remain
Ephemeron

Fiction:
A Floating World (a novel)
Convergence - Aspects of the Change

Non-fiction:
Aikido - Basic and Intermediate Studies
Aikido - Beyond Questions often asked
Attributes a Writer Needs
Cinematography Underwater

Dreams of Mars - 130 years of stories about Mars
More Dreams of Mars -

Grab That Moment

a memoir

John Litchen

Yambu

All rights reserved. No part of this publication may be reproduced by any means including photocopying or other information storage and retrieval systems without written consent of the publisher, except for small portions which may be quoted for the purpose of reviewing the work as a whole.

Grab That Moment
First edition, 2021
Copyright © John Litchen 2021

ISBN: 978-0-6488801-2-7 (paperback)

Published by Yambu
PO Box 3503, Robina Town Centre, QLD, 4230
Contact: John Litchen.

Para Moniquita
Mi mejor amiga
y mi esposa para siempre

¡Que felicidad tú me has traído!

Disconnected fragments...

It's amazing how quickly one settles back into old routines.
Barely into 1970 and it seemed as if my year in Mexico was far in the past.
I was back delivering and picking up dry cleaning from our agencies across the suburbs from Williamstown to Sunshine via Footscray, Yarraville and North Altona. The shop in Williamstown was the same, the people who work in the dry-cleaning factory at the rear of it were the same, going out Friday nights for dinner with my brother in Law Fred and his diving partner Rommy (AKA Ken Johnson) with the occasional other abalone diver turning up, was basically the same. Dropping into Space Age books to buy the latest SF novel and chat with the guys there was again the same as always, although there did seem to be a feeling of excitement in the air as they talked about bidding for a world convention to be held in 1975. A long way off, but none the less... possible.

Although Fred (my brother in Law) had, like me, just come back from Germany after he went there with Zara and their first born David, to see his parents whom he hadn't seen since he left Germany in 1955 to ride his bicycle to Australia for the Olympic games, he too was beginning to feel as if his recent trip was so far in the past as to be almost forgotten. But that's life, always full of routine stuff that becomes monotonous over time. You need the occasional adventure to spice it up, to take you out of the box, and into the unknown. This is of course why people take annual holidays, but sometimes you need more than that. You need something unexpected, something out of the ordinary, so beyond regular routines that it never previously could have entered your mind. These spontaneous adventures can be sparked by the tiniest moment, the sudden realization that something never considered, or thought to be impossible, is after all quite possible.
You have to grab that moment and run with it.

Fred's life as an abalone diver was far more interesting than mine as a dry cleaner. He got to dive in different locations in Port Phillip Bay as well as along the coast towards Apollo Bay. He even dived with a team from a larger boat in Bass Strait where they once became shipwrecked, so his life seemed much more exciting. There were moments when I envied him and Rommy as they dived together. I even accompanied them sometimes on my days off. But being a professional diver was not something I had considered. Scuba diving and skin diving, or diving with a hookah from a boat was for me a leisure activity usually combined with taking photos or shooting film underwater.

I was lucky in that I worked in a family business and could take time off to pursue other activities. I sometimes had to leave early so I could travel across town to channel 9 or channel 10 to rehearse for a TV show in which I played in the studio band or orchestra as a fill in percussionist when the regular percussionist (Garry Hyde) was unavailable. As such I participated in the Don Lane Show, on channel 9, and the Peter Couchman Show on channel 10 as well as the odd studio recording session. Or I could take time off to do some underwater filming for channel 9 news which I did with Fred on a report about Starfish infestation in Port Phillip Bay. On another occasion one morning very early, I heard on the radio about a pod of whales that had beached themselves at Gunnamatta Beach which is not far along the coast from Port Phillip Heads, so I called Fred and said we should go and look at that, and off we went for the day.

But I am getting ahead of myself…

As kids, we used to holiday at Portarlington on the Bellarine Peninsula.

You followed the road from Geelong as it went around the peninsula towards Port Phillip Heads and Queenscliff. Portarlington was half way around and sheltered by rising hills behind. Geographically it overlooked Corio Bay which was a more protected section of Port Phillip Bay hidden behind the Bellarine Peninsula. The beach, a shallow slope out to deeper water, was almost always calm with only the gentlest of waves and as such was a safe place for children to swim. Set back and stretching from the pier along the beach towards Geelong was a camping area full of tents in the summer, and they were usually there until after the Easter long weekend. They were all gone before the winter would begin. As a family we camped there every summer, as did many other families. We had the same spot every year and we got to know those in the neighboring tents who also had the same spots every year (booked always in advance at the end of the holiday season). After many years, as I imagine other families also did, Mum and Dad bought a block of land on the hill rising behind the township and built a holiday house there. It overlooked the town and we could see the whole of Portarlington laid out below as well as Geelong to the west, and on a clear day even Melbourne was visible in the distance if we looked beyond Portarlington to the north. It was a big holiday house with five bedrooms and two living areas, because Mum and Dad had looked to the future when all their children would be grown up and had families of their own. They needed a place to get together for Christmas holidays, Easter breaks, long weekends, or just whenever any one of us wanted to go there for a break. It was an hour's drive from Melbourne, starting as we did from Yarraville, along Geelong Road (Princes Highway) through Geelong and along the edge of Corio Bay around the Bellarine Peninsula.

During the summer at the beginning of 1971, we were sitting on the veranda, looking out over the town below when we saw a small plane come down and land in a paddock beyond the camping area. A landing strip had been graded in the paddock parallel to the beach. We went down to have a look and that's when we met Theo van Loenen. He was doing joy flights over and around the Bellarine Peninsula in order to build up his flying hours as part of his training to upgrade his commercial pilot's license. It was a good location, right next to the camping area and many holidaymakers were eager to take a short flight. We all took a flight with him which is how we became friends.

January 1971... Portarlington - looking across the campsites on the beachfront - part of the view from our house on the hill behind the town centre.

*Images from the 16mm film of our journey to New Guinea.
The small plane Theo Van Loenen used for the joy-flights taking off.*

*The camping area along the beach at Portarlington in 1971.
The small dirt airstrip used by Theo for his joy-flights was beyond the left
edge of the camping site.*

Part One
New Guinea

A Hop, skip, and a 10,000-year Jump.

An idea is born

At the end of January 1971, we were spending a hot summer's long weekend at the family holiday home in Portarlington, on the Bellarine peninsula. The house was half way up a hill overlooking the town, the holiday campsites and the beach. Sitting on the veranda, reading a new skindiving magazine, and looking down over the holiday tents pitched along the beach, I watched a small plane take off and land on a makeshift airstrip just beyond the campsites. This was the first-time joy-flights were conducted in Portarlington. The plane shimmered as waves of heat rose up from the land making it look as if it had emerged from a mirage.

I tossed the magazine over to Fred. "Have a look at this."

The magazine was Fathom, volume one, number one, the very first issue.

Fred opened it to a double spread showing a low-lying coral atoll in which a dugout canoe was paddled by two beautiful native girls, but the other shots taken underwater showed prolific coral reefs teeming with colorful fish. It was a place called *Kapingamarangi*, and it was one of only two inhabited islands in a group of twenty-nine atolls and islets in the southern part of the North Pacific Ocean; a part of Micronesia which is administered by the United States of America.

"Wouldn't it be great if we could go to place like that? Just think of the diving... the film we could shoot."

"Unreal," Fred replied. It was his most often used expression.

"But," I said to bring a touch of reality, "The only way to get there is by boat. It could take a couple of months."

Flicking the pages over Fred saw photos of the divers using a US Navy sea-plane which was put at their disposal by the US Government for them to conduct a survey of Crown of Thorns starfish depredation. Other underwater photos showed bleached reefs swarming with thousands of massive ugly starfish.

"What about a seaplane," Fred said, "like the guys who wrote the article used?"

"Where on earth would we get a sea-plane?"

Fred pointed towards the distant beach where on the airstrip at the end of the camping area a small single engine plane was just taking off on another joy flight. "We could ask Theo. He would know."

Theo landing behind the campsite.

The pilot

I had already shot some film of Theo Van Loenen taking joy flights in a rented Cessna single engine aircraft from the gravel strip at the end of the camping area. We had taken a joy flight as well to look at Portarlington from the air. Theo had become an instant friend and had been several times up to the house for drinks and a meal or two. He told us that he came here this holiday season because he needed to fly as much as possible so he could build up enough hours to qualify for a commercial pilot's license. He was doing quite well with the joy flights.

I watched him check over the plane in between flights and he seemed quite efficient as he measured the fuel used, checked for condensation in the tanks, checked the tyre pressure and other things needed to be certain the plane remained airworthy.

"Can you fly a sea-plane?" I asked.

"Not legally. I haven't been certified. Why?"

We showed him the magazine and the article about Kapingamarangi.

"Why do you want to go so far out? That's more than half way across the Pacific. If all you want is to see something of Micronesia or Melanesia why

— Grab that Moment —

not try one of the islands off the coast of New Guinea?"
Fred and I looked at each other as we considered that idea.
"There are plenty of wartime strips on almost all of the islands in and around New Guinea. And you can get to them in an ordinary twin engine plane. I'm not endorsed to fly a sea-plane, but I am for a twin-engine plane."
"It was a day-dream," I said. "I doubt we could afford to hire a plane and fly off like that."
"Why not? It's done every day. I can find out how much it costs. What harm will that do?"
"Bloody hell!" I said. "Why not?"
If it hadn't been for the joy-flights with Theo flying kids and their parents over and around the camping areas and the beach we would never have thought of hiring a plane.
"Let us know when you find out and we'll talk about it, okay?"
Theo smiled at us.

Niu Gini

Papua New Guinea is the second largest island in the world, straddling the equator immediately North of Australia. It is a land of dense jungle, mountains that almost rise three miles high, thousands of rivers that boil over ridges as cascading waterfalls until they reach low lands where they sluggishly drift through swamps of mud, sago and slime, where malaria is endemic and crocodiles eat people. It is a place of tremendous tropical rains during the wet season, of cannibalism and other strange burial practices, of primitive people who have yet to see a white person, a place where more than ten thousand tribes speak more than seven hundred languages and countless dialectical variations, a place where genuine exploration still occurs and where new tribes of stone age people are occasionally discovered.

The first white man to land in New Guinea was *Dom Jorge de Menezes*, the Portuguese governor of the Moluccas. He went ashore at the Vogelkop Peninsula in Western New Guinea (West Irian) and named the country *Ilhas dos Papuas*, from the Malay term *orang-papuwah* which meant fuzzy-haired man. After several Spanish ships visited the place it wasn't until *Ynigo Ortiz de Retes* bestowed the name *Nueva Guinea* —because it reminded him of Guinea in West Africa— that this name became recognized.

It appeared with this name on Mercator's world map in 1559.

Colonial occupation

In order to forestall any rivals, especially the Portuguese, the English and the Dutch (who had control of the spice trade in the East Indies) annexed all of New Guinea west of the 141st meridian in 1828. This left 183,435 square miles of vacant country to the East which included a maze of offshore islands. The Germans grabbed most of these and Britain got the rest.

In 1901 Britain transferred British New Guinea to the newly established Commonwealth of Australia. It took five years before Australia formally accepted and named the area Papua.

After the Second World War, German New Guinea became a part of Australia's mandate and the whole area was renamed TPNG, Territory of Papua and New Guinea, later shortened to PNG.

Indonesia took over the former Dutch held area and called it West Irian.

Papua New Guinea is now an independent country not administered by any foreign power, but West Irian still remains a part of Indonesia even though geographically and culturally it has no connection to Indonesia at all.

Pidgin English

English is the official language but Pidgin English is the common language used because there are several major languages like Motu spoken, along with more than 700 minor languages, and who knows how many dialects. Until Europeans came each tribe was isolated from the others. Each developed their own language which was not understood even a few kilometres away by other isolated tribes.

The British introduced English and a corrupted form became commonly used across the whole country. The writing of this language is phonetic, reproducing the sound as it is spoken in letters so New Guinea is spoken and written as Niu Gini. Over time, Pidgin has evolved as a complete language.

Cannibalism *'is not a crime'*

The headline of an article in a Port Moresby Newspaper: Wednesday (early 1971)

A judge ruled today that Cannibalism by seven tribesmen was not a crime. He cleared them of charges of indecently interfering with a corpse. The men had cut up the body of a fellow tribesman and eaten it cooked with sago, the Supreme Court in Port Moresby was told.

Their victim was considered *Long Long* — meaning a bit crazy in the remote part of Western Papua where the tribe lived. He had attacked a fellow tribesman with an axe and killed him. The man's brother in turn had killed the Axe-wielder by shooting him with an arrow. Seven of the tribesmen then disposed of the body by cutting it up and eating it.

Because there is no specific law in New Guinea against cannibalism, they were charged under a Queensland law forbidding interference with a corpse.

In judging the men's behavior, the presiding judge considered tribal customs in that remote area and ruled that *cannibalism in this case was a legitimate means of disposing of a body.*

The case was dismissed.

A decision made

By the time I got back home from Portarlington I knew we would be going to New Guinea. I had no idea of the costs involved, but the excitement of going to a really strange place, and of doing something none of us had ever considered before, like hiring a private plane to get there, was what convinced me. I was sure Fred felt the same.

We got some charts of New Guinea and tried to decide where would be a good place to go once we were there. We still hadn't decided when Theo rang to tell us about the types of planes we could use and the prices per hour (*wet hire — that is including fuel as well as time in the air*) each plane would cost.

"I'm happy to pay for my share," Theo said. "I need the extra flying hours anyway and would have to hire a plane to do it, so this is good for me."

The plane finally decided upon was a four-seater with twin engines.

"You need twin engines," Theo explained, "because we have to fly over water from Cape York to Daru in Papua and then from Daru to Port Moresby, and to go the Trobriand Islands as well. It's a safety thing. If one engine cuts out, we still have the other to keep the plane flying."

But with only the three of us it would cost too much. We needed a fourth person to share the costs.

"What about Rommy?"

Rommy, aka Ken Johnson, was Fred's abalone diving partner.

"Yeah, He'll go for sure," Fred said.

We told Theo to go ahead and charter the plane and that was it; a decision made.

It was a month before we heard back from Theo and it was the first week in March when we finally took off.

Sierra Kilo Lima

SKL, Sierra Kilo Lima was our call sign.

The chartered plane was a twin-engine Piper Comanche... a beautiful little plane capable of flying at 160 knots while carrying a pilot, three passengers and 200 pounds of luggage most of which was diving gear and cameras.

"Shit, that's no more than a *Mixmaster*," Rommy's wife Julie said when she saw it. "And you're going to fly that to New Guinea!"

The Altona Star

Wednesday, March 3, 1971   THE ALTONA STAR   Page Three

7000 miles to the islands on two engines

By Michael Stevens

A North Altona professional skin-diver is one of four men who last week set out on a 15-day, 7000-mile return trip to the Trobriand Islands in a twin-engine Piper Commanche.

The islands are 100 miles off the northern coast of New Guinea. The men hope to film the trip as a documentary and sell it overseas.

The Altona man is Fred Glasbrenner, 34, of 88 May Street, North Altona.

He will make the trip together with his partner, the four-seater, twin Rimantis Statkus, 30, of engine Piper Commanche, Flat 12, 20 Eldridge Street chartered for the trip. Footscray; John Litchen. The men hope to take a

incidentally is married to John's sister Zara (an original Lido dancer), was born in America of German parents.

He made headlines in Melbourne in 1956 when he and two friends pedalled from Germany for the Olympics.

● Armed to the hilt with baggage before they load on to the Piper Commanche at Essendon Airport are from left, John Litchen, Fred Glasbrenner, Rimantis Statkus and Theo Loenen.

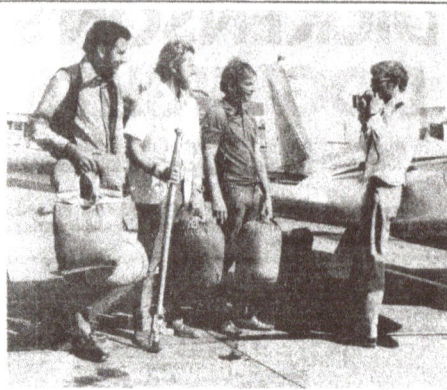

The reporter from the Altona Star taking pictures as we prepared to load our luggage into the 'Mixmaster'.

Rommy's wife Julie and Fred's wife, my sister Zara, are watching as we load up to take off on our epic journey.

Climbing aboard

Climbing aboard seemed a bit of a struggle.
Fred decided the easiest way to get in was to go backwards so he could move forward into the back seat. Rommy followed. Theo was already seated in the pilot's seat and I was the last one in, sitting next to Theo in the co-pilot's seat.

Up and away

Essendon Airport was full of people on the day we staggered through the terminal dragging bags of equipment behind us. They stared at us and wondered, because we were followed by a gaggle of photographers from two suburban newspapers doing a story on our expedition to the Trobriands, as it was now called. Fred had called them. The papers were the Footscray Mail and the Altona Star, both owned by the same company. Both stories were virtually the same. Fred was familiar with using newspaper stories to promote his activities from the time he traveled by bike from Germany to Australia for the Melbourne Olympics... and this little 7000-kilometre trip was certainly worth a story or two.

Theo wasn't with us in the terminal because he had flown SKL from Moorabbin to pick us up at Essendon. He was with the plane waiting for us, dressed as a pilot and looking officious as he completed the flight data sheets for the airport traffic controllers. We posed for photos for the reporters and photographers beside the plane after which we loaded SKL with our gear and climbed on board.

Theo must have been nervous because he flooded one of the engines and it wouldn't start. He quickly fixed that and with the engines roaring we taxied onto the tarmac and moved cautiously along until we reached our take-off position.

A TAA flight landing directly in front of us.
Both airlines Ansett - ANA (formerly Ansett Airlines and Australian National Airlines) and TAA (Trans Australian Airlines) no longer exist. Ansett had merged with ANA to form one airline in order to maintain the 2 airline Policy. Only two major airlines were allowed by the Government to operate domestically. Qantas at that stage was the only Australian International Airline.
There were smaller airlines that served regional centres and there were private charter lines. Our flight was a private individual charter, which was why we were allowed to depart from Essendon airport instead of Moorabbin where Theo had gone to collect SKL.

We had to wait while two huge passenger jets came down for a landing right in front of us. SKL shook in the turbulence produced as each screamed past. a few minutes apart. A moment later Theo was given the all clear and he taxied out onto the runway which stretched so far in front of us we couldn't see the other end.

"Here we go," Theo said. He revved the engines.

SKL leaped forward, and within one hundred and fifty metres we were airborne.

Wow! The feeling of lightness was incredible.

We just floated up into the air.

Essendon dropped below behind us, disappearing into the haze that covered Melbourne as we climbed to 5000 feet.

We headed north and soon we were over dry farmlands surrounded by faded green trees (it had been a long dry summer, as usual). Theo took us up to 9000 feet, our cruising height while flying north. And then it finally sunk in: We had our own plane and could go anywhere we wanted, as long as we came back within fifteen days.

It seemed too good to be true.

The intrepid four

Fred Glasbrenner

Rommy Statkus

John Litchen

Theo Van Loenen

Sierra Kilo Lima looking very small at the end of the runway in Bourke.

Theo and Fred dragging SKL over to the fuel pumps. It was easier than driving over.

Bourke and Charleville

It took three hours to reach Bourke, in north central NSW, our first refueling stop. When we stepped out of the plane and stood on the tarmac while Theo refueled, the dry heat seemed to suck all the moisture out of us. Summer had finished in Melbourne and the weather was becoming pleasant but cooler, but there was no relief from the heat up here in Bourke, and it would only get worse the further north we went.

Once refueled, Theo filed a flight plan for Charleville in central Queensland, and we took off, climbing up to our cruising height, 9000feet. Several hours later we landed at a deserted strip outside of Charleville. Theo refueled and locked the plane which we left beside a small hangar. We were going to stay overnight in Charleville.

The airstrip was about ten kilometres out of town. There was only one person in a small Office beside the hangar where pilots filed flight plans and other business took place. There was no one else there.

Theo went inside and spoke to the person, coming out a few moments later. "Looks like we'll have to walk into town," he said.

"What about our gear?" I was concerned about the cameras and underwater housing more than anything else.

"Nobody comes out here at night. It should be fine. Do you want to carry all that stuff and walk into town?"

"No way..."

"Then don't worry about it."

Fred and Rommy had already walked out to the road and were waiting for us to catch up.

Bitter pills

When we started along the road Theo asked us if we had taken our Malaria pills.

The others had but I had forgotten. "I haven't," I said.

"You should have started a month ago; two tablets twice a week for a month before entering malaria affected area."

"I'll start right now."

I can usually swallow pills or tables without water so I popped the first two Malaria pills into my mouth, without realizing that after several hours of flying in an unpressurized plane at 9000 feet I would be dehydrated. My mouth was dry and the damned pills stuck in my throat. I couldn't produce enough saliva to swallow them. They were the worst, most vile tasting tablets I had ever taken.

A Ride

We had walked just over a kilometre when the DCA guy who had been the only person at the airstrip drove up beside us in his ute.

"Jump in the back. I'll give you a ride into town."

We scrambled aboard and stood up and hung on behind the cabin as he drove along. The wind blew into our faces and evaporated the sweat from the walking.

The first thing I did was to dive into the nearest bar and order a beer. I needed something to wash away the revolting taste of the Malaria tablets still stuck in the back of my throat. Meanwhile Theo booked a room. It was upstairs and though only for two it was huge. It had twin beds, one for Theo, one for me. French doors opened onto a long balcony that ran the whole length of the hotel where there were many beds lined up. Sometimes it was too hot to sleep in a room and guests would find themselves sleeping in the beds on the veranda, more or less out in the open where the chance of a cool breeze was very welcome. Later that night, Fred and Rommy sneaked in and slept on two of those outside beds.

Not so quiet

We thought Charleville was a quiet cattle town until about 2 am. We were suddenly woken up by the loud clanging or fire engine bells as two fire trucks raced along the main street right past the hotel where we were trying to sleep. Trouble is they didn't do that once as they would to put out a fire. There wasn't actually any fire. The damn trucks turned around and came back with bells clanging and sirens wailing. They did this for about an hour until a police car arrived on the scene and the fire trucks went away.

Feeling seedy early in the morning, the four of us had a quick breakfast in the hotel dining room and then thumbed a lift out to the airstrip anxious to be on our way again.

Townsville

Flying north East towards the coast we headed for Townsville where we had to refuel. It was overcast and we flew through several minor rainstorms. The closer we got to the coast the worse the weather became. Oddly enough, Townsville was clear and sunny, but very humid we discovered once we had landed.

Theo was navigating by sight and taking directions from the control tower. They told us to follow the highway and when we got to the drive-in theatre to turn and fly around the mountain that dominates the city landscape. We would find the airport snuggled in behind it.

We did, we landed safely, refueled, filed a new flight plan for Cairns and took off to fly along the coast north to Cairns.

Cairns

The weather was worse than we expected and so we had to fly much lower to stay under the cloud cover. It was dark and ominous when we landed in Cairns. A huge wall of blackness was slowly drifting in over sluggishly heaving seas.

"I don't like this," Theo commented. "If it starts raining heavily, we could be stuck here for weeks."

This was the tail end of the wet season and there was not much we could do about that.

"We should have waited another month before leaving," he said as we took SKL over to be refueled.

We always refueled immediately upon landing to prevent any condensation in the fuel tanks. It still formed a bit, but was easily drained off first thing before taking off. Theo was fastidious about checking everything on the plane before any flight. And as for the weather, we would just have to wait and see how it looked the next morning.

We bummed a ride into town and the driver told us of a cheap place to stay; a boarding house that costs us each a dollar-fifty a night. It was off-season and no one else was staying there. Theo wasn't too happy, but we didn't care. It was clean and that's all that mattered.

It rained cats and dogs all night, and in the morning it was incredibly windy; too windy to take off, so we had to stay another day. We went to the Cairns Aero Club where we stared out disconsolately at the rotten weather. It rained intermittently and the wind smashed the rain into the club windows so at times you could hardly see through them. Nobody was flying anywhere.

Another pilot who worked for a cattle station inland took us for a drive around Cairns but we weren't particularly interested since the rain and the wind battered us all day. We had dinner that evening at a hotel restaurant where we discussed going back to the boarding house for another night. Theo wouldn't have a bar of it so we found a half empty motel where we got a room for the four of us and it only cost two dollars each. It was a much better room than the one we shared the previous night.

Theo's bombshell

While having dinner before going to the motel Theo casually dropped a bombshell. "I don't think we'll get through the Zone of Convergence." He didn't look at us but focused on eating his dinner.

"What the fuck is that?" Rommy asked.

He looked up and said, "That's where the winds from the Southern Hemisphere blowing towards the equator meet the winds from the Northern Hemisphere which are also blowing towards the equator from the other side. There is one hell of a storm where they meet. It's like a wall of massive storm clouds that stretches right around the world."

"I never heard of that before," Fred said.

"The zone moves from the North to the South, and then later from the South to the North. It crosses the equator going both ways. It follows the sun as the seasons change and right now it is sitting about eleven degrees south of the equator."

"Which puts it where?" I asked.

"North of us, just past Cooktown."

"Can we get through it?" Fred asked.

"God no! There are hundred mile an hour vertical winds inside the zone. A small plane like ours would be torn to bits. Even bigger planes don't fly through it."

"Why can't we go over it? Rommy said.

"Because it rises up forty thousand feet or more. We're not pressurized. We can't go any higher than thirteen thousand feet, so as far as we are concerned it's impenetrable."

"What can we do?" I was thinking that instead we could visit some of the Barrier Reef resort islands. Most of them have airstrips for small to medium planes. It would be a letdown, but at least the trip would not be an entire waste.

"There is always a chance though..." Theo started.

"What Chance?" We practically jumped down his throat.

I could see he was reluctant to comment further and was regretting having opened his mouth. "Well, if we could leave early enough, we might be able to get through."

"How early?" Fred said.

"If we can get far enough North before it starts forming for the day."

I could see him thinking about that.

"By nine or ten it would be impenetrable so we would have to go very early."

"And by 'very early' you mean...?"

"Between five and six AM..."

He was obviously reluctant to fly anywhere into storm weather, and quite rightly so. He was the pilot and the person who had chartered the plane. It was his responsibility to look after his passengers and the plane. But if he thought there was remote chance we could get through the zone before it was fully formed for the day, then I was willing to give it a go. I'm sure the others would concur.

"It's up to you guys," he said after a long pause.

"We'll try," we said simultaneously.

Theo nodded, but looked miserable.

"We can always turn back if it gets bad," I said.

Very early

We felt uneasy as we arrived at the airport a bit before 5:30 in the morning. It had rained steadily all night and was still raining though the wind had dropped. Towards the East, out over the ocean the sky seemed lighter than it should have been so perhaps it was beginning to clear. But it was still not good enough to take off. We would have to wait awhile.

It did improve enough to encourage Theo to file a flight plan from Cairns to Daru in Papua, via Coen in the middle of the Cape York Peninsula. He explained to us if we couldn't get through then we would return and if Cairns was closed by bad weather then our alternative was to land in Cooktown. He notified Customs and an officer was sent to check SKL and to whom we made declarations regarding what we were carrying on the plane as well as giving our reasons for flying there... all routine, and once that was done with our passports stamped, we were free to depart.

Coen

By the time preparations were complete it was clear enough in Cairns to take off. We could see far out to sea there was a huge dark storm which would no doubt envelope the city in a few hours. We headed out a bit over the sea and turned north to follow the coast up to Cooktown. We weren't going to land there, but would use it as a reference point for direction inland to Coen.

We stayed at five thousand feet to keep under the developing cloud. To our left the coast was a dark impenetrable green jungle. Inland closer to the coastal ranges it was black with massive storm clouds. The sea to our right looked grey and choppy, uninviting, already responding to the distant storm further out. The plane shuddered intermittently as wind gusts buffeted it. And it was cold. No matter how warm and humid it had been on the ground, up here it was icy cold and we couldn't stop shivering.

Barely fifteen minutes into the flight Theo said, "I just got a message that Cairns airport is closed to all traffic."

"I guess we're lucky we got away in time, or we'd be stuck there for who knows how long," I said.

"I'm not so sure about that. The storm is moving in faster than anyone expected," Theo told us. "Cooktown is also closed to air traffic. We have to turn inland."

"Wasn't Cooktown our alternate in case we had to turn back?"

"Yeah, but we can't go there now."

Theo turned the plane inland heading west. It was almost a right-angle turn.

"The clouds up there ahead are not so dense and we can probably go over them without too much trouble."

We could feel the plane rising as Theo gained height.

"We should clear them at ten thousand feet."

Once we got over the clouds and further inland, he turned north dropping back down to about five thousand feet. He pointed down to a road cut through the bush. "We'll follow this road north to Coen. I want everyone to watch out for the junction of that road below us with a telegraph line. I need that to give us a fix." He had a chart of the land below on his lap.

I saw where the telegraph line intersected the road. It ran all the way to tip of Cape York.

"We won't get lost if we follow that."

But before that point arrived, we had to detour a bit south and further west around a massive rainstorm that extended for miles. It took some time to go around it and to find the road north again.

If it continued like this it seemed unlikely that we would get through the Zone of Convergence.

"We may have to land at Coen to refuel,' Theo told us. "It's against regulations though. We're not supposed to land anywhere until we get to Daru and can go through PNG Customs for clearance to enter the country.

"Don't we have enough fuel?" Rommy asked.

"We do, but I would like to top up at Coen in case we have to make more divergences as we get near the Zone. We may have to go around a lot of thunderstorms."

Coen was little more than a grass strip and once we landed, we had to wait for the Shell agent to come out and sell us some av-gas. He knew if a plane other than the flying doctor or the mailman landed it was because they needed fuel. No one landed there otherwise.

The local agent looked a typical country man. He wore overalls, had a cheerful ruddy face, and was happy to see us because we were someone new to talk to.

"Haven't seen a plane land here for four weeks," was the first thing he said after 'G'day.' The weather has been revolting."

Everything around us was super green and wet. Even the ground was soggy once you stepped off the compacted runway. No one could drive through this way during the Wet. All the creeks and rivers were overflowing and vast areas were flooded. Flying was the only way in or out, and if the weather was really bad, there was none of that either.

"Where are you bound?"

"Daru" Theo said.

He nodded. "You know Customs have asked me to file reports on any planes that landed no matter which way they were headed."

"Really..."

"But they haven't given me any forms to fill in yet."

"Maybe they're not all that serious," I said.

Theo started to explain about how we had to go out of our way to avoid some storms which used up more fuel than expected.

"Don't worry," he said reassuringly. "I didn't see you land. I didn't even hear you going by overhead. There's nothing to report is there?"

"If you don't say anything, then we won't either." I said.

We chatted while he filled the wing tanks and Theo signed the credit forms.

"I hope the weather doesn't get any worse," he said as we climbed back on board.

He waited there while we taxied over to the runway and then took off. We circled the airstrip once and he waved goodbye, then we went through a light cloud and Coen disappeared.

The Zone of Convergence

By 9 am Coen was well behind us. The east coast was closed to small aircraft because the weather had worsened. There was no going back, but if it was our only option, we could have flown straight south along the York Peninsula into central Queensland's gulf country. There were many small landing strips scattered all over, but most of that area was inundated by flood waters. The only real choice was to push on northwards and hope we were still early enough to get through the Zone before the storm clouds built up.

I'm sure Theo was now wishing we had not decided to try our luck. We should have stayed back in Cairns. More often than not we were forced to fly around big thunderstorms that suddenly bubbled up in front of us. We zigzagged east and then west as we flew around these storms without making much headway. But looking back it seemed even worse. There was no way we could turn around and fly back to Coen or anywhere else further south.

"Hey guys, keep your eyes peeled for any flat land or emergency strips in case the weather forces us down," Theo said. He was definitely worried and that made us very nervous.

SKL was buffeted from both sides and sometimes it rose up suddenly or dropped so fast we felt dizzy; not good at all.

About 10 am we entered a clearer zone with the worst of the storms behind us.

"Look at that," Theo said as we flew more smoothly, because the wind was now behind us and travelling in the same direction, pushing us forward.

A huge wall of cloud stood clearly across out path. It stretched as far as we could see to the west, (our left) and similarly to the east, although there seemed to be broken sections and gaps. It was absolutely black at ground level, and torrential rain filled the space between the bottom of the cloud barrier and the treetops of the jungle beneath. Layer upon layer of thick cumulus clouds boiled up above; stretching so far up into the sky we couldn't see the top.

"There's no way we will get through that," I said.

Theo didn't say anything. He took the plane up higher until we were nudging the limits we could go, just above 12,000 feet. From this height because we were far enough along Cape York, we could actually see the Coral Sea on our right with the wall of cloud extending far out across the ocean disappearing into a hazy horizon. To our left there was so much haze we couldn't see the waters of the Gulf of Carpentaria, but we knew they weren't too far away.

Feeling the wind pushing us and seeing how violently the clouds formed and rolled upwards was frightening. We couldn't go back, too stormy, we couldn't land, nothing but jungle beneath, the only choice was to keep going forwards. Theo took us right up until we were forced to turn slightly eastwards and fly along the wall of cloud. This close we could see it wasn't as dense as it looked from further back. There were small gaps that opened briefly before closing again. The Zone was still forming. As the moist wind that had been pushing us from behind started rising the moisture it contained was released forming clouds that boiled upwards at phenomenal speed.

We stared at the visible violence of the wind too numb to feel scared.

"We might still be early enough to get through," Theo said, though not very hopefully.

There was nothing we could say as we flew along this immense wall feeling that we could be sucked into it at any second and torn to pieces by violently rising winds or shredded by the hailstones inside the clouds. The further along we flew the blacker the wall seemed to get.

A hole

Suddenly Theo turned SKL around and shot towards the blackest clouds I had ever seen.

"Shit!"

"There," Theo yelled. "There's a gap."

And the instant he said that I saw a tiny V shaped blue hole between two black thunderheads.

We hurtled towards it.

It seemed to be shrinking the closer we got. Hardly daring to look, fingers crossed, breaths held, this was the point of no return.

If the hole closed suddenly, we would be torn to shreds before we knew it.

Inside the hole it was ominously dark, icy cold, and SKL vibrated and shook so much we expected it to fall apart at any second. We shivered uncontrollably.

Suddenly we shot through to be bathed in sunshine.

The hole behind us closed up like a goosed arsehole. I couldn't see where we had come from. There was nothing but writhing dark grey and black clouds boiling upwards to tower over us. But the sky in front was clear, and just ahead the tip of the Cape York Peninsula looked as sharp as it does on the navigation charts. This was the very northern end of Australia. Beyond it the sea sparkled.

We all started laughing as the cabin warmed up again.

Moments later we passed over the top end of mainland Australia.

Several islands, one of which was Thursday Island, drifted by underneath as we crossed Torres Strait heading towards Daru.

Out of The Zone of Convergence and heading across Torres Strait to Daru.

Approaching the airstrip at Daru

Hot and deserted

Daru is a tiny island on the edge of the Gulf of Papua only a few miles from the massive mouth of the Fly River. It is very hot and humid. Most of the mainland behind the island is swamp and almost uninhabitable, although there are lots of villages along the Fly River.

It was just after 11 am when we landed and found the small airport deserted. There was one large building with a few small offices and that, we assumed, was the airport terminal. There were also several fibrocement huts nearby, each bearing the name of an airline painted on the front. Some distance away from the other buildings was another smaller fibrocement structure that looked like a toilet.

Suddenly feeling the urge to urinate I wandered over to it. Fred followed me. The smell should have warned us, and the incessant buzzing, but we didn't think of that until we entered. I almost vomited on the spot. The walls and floors were covered in dried shit. It even obscured some crude graffiti on one wall. The toilet bowls were caked with shit and piles of crumpled newspapers were scattered all about. Clouds of massive blowflies hovered and zipped about everywhere. I staggered back, bumped into Fred who was behind me.

"Shit," he said as he rapidly backed out the door.

"What kind of dump is this?" I muttered once we were far enough away to be able to breathe again. We walked over to the terminal and pissed against the side wall where no one could see us. There wasn't anyone there to see us anyway.

Meanwhile, just inside the terminal building Theo had discovered a telephone and a notice directing pilots of unscheduled craft to call a particular number if no Customs Officers were on duty. He called the number, as well as calling the refueling agent to ask if he could come out so we could refuel and be on our way as soon as possible.

While we waited for the Customs and the Fuel agent to arrive Theo radioed Port Moresby Traffic Control and asked for permission to fly directly across the Gulf of Papua to Port Moresby rather than having to go by the much longer route following the coastline all the way around. They gave permission which made Theo happy. We would have preferred to fly along the coastline to see something of the country but it would take a lot longer and Theo was exhausted after an already long hard flight, and just wanted to get there as quickly as possible.

We waited an hour for the Customs Officer to arrive and all he did was to check our papers, stamp our permits and ask if were carrying any contraband or prohibited items like packs of playing cards. We could have unloaded and reloaded SKL several times before he arrived and he would never have known.

The fuel agent didn't arrive until the Customs man had gone, but once the plane was topped up Theo radioed his new flight plan to Port Moresby Control and we took off, glad to be flying in the much cooler air at 9000 feet.

Banned in New Guinea

Playing cards are banned.

Oddly enough you can buy souvenir packs of playing cards designed with characters from regional areas across the country... (*made in China*) but you are not allowed to use them.

It is illegal everywhere in PNG to play cards for money, publicly or privately, and to prevent gambling problems the government banned playing cards. Bringing packs of playing cards into the country incurs a heavy fine, and they will be confiscated or worse still you will not be allowed to enter.

Playing cards have been around in one form or another since the 14th century which makes this ban seem rather odd to us.

The most smoked newspaper

According to the Guinness book of Records (October 1971) New Guinea's **South Pacific Post** which circulated only 5200 copies over 178,000 square miles had been the most sought-after newspaper for smoking and sold at 6 pence per pound for this purpose. In 1962 the arrival of the *Niu Gini Toktok* eased the paper shortage.

Approaching Port Moresby after flying across the Gulf of Papua from Daru.

Welcomed with a cold beer

It was 4:30 in the afternoon when we finally landed at Port Moresby's very long International airstrip.

We were directed by Traffic Control to the Aero Club. The moment we stopped Theo got out to do his basic checks. Just as we climbed out of the plane someone came out from the club rooms to welcome us. He dragged us inside where a number people enthusiastically guzzled cold beer. We each had a massive glass of icy beer thrust into our hands which we downed with relish. The club rooms were air-conditioned so it was relief to get out of the humid heat outside.

Relieved to be climbing out of SKL at Port Moresby

As always, SKL is checked over immediately after landing, refueled and prepared for the next flight. It was especially important to top up the fuel tanks to prevent any condensation from forming while the plane was sitting on the tarmac.

Our contact in Port Moresby

We had one contact in Port Moresby, Charles Cepulis, or Charlie as we called him once we met. He was Sports Editor of the *Post Courier*, PNG's major newspaper.

Charlie was my brother Phillip's brother in law and I had sent him a telegram to let him know we would arrive on Sunday. It had been imperative to arrive on Sunday because Theo had been booked in at DCA to sit for three exams to upgrade his pilot status, and the first of these was on Monday.

After downing a second beer I called the *Post Courier* to speak to Charlie and he told me he would be tied up for a couple of hours.

"Don't worry, give us the address and we'll get a taxi from the airport."

"I'll see you when you get here," Charlie said.

I used the phone in the club room to call a taxi and was told one would be there in half an hour.

I thought that was a bit of a wait; after all we were at the airport and there should be plenty of taxis somewhere there.

It actually took two hours before a taxi pulled up in front of the Aero Club by which time we'd had a few more beers. When we arrived at the *Post Courier* offices Charlie was just knocking off and we were decidedly tipsy.

"You're early," he said. "I didn't expect you for at least another hour."

"You're kidding."

"Obviously you don't know how efficient the taxis are in Port Moresby," he said.

We followed him out to a car park where he indicated a beat-up old Peugeot.

"Pile in. We'll go and get something to eat."

That was a great idea because we were very hungry having eaten nothing all day. We were also a little drunk after those beers at the Aero club. We only went a short distance before stopping at what looked like an RSL club where we discovered that 'dinner' for Charlie was several cans of beer, with food an afterthought.

According to Charlie, each can of beer has the equivalent number of calories as does one pork chop. It was the reason he preferred drinking beer to eating food. "There's a pork chop in every can," he told us several times.

Even though we ate something, we still were drunk when we got back to the flat which Charlie shared with two other journalists. They insisted we celebrate our arrival, instantly producing a large bottle of whiskey while Charlie found a number of glasses which he passed around.

Eventually we collapsed onto the floor, which was fine since that was where we were going to sleep anyway. We never noticed how hard the concrete floor was until we woke up the next morning.

John and Fred with Charlie in a festive mood at his flat.

Charles Cepulis at the Aero Club when we were about to leave for the Trobriand Islands 3 days later.

Out and about

When we picked ourselves up off the floor in the morning the other two journalists had gone and Charlie was in the kitchen looking as fresh as…

He was drinking a glass of artificial orange juice. He made this by putting two teaspoons of orange coloured powder into a glass, filling it up with water while stirring vigorously with a teaspoon.

"Want some?" he asked as she held up the glass for us to see.

"I don't think so," I muttered.

"There's nothing in here to eat, but there are some cans of beer in the fridge."

"We'll give them a miss," Fred said.

"You can borrow my car while you're here," Charlie said. "Keys are on the table. I'll walk to work."

Since Theo had to sit for three exams with the Department of Civil Aviation, we had three days to spend in Port Moresby. Having use of a car to get around was fabulous. Before we had a chance to thank him, he was out the door and gone.

Our first impression of Port Moresby was that it is a beautiful city built on hills that gently roll down into a sea of scattered islands and very tropical. It was the nerve centre of PNG, and you could feel the sense of development and the growing pains of this young and vibrant city. It was a mixture of modern, and primitive, with new steel and glass structures glistening in the sun while at Koki by the sea and the town's major market there were innumerable houses built on stilts out over the water. There were houseboats that seemed totally unseaworthy moored beside them.

Houseboats at Koki.

Women fishing with seine nets.

Koki, with its women fishing with seine nets in shallow water, with groups of children running about happily playing, and the nearby market, was a fascinating place for a photographer. I was happy to spend time here. People from all over PNG could be found here. Unfortunately, we also saw a lot of people, especially men, who seemed lost, bewildered by the impact of civilization, who were often drunk, belligerent or apathetic.

Koki

At Koki, a residence of woven coconut palm mats

On the other side of Port Moresby was Poreporena in the district of Hanuabada, a village built on stilts in the traditional style but using modern materials like corrugated iron for walls and rooves rather than strips of wood and banana leaf thatching. Like most villages built on stilts over water, sewerage, and all the rubbish was simply dumped into the water through holes in the floor of the various houses, to be washed away by the sea. Up close it was a bit smelly but nonetheless picturesque.

Poreporena

— Grab that Moment —

Bolted to the floor

The ugly side of Port Moresby were the local pubs. We discovered in one that all the tables and chairs were made of concrete and bolted to the floor so the drunks couldn't throw them at each other during the daily drunken brawls. The bar itself was protected by a wire mesh screen to protect the barmen from attack, and all drinks were served in plastic containers: No glass to break or to be used to slash someone in a fight.

Most tourists and expatriates stayed out of these pubs.

An interview

Charlie had told his mates at the newspaper about our film-making holiday to the Trobriands and one of them wanted to interview us for the social pages. Charlie took us to a restaurant out of town where we were interviewed for a story that was published in the **Post Courier** (*Scene 71 - Friday March 12, 1971*).

He asked lots of questions and was fascinated by Fred's epic bike ride from Germany to Australia for the 1956 Olympic Games. He began his article with the headline *Fred road a bike to Australia*: and underneath the lead in was *Fred Glasbrenner had a lot of fun pedaling a push-bike from Germany to Australia in 1956.*

The rest of the article was so full of imaginary embellishments that it was embarrassing to read. It had elements of truth in it, but exaggerated to a point of ridiculousness. It was published after we took off for other parts and we didn't see it until we came back through Port Moresby a week and a half later.

It talked about Fred staying with Princess Soraya and The Sha of Persia, of Fred's meeting with the wife of President Sukarno, Ibu Fat Mawati, in Indonesia and how she paid for his and his companion's air fares from Indonesia to Darwin and among other things, of Fred and Rommy jumping over the side of their boat to go fishing for abalone off the coast of Victoria... fishing!

I don't think he knew what an abalone was. He also said something about a film I shot of Fred and Rommy diving for abalone being seen on TV by *45 million people in Germany...*

But that's what the social pages in newspapers do; they make up entertaining stories for people to talk about.

— Grab that Moment —

Charlie with us at the Aero Club as we loaded our gear onto SKL for the next part of the journey.

Theo preparing the flight plan for the next part of the journey:
Port Moresby to Popondetta to Kiriwina in the Trobriand Islands.

The Gap

You can see The Gap quite clearly from the Port Moresby airstrip. It is a shallow V shaped ridge with towering mountains on either side.

These mountains on either side that stretch along the whole length of the island divide Papua from New Guinea average around 12,000 feet in height. The Gap the smaller planes fly through is really a series of low ridges 7000 feet above sea level. If you are going from Port Moresby to anywhere in New Guinea in a small plane, you have to fly through that gap.

Once airborne and approaching the Gap it becomes much more difficult to see than it is from ground level.

16 mm frames...
Approaching The Gap. We had to climb another five hundred feet to clear the ridges which meant we were scraping the bottom of the cloud layers above.

In the middle of The Gap; clouds are already forming between the ridges as we fly over them. In another hour they would merge with the heavier cloud above and The Gap would be completely obscured and impassable for the rest of the day.

The clouds have rocks in them

It's a common phrase often heard in the aero club as people remind themselves about the dangers of flying in New Guinea in a small plane.

New Guinea's climate is equatorial and is particularly dangerous during the wet season. All flying is done as early as possible in the mornings. As warm damp air rises it condenses and forms massive clouds which settle around and over the mountain tops. Except for International flights that land in Port Moresby or Lae (usually pressurized passenger jets that can fly at thirty or forty thousand feet), all local flying is done visually and pilots are familiar with the routes they fly. They are not allowed to fly by themselves until they have completed a number of flights with a more experienced pilot who knows the routes being flown.

Most of the routes to small towns, settlements and villages require flying between mountains and along valleys and rivers so it is essential the pilots become familiar with the landscape. Once the cloud cover builds up it is impossible to see anything, so no flying is done after mid-day.

Theo had no idea of the route we needed to take to go over the mountains other than what he could see on his navigation chart. He was told to take part in a convoy so he could follow others who knew the way up through the Gap. There were four other small planes in the convoy and each took off a minute after the one before. We were the last one on the end so it was easy to follow the others.

Even at 10 am when we took off there were layers of low cumulus cloud forming around the mountains on either side of the Gap so we couldn't fly higher than 7500 feet. As we rose up to the designated height, we were buffeted so alarmingly I thought the wings might fall off and we would crash into the tree tops barely 500 feet beneath us. The heavy clouds sat just a couple of hundred feet above us

Theo's hands were absolutely white where he gripped the controls.

Some of the trees below reached up 200 feet. If we hit an air pocket and suddenly dropped, we would certainly scrape the tops of them.

A moment later we were through and the planes ahead peeled off to fly in other directions. We were left to follow a cascading river down into the low plains ahead. I could see the far distant shimmer of water where the land touched the sea.

The shuddering stopped and flying was smooth once again.

Coming down the other side

Theo throttled back so we wouldn't fly faster than 270 mph. We flew over the odd tiny village stuck on a ridge or a mountain top. Each of these tiny settlements had an area of cleared space around it for cultivation of food crops, and some even had small airstrips.

"How would you land there?" Fred asked.

"With a lot of skill," Theo who seemed much more relaxed now we were on the other side of the mountains joked.

Seeing one little airstrip along the top of a ridge beside a tiny village I said, "I reckon taking off would be harder."

"Yeah, a lot scarier than landing… you keep going until you reach the end and then if you are not airborne you fall over the end of the ridge. Falling should give you enough speed to fly properly before you hit the bottom on the valley."

"Bloody good thing we're not doing that," Rommy commented from the back seat.

Charlie told us before we left that not so long ago a plane crashed high in the mountains in Chimbu country. It took weeks to find the wreckage in the jungle covered mountains, and then the investigating team which had to drop in by parachute since they couldn't land a helicopter, managed to lose themselves before reaching the crash site.

Suffering from exposure (it's very cold and wet in the perpetually cloud covered high mountains), lack of food, and ulcerated legs, it was another two weeks before more rescuers found them.

Charlie wasn't clear on whether the original plane crash site was ever found again.

The airstrip at Popondetta.

Popondetta

It wasn't long before we saw the Popondetta landing strip surrounded by dense bush. We had no trouble landing. The first thing we did on landing was to refuel, but we had to pay cash here because no credit was extended to anyone for any reason. Everything has to be ferried in by plane and paid for in cash.

After refueling and the usual pre-flight checks, Theo called us back and boarded SKL to continue our flight. Firstly, we headed towards a village on Dyk Ackland Bay called Tufi. Theo would take a navigational bearing there before flying out over the Solomon Sea to the Trobriands.

Tufi is a small coastal village snuggled up against Mount Victory. We were flying over the village when suddenly Theo turned SKL around and headed back to Popondetta.

"What's going on?" I asked.

"We're not allowed to fly to Kiriwina."

Kiriwina is the only town in the Trobriands.

"Why not?" Freddy and Rommy said simultaneously.

"Moresby Control told me to switch to a different frequency, but we don't have the crystal for it. They won't let us fly in that area if they can't be in contact with us."

"I'll be stuffed."

"What are we going to do, buy another crystal in Popondetta?"

"Fat chance of that," Theo said.

Of course, there was no crystal to be had in Popndetta and it was too late to go anywhere else, so we ended up at the only hotel in the town.

The cost of the room for the four of us included breakfast lunch and dinner. We had the dinner later and of course, breakfast in the morning. There was nothing to do other than wander around the very clean but small town and we soon found ourselves at the aero club where we had a few drinks before returning to the hotel.

We spent the night trying to sleep in the extreme humidity while swatting mosquitoes and listening to giant frogs or cane toads which looked big enough to weigh a kilo calling to each other while they sat ponderously on the veranda snatching and eating insects attracted by the outdoor lights.

A weekend to kill

It was Friday, and in the morning, we flew to Lae which was a long way north in the Huon Gulf. The weather was beautiful, clear sky a deep blue, and the sparkling ocean below with all shades from the palest blue where it was shallow to patches of deep ultramarine between scattered reefs and small islands. We flew only a couple of thousand feet up and it was so clear we could even see fish swimming in schools along the reefs. There were an untold number of shipwrecks clearly visible just beneath the surface. It would be fantastic to dive there but there was no way to get there other than by seaplane, or some kind of boat. Most of the coast as far as we could see appeared uninhabited. Inland to our left clouds were already building up along the mountains and by midday we couldn't even see them.

The first inhabited place we saw was a town called Morobe. It was half way from Popondetta to Lae. Theo took a bearing to confirm we were flying in the right direction, and reported our position to Port Morseby control.

Of course we were flying in the right direction, we were following the coast. The only other town we would see before landing at Lae in the Huon Gulf would be Salamaua.

"Now there's a place we can come back to," Fred said. "There's probably a road of some sort from Lae."

"Have a look at the ship wrecks down there," Rommy added.

There were a number of small wrecks in the shallow water only a few miles away from the town.

"They're all left over from the War," Theo said.

He meant the Second World War. Japanese and American forces fought many battles in the Coral and Solomon Seas and there are thousands of shipwrecks scattered all through the reefs along the coast.

"If we can't get the required crystal we can always fly back here and dive," Theo said. "It won't be the same as going to the Trobriands, but as an alternative it looks okay."

He was hoping we would agree. I think he was nervous about flying over open sea without any visible land which is what we would have to do to get to the Trobriand Islands.

On the maps and charts, it looks like there are thousands of little islands and atolls scattered across the sea between the larger inhabited islands, but when you fly over the area there is still an awful lot of open water to traverse. If his navigation was a bit off, we could miss our destination altogether and then we would be in trouble.

It was late afternoon when we landed at Lae.

It was too late to do anything much, but worst of all, Theo found that the crystal we needed for the radio wasn't available.

"They're going to send one up from Melbourne," he informed us.

"When will that get here?" I asked.

"Unfortunately, not until Monday morning."

"That's a bummer," Rommy said.

"Well we can't dive here," Fred said. "The water is the colour of shit."

We had seen the brown smudges of silt flowing into the bay around Lae from the many rivers that were overflowing with the runoff from heavy rain in the mountains surrounding the Huon Gulf and Lae itself. The town is situated in the Markham River valley, a low-lying basin carved out by the Markham river between two incredible mountain ranges; the Finisterre Range on the Huon Peninsula and the Kratke Range which is part of the Eastern Highlands.

The town didn't look all that exciting either.

Before we could say anything, Theo said, "Someone at DCA suggested we fly to Finschhafen for the weekend. It's only forty-five minutes from here. A lot of guys go there for the fishing."

"Why not? It's a good as going anywhere else, and probably a lot better than staying here."

Finschhafen

Situated right on the tip of the Huon Peninsula and protected by Cape Cretin, Finschhafen is a tiny town cut off completely by mountains and jungle on one side, and the Solomon Sea on the other.

The only way to get there is by small plane or by boat.

"What are we waiting for?" Fred said.

"As soon as I can refuel and check everything," Theo said.

From the air, as we flew in to land, the water looked clear and there was a row of tiny islands stretched along the coast as far as we could see separated from the mainland only by a couple of hundred metres which looked ideal for diving and filming. It did look as if a strong current ran along between the islands and the land's edge so it wasn't possibly as clear as it looked. Strong currents often carried fine sand which reduced visibility and there were lots of creeks with fresh water running down off the peninsula into the sea.

"I'll bet they do big game fishing along that channel," Fred said.

There were several rusty hulks of square looking ships sticking out of the water at one spot and there were kids playing in the water that covered parts of the wreckage. They waved to us as we flew over.

The landing strip was a fair distance out of town and we managed to get a lift from a guy working there who was just knocking off for the day. I suppose they always put these landing strips way out of town in case there is an accident on landing. The planes would be less likely to crash into residences and injure other people that way.

An offer we couldn't refuse

We were dropped off in front of the only community club in town. It looked like an RSL club but I couldn't see any signage. There were several people inside as we entered but the place was very quiet. Everyone stared at us as we walked to the bar and ordered beer.

It was obvious we were strangers.

"What's going on?" I asked the barman. I could see a guy setting up a large film projector on a heavy table at the far end of the room.

"It's Friday night… film night. Everyone in town turns up to watch the movie whatever it is."

Everyone meant the town's European population, not the local indigenous people.

And as it turned out quite a few people arrived not long after the projector and the screen were set up.

We had barely finished our beers when a clean-cut young man dressed in immaculately pressed shirt and shorts, with calf length white socks and black polished shoes approached. He was studying us with far more interest than anyone else there had.

"I'm Colin," he said, "I haven't seen you around here before"

He didn't seem at all friendly.

"We just flew in from Lae," Theo explained. "They told us there that this was a good place to come for a weekend."

"We're actually on our way to the Trobriands to shoot a film," Fred added.
"But they wouldn't let us fly there until we obtained another radio crystal. We were told to fly to Lae to get the right frequency set up but unfortunately DCA here doesn't have a spare crystal so they are sending one up from Melbourne. We have to wait until Monday before we can install it."

"So here we are," I said. "Is there a decent motel or someplace like that here?"

"You came in your own plane?"

Suddenly Colin became very friendly. The moment he knew we had our own plane his attitude changed. No longer stiff and suspicious he suddenly acted as if he had known us for years and was happy to see us after a long absence.

"Look. I'm the local police chief, and it's my job to check out any strangers who arrive in town."

Theo nodded.

"Why don't you all stay at my place? I've got lots of room. There's plenty of time before the film show starts. I'll run you out to the airport and we can collect your luggage."

"Fantastic," Fred said.

A good way to see if we really did have a plane, I thought.

"Why don't I get some beers to take back to your place?" Rommy suggested.

"Sounds good," Colin said.

With our luggage loaded we went to Colin's place where we had a shower, put on some fresh clothes and joined Colin and his wife Fran for dinner. After that we went to the club to watch the movie and had a lovely evening and quite a few beers with the other club members. Actually, there was no hotel or anything like that in Finschhafen, and visitors stayed with people they knew, or perhaps bunked down at the community club. We were lucky Colin was kind enough to offer us accommodation.

The weekly market

Every Saturday there is a market in Finschhafen where tribes-people come down from the mountains and the villages in the jungle with goods to exchange and sell. It starts early and is over by 9 am after which people rapidly disappear back into the jungle.

When Colin woke us up at 6 am it seemed as if we hadn't slept at all.

"Grab your cameras," he said as we splashed water onto our faces to help wake up.

"We're off to the market. It only happens on Saturday mornings so you timed your visit perfectly."

It was 7-30 when Colin dropped us off.
"I've got to see about getting a boat so we can dive in the channel. I'll leave you here to have a look around and I'll be back in an hour or so."

The Boung or market was in full swing; a cacophony of noise with hundreds of women and men bargaining over the goods displayed by the sellers. Many of the women carried stuff they bought or wanted to sell in a woven bag they hooked over their head so it hung down on their back.

I shot some movie footage as surreptitiously as possible. I would walk behind Fred and Rommy so I couldn't be seen and pointed the Bolex camera zoom lens just over Fred's shoulder.

— Grab that Moment —

Anyone looking at Fred would only see the lens on his shoulder and not the camera I held behind him. In fact, hardly anyone saw the lens at all; they would see a jolly bearded face, an obvious stranger and not look beyond.

Rommy standing next to Fred held his 35mm SLR camera at waist height. It was self-focusing and he didn't need to look through the viewfinder. He would pause a moment, press the shutter button, then move on again. He thought he was being unobtrusive, but looking at the film I shot of him doing this, it was obvious what he was doing.

Apart from the odd glance, no one at the market took any notice of us; they were focused entirely on bargaining, buying and selling, catching up with gossip and sharing betel nuts.

People at the market.
Note the women in the photos above carrying their goods bought in' bilums' (bags) draped across their head or forehead. Men on the other hand simply throw it across their shoulder. The market only goes until 9-30 am so if you want anything you have to get there early.

— Grab that Moment —

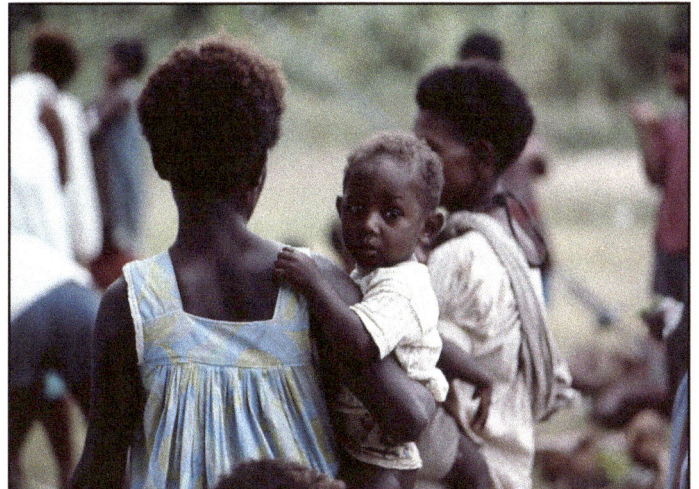

— Grab that Moment —

Above, Rommy and Fred with fresh mangoes.
Selling stuff can be hard work and a good rest is exactly what is needed.

Betel Nuts

Betel nuts, the seeds of the Areca Palm —common everywhere in South-East Asia— are consumed with enthusiasm by young as well as old.

Chewing betel nut in PNG is known as *buai*. The nut is consumed with a mustard stick dipped in slaked lime. It turns the lips and teeth bright red so when someone chewing opens their mouth to speak it looks as if the mouth is full of blood. It has a euphoric effect, and is more often than not an addiction. The PNG government has attempted to ban the chewing of betel nut but no one wants to pass this legislation so the practice continues.

The only downside is that wherever the nuts are consumed, where consumers spit out the residue and the excess saliva produced by chewing, the pavement, tree trunks, lower parts of walls and fences are stained a dark red which eventually darkens to almost black. It's not nice to see someone spitting out copious amounts of what looks like blood as they walk along the road.

Dive boats

Colin returned as the market was closing and people were packing up unsold goods.

"I've organized a couple of boats with Tony Tonks. He's the school teacher. He'll come with us to drive one of them."

"Sounds good," Fred said.

We piled into the car and Colin took us to the airport to collect our diving gear from the plane. We then went back to his place to collect his wife Fran who was also coming with us.

At the boat ramp Fred and Rommy went with Tony in his smaller 'tinny' while I went with Colin, Fran, and Theo in the other boat. Colin took charge of driving the boat.

Stopping beside one of the small islands on the other side of the channel. Colin is driving the boat.

Into the water

Fred and I decided to have a quick paddle in the water off the beach while the gear was being loaded. The sand was gritty and rapidly dropped to a reasonable depth visibility was poor. From the air as we flew in it had looked very clear, but it was different under the surface. A strong current ran along the channel carrying sand and silt from nearby creeks. The bottom was littered with dead broken coral bleached white, blocks of concrete and other wartime debris. There were hardly any fish.

Rommy swam across the channel to the nearest of a row of small islands and came back to report lots of fish, plenty of live coral, and lovely clear water.

On a small island of broken concrete and coral which delineated one side of the boat entrance a bunch of local kids sat and watched us with interest. A few hundred metres along the channel huge blocks of concrete and a series of rusted boxlike structures jutted out of the water. A number of kids were jumping off these blocks into the water, swimming around, and climbing back up again, having a great time.

Once we got across the channel close to the nearest of the row of islands scattered along the coast for several kilometres the water became much clearer.

Sunken hulks lay at various depths beneath us and we stopped alongside one where the back end of it was less than a metre beneath the surface. We could stand on it without any problem.

"There's probably a hundred or more barges along this channel," Colin told us. "When the Americans pulled out because the Japanese were coming, they deliberately sank all of them so the Japanese would not be able to use them."

By this time, I had the Bolex inside its underwater housing and had stepped over the side and was standing on the top of the sunken barge.

"There were over two thousand Americans based here at Finschhafen during the war. They built all the roads here with crushed coral and cement mixed together. Most of their base has disappeared, but the roads are still here."

Theo stayed in the boat with Colin and Fran while Fred and Rommy joined me in the water to swim around the sunken barge. Colin also stayed in his boat.

"Are you coming in?" I asked Colin.

"I don't swim in this channel, or anywhere around here," he said "too many sharks."

No sharks this time

We didn't see any sharks. We swam the length of the barge diving down to 10 metres at the deepest end and I shot a complete roll of film. Back on the tinny I changed the roll of film, which meant taking the camera out of the housing, extracting the roll of film and replacing it again. Each roll of film only lasted four minutes.

We didn't have the HD digital video used today. We didn't even have video cameras back then. What a difference a couple of decades makes! With a decent digital video camera, you wouldn't have to return to the surface after every four minutes of filming, and could stay down there as long as it took to shoot whatever footage you needed.

On the outside of the islands the water dropped down into deep blue depths where we couldn't go. We were limited to the top 10 metres, basically the depth we could dive down to holding our breath, and that meant barely two minutes at a time before we had to resurface to breathe. The reefs along the outside edge of the islands were alive with coral of all colours and shapes, swarming with fish, and shrimp and Fred prised off some pearl shell oysters which he later opened but unfortunately didn't find any pearls. I filmed a school of giant Maori Wrasse as they came up out of the deepest blue depths to cruise along the edge of the fringing coral. I was fascinated by the huge bumps on their heads which apparently, they used to smash the delicate coral so they could eat the living polyps inside.

This time Tony went into the water with Fred and Rommy. Like Colin, he normally never went into the sea here because of the sharks, but he must

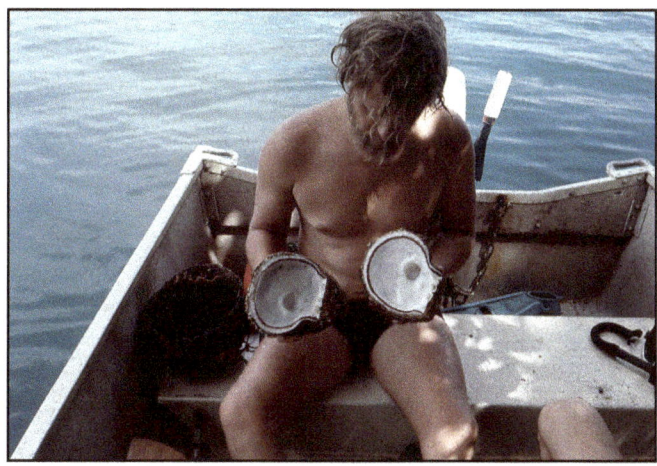

have felt emboldened by the fact that three of us were in the water diving and filming, and that we hadn't seen any sharks at all.

It never occurred to us that there could be crocodiles in this water along the coast. There are certainly plenty of them in PNG's many rivers and creeks, swamps and bays.

We spent several hours in the water along the outside of the islands and although we saw lots of fish, only once did we see a small reef shark. We were exhausted and decided that was enough for one day.

"The channel is very clear early in the morning," Colin said as we headed back to the small beach where we'd launched the tinnies, "if the tide is coming in."

And that's exactly what we did. We were there again the next morning as soon as the sun started to come up, and the water was crystal clear.

We went back to the sunken barge and dived there again, filming it in detail.

"The locals have been diving here for years," Colin informed us, "and they make a good living bringing up old wartime ordinance to recycle the brass. The Americans sank everything, all the bullets, weapons, tinned food, whatever they had, rather than pack it up and take it with them. Wherever they went there would be more than enough, so why bother with this stuff? They dumped the lot. Drove the trucks into the water, sank the barges, blew up the bridges over the creeks and rivers, and got the hell out of here. They left nothing the Japanese could use. But it was a bonus for the locals who for years have salvaged whatever they could. They still find stuff today. God only knows what else is out there in the jungle. Not long ago some villagers blew themselves up trying to dig out an unexploded bomb."

By 10-30 am the water started to get cloudy again as the tide turned. Sand and silt started moving back along the channel, so we called it a day.

Fred with Tony Tonks in the tinny

One of the locals with his outrigger canoe

— Grab that Moment —

Rusting wreckage left over from the 2nd World War makes a great place for children to swim and play.

Children playing on the rusted remains of wartime barges, sunk deliberately so the invading Japanese would not be able to use them. The whole channel between the mainland and a group of small islands a few hundred metres offshore was full of these sunken barges, mostly underwater.

That evening Colin organized a party with all the people we had met in the club. We drank a lot of beer, ate steaks and sausages cooked on a hotplate in Colin's back yard and eventually dropped into bed. When we woke up in the morning Colin had been gone for two hours. He had to work since the weekend was over. He came back around ten while we were having breakfast with Fran. He was wearing his police uniform.

"When you're ready I'll drop you off at the airport."

We grabbed everything, piled into his police Land Cruiser and he took us to the plane. He hung around while we loaded and Theo went through the pre-flight checks. He watched us take off and we circled the airstrip once so we could wave goodbye to him.

Another delay

We flew back up the coast to Lae and found out when we landed that the crystal we needed had not arrived. We would have to wait another day.

Shit! If we'd known that we could have stayed another day in Finschhafen.

We spent the night sleeping on the Lae Aero club floor and when the crystal still hadn't arrived the next morning Theo managed to borrow one from a club member whose plane was being serviced. In exchange He could have the crystal that was being flown up from Melbourne.

Finally, we were airborne and heading back towards Popondetta where we would refuel before heading out over the sea to The Trobriand Islands.

There was only one problem. We couldn't receive with the borrowed crystal. We could send, but to receive we used (illegally) a transistor radio with its long thin antenna stuck out of the window on the pilot's side. Theo tuned it to the frequency used by the Port Moresby control. It was makeshift, but it worked. As long as we could receive instructions and respond with the borrowed crystal everything was fine.

They didn't have to know how we did it.

Out to the islands

Taking off from Popondetta we headed to Tufi where Theo could take a bearing from Goodenough Island from which he would triangulate a course from Tufi to the Trobriand islands. We would fly just north of it keeping the volcanic mountain on our right.

Goodenough Island is part of the D'Entrecasteaux islands which are extinct volcanoes that mimic the terrain of southern new Guinea. They stick up so high above the sea that they have their own weather. While everywhere ahead of us was clear and sunny, the actual peaks of Goodenough and its neighbors were covered with massive storm clouds heavy with rain. I even saw lightning flashes in those clouds as we flew past a few kilometres north.

It didn't take long to leave that massive island behind and ahead the glistening shallow Bismarck sea full of reefs and small atolls stretched endlessly into the distance.

Moments of uncertainty

"How long before we get there?" Fred asked.

Theo was busy relaying our position to Moresby Control and checking his position on the chart he had open on his knees.

"They're about 90 miles out to sea past Goodenough. If we don't see them, we will only have enough fuel to make a couple of wide circles, after which we'll have to return."

There are no refueling facilities on the islands and every flight there had to carry enough fuel to make the return trip.

Theo seemed concerned. He kept studying the chart open on his lap in between staring out of the windscreen to look for the islands. There are no radio beacons out here and navigation is by dead reckoning and sight. A few degrees out when passing Goodenough and you would be far enough off course to miss even seeing the low lying Trobiands.

Now we were worried as well. We stared out of the side windows looking for any sign of the islands. Compared to the many little atolls they would be quite large and easy to see even though they were low lying.

We flew on, and on, and still no sign of Kiriwina, the largest of the Trobriand group.

The chart had a large blank section between Goodenough and Kiriwina stating uncharted coral reefs, so there was nothing we could reference to tell us where we were. Some of the reefs jutted above the surface and had pure white sand around the edges. One I saw even had a small coconut palm growing on it. The water was full of coral reefs many of which broke the surface. It would be almost impossible to take anything through these waters that wasn't a flat-bottomed boat or a dug-out canoe, and even then, someone would have to stand on the bow and look for the passages between the reefs.

"If we are on course," Theo said, "we should see them in a few minutes." He sounded uncertain, which didn't inspire confidence.

We reached the ninety-mile mark and kept going.

Now we were worried. We all stared off into the haze.

"Another minute," Theo said. "If we don't see anything in another minute we will have to turn back."

We stared and stared until our eyes watered.

Suddenly Rommy shouted: "Over there…"

We were not heading directly to them and if Rommy hadn't seen them we would have gone past them altogether.

Theo immediately turned towards them and rapidly the question-mark shaped island of Kiriwina grew larger and larger.

What a relief! We had made it.

My estimation of Theo's navigation abilities rose exponentially.

"We'll circle around Losuia before we land so people will know a plane is landing and the hotel will send someone out to collect us," Theo said.

Losuia

Losuia was the only 'European' settlement on the island. There were a few large as well as small villages over the several islands that made up The Trobriands, but Losuia was where everyone visiting went.

The airstrip. as always, was several kilometres away from the town. It had been built during the Second World War and was enormous, far bigger than what was needed for the small planes that serviced these islands.

Flying over the island we passed over what was obviously a resort with a number of modern buildings, all with thatched roofs, and a swimming pool that was empty. It was the wet season, off-season for tourists because it was too hot and humid, so there probably weren't too many guests there.

We followed a dirt road out to the airstrip and there was nothing in between the hotel and the airstrip but jungle. If no one came to pick us up we would be in for a long walk.

The hotel

We hadn't been out of the plane for more than a few minutes before a Chinese guy drove up in a mini-moke.

"I've come to take you to the hotel," he said as he jumped out and shook hands with each of us.

"How do you know we want to go there?" I asked.

"Where else can you go?"

"Losuia," I suggested.

"It's a government administrative centre, that's all. I've got a general store there, but that's it. The only place to stay is at the hotel."

He was telling us this as we unloaded our gear from the plane.

"I assumed you want to go there because you circled around before landing. The weekly charter from Port Moresby does that and I drive out to pick up the guests or to unload stuff for the store."

We shoved our gear into the back of the mini-moke and jumped in. There was not a lot of room but we managed to squeeze in.

"We haven't seen a charter for a month," he said as he drove along the tarmac to the dirt road. "The weather's been shit-house for weeks… middle of the wet season. This is the first clear day we've had. It should get better from now on since the season's about over."

The dirt road was a mess, rutted and full of puddles. We crossed a creek of brown water, and thought there'll be no diving here with all the wet season runoff. We came at the wrong time. We should have waited another month.

"You were lucky to get down," he said as he slowed down to go around a huge puddle.

We looked at each other realizing it was a mistake to have come here.

As we whipped around a bend slipping and sliding, we almost ran into a group of native women wearing nothing but grass skirts. Some of them had baskets full of stuff balancing on their heads. They frantically jumped off the road into the tall grass along the edge. One of them screamed at us as we slid past.

The hotel was a ramshackle joint and we were the only guests. The guy who picked us up along with his wife were the owners of the hotel as well as the general store. They were both about our age and had originally come from Madang, much further up the coast of PNG from Lae. They were recently married and the hotel and the general store had been wedding gifts from the man's father. The swimming pool was empty because a recent earthquake had opened a big crack in it and the water had drained out.

The women forced to jump off the road as we came around a bend; not looking happy...

The Sing Sing

"Are you here for the Sing-Sing?" The young man's wife who was the receptionist at the hotel said as we signed the register. "It's on at the weekend to celebrate the end of the wet season."

"We didn't know about that," I said," but since the water inside the lagoon is so muddy and we can't dive, we might as well wait for that."

It was Tuesday afternoon and we had to wait until the weekend.

I was happy to stay for the Sing-Sing but Theo didn't look so happy. He looked quite uncomfortable. It must have been the heat and the humidity getting to him.

"What is there to do while we wait?"

"We can organize a canoe for you to go up river to the big village where the Sing-Sing will take place."

"Tomorrow?" Fred asked.

"Not a problem," our driver said.

Unrelenting humidity

We hung around the foyer, sitting under big fans to try and keep cool. It was so humid, any movement at all had sweat seeping out all over. Our clothes were stuck to us. It looked as if we had jumped into the river and climbed out without changing. No wonder no one came here during the wet season.

"Do you really want to stay here until the weekend?" Theo asked us with a hint of desperation in his voice.

Grass skirts and souvenirs

There were a lot of native women only wearing grass skirts hanging around the hotel. I wondered if that was for the tourists because elsewhere, the women we passed while driving from the airstrip all wore ragged cloth skirts. These women had brought artifacts that were made in their village to sell to tourists, or alternatively to the hotel gift shop which would re-sell them to the tourists that come in on the charter flights. Perhaps they had seen our plane circle around before landing and must have thought there would be a lot of tourists. Unfortunately, there were only the four of us, not a big planeload of tourists.

I bought a small drum with a snake's skin head and carving of a female figure both made from teak. Both the drum and the figure were quite different in style to other artifacts we had seen in New Guinea itself.

An Outrigger canoe

The next morning, we followed the hotel owner down to the water's edge where a long outrigger canoe and a tall islander was waiting for us. The canoe was the largest I'd seen and looked very heavy. Bamboo slats had been tied along the outrigger side which acted as a space to transport goods. We put our gear and the lunch provided by the hotel on the bamboo slats. The guy with the canoe was our guide. He would not paddle, but using a long pole would push us along through the shallow muddy water.

Rommy went in first and walked along the full length of the canoe. Fred sat in the middle and Theo was behind him. I hopped in last. The hotel owner gave us a push to send the canoe out into the water while the guide in front pushed his long pole down into the mud underneath the surface.

Getting into the outrigger canoe.

Heading across the wide lagoon towards mangroves and jungle.
The sky was overcast and threatened to rain.

Heading up a broad estuary through the mangroves to the village we visited.

Incessant rain and mud

The canoe moved slowly out across a wide expanse of water. The guide was glistening with sweat. Our shirts stuck to our backs. The air was so dense with entrained water it was hard to breathe. God only knows how the guide managed to continue pushing the pole into the sea floor to propel us across the bay. The pole was about four metres long so the water we crossed must have been quite shallow.

It took about an hour to get across the bay to where jungle and palm trees over hung the edge. There were a few smaller outriggers pulled up on the shore beside a small village with huts made from cut tree branches. The huts had roofs made from overlapping palm tree fronds.

We passed by soon enough and entered a long narrow estuary which looked more like a river the further in we went. The trees on either side started to overhang us the further up this river we went. A couple of kids in a small outrigger canoe passed us heading downstream. They waved as they went by, yelled something to which the guide responded to without slowing his steady pushing.

A typical Trobriand Island village.

Two boys in a canoe passed by heading downstream towards the big lagoon.

A moment later it started to rain. Down it came, so heavy it felt as if we were standing under a waterfall. We passed a group of men and women and children in a muddy clearing. They had cut huge banana tree leaves and were holding them over their heads to keep the water off.

And the rain kept pounding down as we approached a much larger clearing where hundreds of very tall trees with white trunks were clumped in patches around numerous thatched-roof wooden huts on stilts. This was the village.

— Grab that Moment —

Trying to protect themselves from the rain with banana tree leaves.

We also used banana tree leaves for protection as we unloaded gear from the dugout outrigger canoe.

The smoke haze was from a fire burning under a lean-to made of woven grass and wood. They managed to keep it burning despite the heavy rainfall.

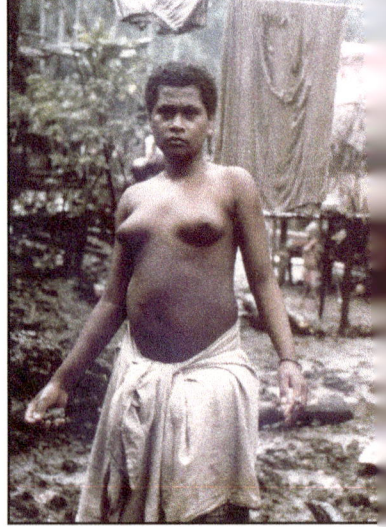

Washing in the creek, an unenviable task in the rain.

Young woman hanging her washing in the village.

Next page: Two girls ran off into the jungle when they saw I had a camera.

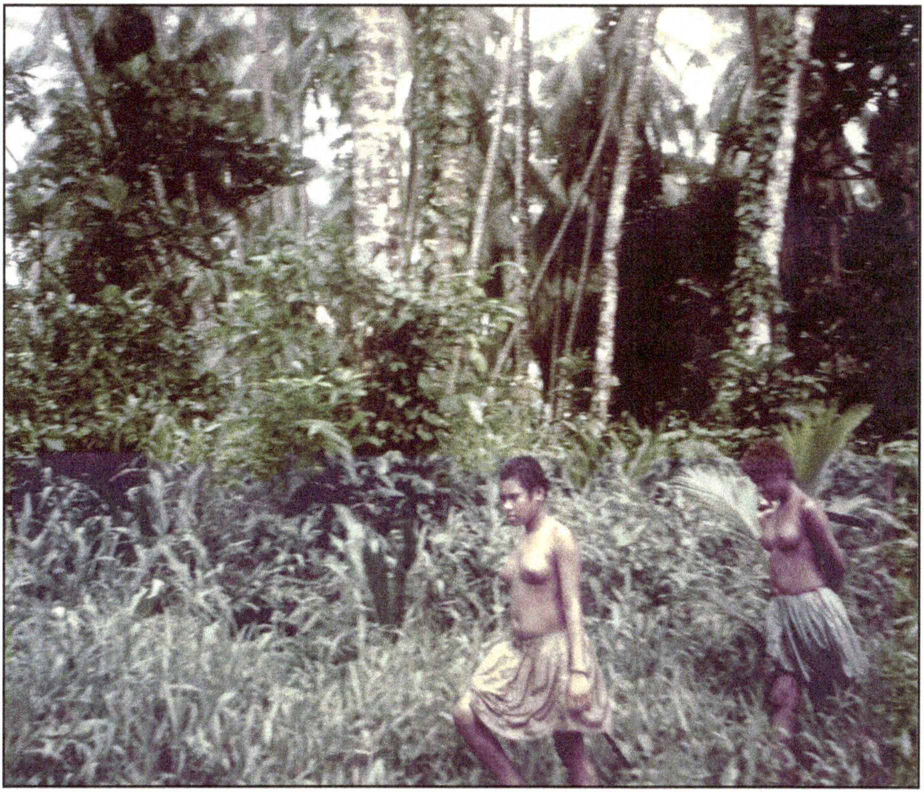

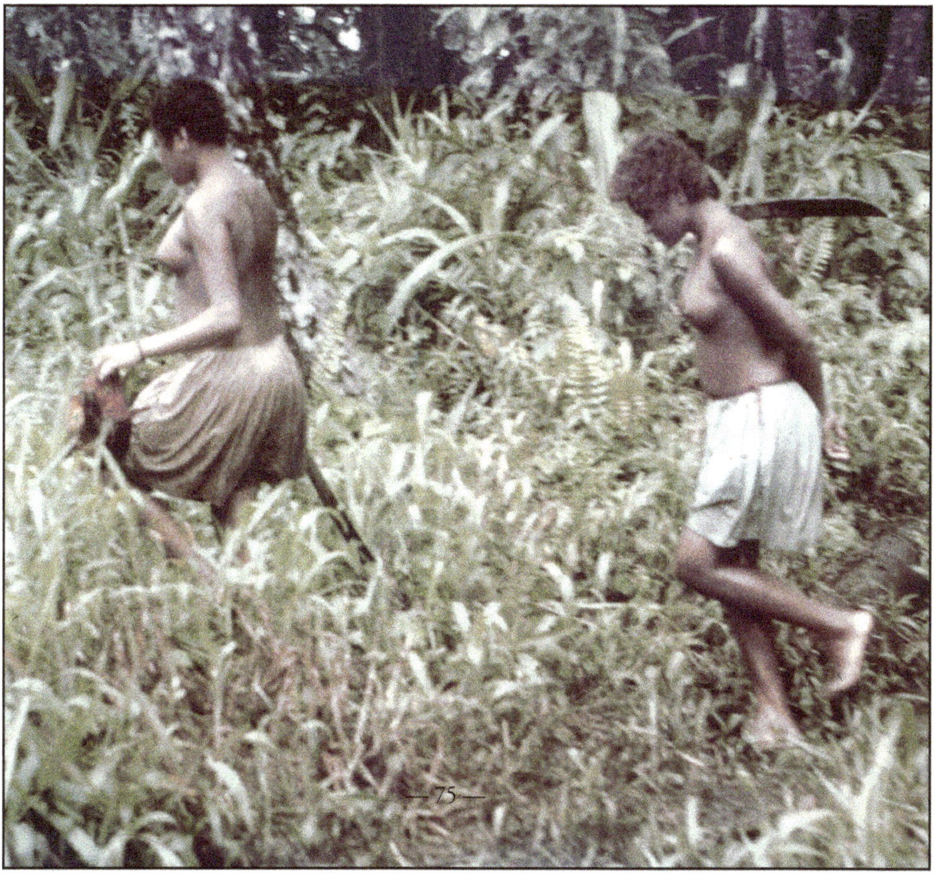

Mud and slush

No wonder the huts in the village we went to were on stilts.

The ground in the clearing was covered with running water. The rain couldn't soak into already sodden ground and simply ran off and drained into the waterway where we left the canoe. The large area around which the huts were located was normally hard packed earth.

With the unrelenting rain from the wet season it had turned into slippery slush and we had difficulty trying to walk without falling over. It was worse than being unable to skate on a skating rink. The only way to move was to slide one foot forward and then bring the other one up while trying to maintain balance. If any of us tried to move too fast our feet would slip out from underneath and we would crash down with a big splash.

I couldn't get over how easy the villagers, the few we saw, could move across this slippery muddy space. A couple of men actually ran across it from one hut to another on the other side of the open space. We could barely move without falling over.

The only good thing about the rain was it washed off the mud we accumulated from falling over.

There were a group of bare breasted women, none of whom wore grass skirts: that's more formal wear, something they put on to impress visitors, or while participating in a sing-sing. These women by the water's edge at the far side of the clearing in front of the village wore ragged cloth skirts. They had metal bowls and were attempting to wash clothes in the river, but had temporarily given up because of the rain. A couple of little kids were in the water beside their mothers. As soon as the women saw me approaching with my cameras they ran off into the jungle, disappearing beneath giant palm fronds and scruffy bushes.

Obviously, there were no crocodiles out here on these islands, or they would not have been so casual about washing clothes in the river or letting the kids splash about in the shallows.

Just over 100 kilometres of ocean separated The Trobriands from the New Guinea mainland and it was unlikely crocodiles would swim that far, although it's not unheard of.

We spent half an hour at this village before slithering slowly back through the mud to the outrigger canoe.

Once on board the guide pushed us away from the edge and we started back down the river to the bay and the hotel on the other side.

Fred, struggling to walk across the open space in the middle of the village. It rained continuously while we were there, but the rain doesn't show in the images except for where it hits the waterlogged ground.

— *Grab that Moment* —

— John Litchen —

A tropical ulcer

When I got back to the hotel, I noticed a small scratch on my shin just above the ankle joint. I don't remember scratching myself against anything, but it could have happened getting in or out of the dug-out canoe. There was a trickle of blood seeping out so it was very recent. I got some antiseptic powder from the hotel staff and put that on the wound. It wasn't much of a scratch, and it was something that normally would scab over and heal very quickly. But here in an atmosphere that was so humid it seemed as if we were breathing underwater, the scratch wouldn't dry out. It very quickly got worse and within a day had turned into an ulcer. It wasn't bleeding anymore but it looked like there was a hole in my shin with necrotic skin surrounding it. Perhaps an insect had bitten me in that swampy village.

I kept putting the antiseptic powder on it.

An unlucky tourist

The next day a planeload of tourists arrived on board an ancient DC3 aircraft. They were ferried to the hotel and tried to settle in, but it was obvious they were affected by the extreme humidity. The mainland was nowhere near as bad as out here on the island of Kiriwina. There was no movement of air, not a breeze off the ocean to make the air lighter. It weighed you down and it was hard to breathe. Any movement you made erupted in sweat all over. T shirts stuck fast and our shorts felt uncomfortable to wear. No wonder the native dress was a kind of grass skirt for the women or a bamboo or grass codpiece for the men. Kids ran around naked.

One of the tourists, an overweight middle-aged man seemed particularly bad. His breathing was labored. He looked pale and kept clutching his chest as if he was having a heart attack. He told the hotel manager that he wanted to return to Port Moresby but the plane that brought them had already taken off and gone back. He was stuck there until after the Sing-Sing on Saturday, when the plane would return on the Sunday to collect them.

He was desperate.

The hotel manager, knowing that the only plane on the island was our little four-seater Piper Comanche, approached Theo and asked if he would fly the man back, at least to Popondetta where there was a small hospital. There were no medical facilities on Kiriwina.

Theo was happy for an excuse to leave. He also found the humidity unbearable. But we couldn't all leave and take the sick tourist with us. There was only room for four passengers. One of us would have to stay in order for him to go.

"I'll stay," I said. I wanted to shoot some film of the sing-sing. It was not something I had ever seen before. I said that without thinking about how I would get back. I looked at the sick tourist, about to reconsider my impulsive decision.

"You can have my ticket." The man said becoming momentarily animated. He didn't want me to change my mind. "It's a return ticket on Sunday's flight."

"Okay, sounds good." Well, that was that. It had been decided.

Fred and Rommy were delighted to be leaving as well. There was nothing they could do here. Diving in the lagoon was impossible because the water was brown from the muddy flood waters that kept pouring into the bay. Nor were they interested in watching the sing-sing, especially if it continued to rain as it had been doing since we had arrived.

"That's it," Theo said. They would take the sick tourist back to Popondetta and then fly on to Port Moresby where they would wait for me to arrive on Sunday when the next commercial flight flew in and out.

The man gave me his ticket. He looked relieved even though he still had trouble breathing.

"We'll go and pack," Fred said.

"Right," Theo said. "As soon as you're ready we'll get the manager to take us to the airport."

And then they were gone.

A frightening flight
Fred's account…

They had no trouble returning to Popondetta where they dropped off the sick tourist who immediately went to the local hospital.

They took off, but before heading up the mountains behind Popondetta towards the pass everyone used Theo had to circle several times to gain height. In doing so he lost his view of where the pass was. It looked different from this side, especially once you were up in the air, and there were no other flights coming or going which would have indicated the exact position of the pass. All the three of them could see were layers of jungle covered mountain ridges rising endlessly towards the dark cloud layer that obscured the actual tops of the mountain peaks. There was no obvious pass between them.

Theo didn't want to acknowledge that he had no idea where the pass was, so he kept flying towards the higher mountains in the hope that the pass would become visible as they got closer. If it didn't become visible within another ten minutes he would turn around and fly back to Popondetta where they could wait until another plane with a pilot who knew the area would be returning to Port Moresby and they could follow that plane. It wouldn't matter if they had to wait all day, as long as they could follow someone who knew the route.

What Theo hadn't realized was that the winds blowing along the coast which were eventually funneled up into the gaps between the mountains had pushed the plane slightly south of the course they should take. He wasn't flying straight towards where The Gap should be, but diagonally south of the course he needed to take.

As they got closer to the last of the big ridges that gave way to the actual mountains Theo saw a wide gap between two large mountainous masses right ahead of them.

"There it is," he yelled over the top of the engine noise.

He flew straight over the ridge and entered the gap. The plane shuddered.

Sitting in the back Rommy and Fred looked out of the side windows at the layers of mist shrouded jungle flashing past.

"This doesn't look right," Fred told Rommy.

"It definitely doesn't look like the pass we flew through before," Rommy agreed.

But before they could tell Theo to turn around and go back, the plane dropped sickeningly and slipped sideways towards the jungle sided mountain rushing past.

Theo gripped the controls so hard his hands turned white, like the hands of a corpse. The plane shot back up and shook like a wild animal.

Theo wrestled with the controls, but the plane did what it wanted, jerking up, dropping down suddenly, again slipping sideways dangerously close to the side of the mountain before Theo could pull it back.

The sides of the mountains got closer and closer as the gap narrowed ominously. There was no room to turn around. Any attempt to do so would have them smashing into one side or other of the narrowing gap. They could only continue forwards.

"I've got to get higher," Theo yelled back to Fred and Rommy, both of whom remained deathly silent as they stared out at the sides of the mountains rushing past the tiny plane.

The trouble with going higher was that they were already at 12,000 feet and the height limit the plane could safely fly at was 13,000 feet. A mere few hundred feet above them were heavy clouds, formed by the rising warm sea air rushing up the gaps between mountains where it encountered the cold high-altitude air. If they flew into the clouds, they would be blind. They would never see the mountain side that they smashed into.

Buffeted as it was, the plane struggled to gain further altitude. Beneath them the jungle covered ridges crept closer and closer. Fred was sure that the plane's wheels were brushing the treetops. Theo looked like a wild man as he struggled with the controls, fighting furiously to keep it steady. Ahead, the cloud layer just touched the tops of the trees covering the floor of the ever-narrowing gap they were flying through.

"That's it, we're done for," was the only thing Fred thought as he looked ahead through the windscreen.

Then they were in the clouds, the very bottom of the descending clouds, almost blind. This part was not yet as heavy as the clouds higher up being more like a fog. A couple of indistinct misty trees whipped past one side of the plane as they flew dangerously close to the side of the mountain, but before any of them could react, the jungle covered ground beneath them instantly dropped away into a series of deep ridges.

They were through!

"Jesus! What a ride," Fred exclaimed.

"I never want to do that again," Rommy added.

Theo was absolutely silent. He dropped their height so they were well below the roiling clouds that obscured the mountain tops. Looking back there was no sign of the gap they had flown through; it was inside the lowering clouds.

It was in that moment they realized how lucky they had been.

Later, Fred told me that if I had been with them, the extra weight of one more person would have prevented the plane from gaining enough altitude to get through that unknown gap in the mountains.

Far in the distance a shimmer of light glistened on a wide expanse of sea.

Theo radioed Port Moresby control and told them we had come through a gap but there was no sign of Port Moresby.

Port Moresby informed them that they were about fifty miles south of where they should be.

After that Theo turned north and followed the coast and within a few minutes caught sight of Port Moresby and landed without further problems.

Postponed

It rained without a hint of stopping. The Sing-Sing was postponed. The ground was too slippery, slushy with mud the consistency of thick tomato sauce.

Now what? I thought when the DC3 arrived with a few people to see the postponed performance. They weren't going to do it before I had to use the return ticket. The plane would leave the next morning before the heavier rain clouds could build up. The passengers would be staying for several days until the mid-week flight came to take them back.

One of the passengers on that flight was a photographer, and he had a

16mm movie camera with him. I asked him if he would be so kind as to shoot a couple of rolls of film for me while doing his own filming of the ceremony. He was happy to do that and I gave him 2 rolls of Kodachrome film on which I had already written my return address so when it was processed the lab would post it to me back in Melbourne.

Frames from the 16mm movie sequence of the **Sing Sing**.

Everyone in the village participated including the children.

I left the next morning when the rain was not much more than a preliminary drizzle. The DC3 was noisy but fine until we came to the mainland and it flew over the tops of the mountains to Port Moresby. Coming from the extremely hot humid atmosphere on the island and flying for 45 minutes at a height where the air was absolutely freezing was unbearable. The plane wasn't insulated and I shivered uncontrollably all the way. I never felt so cold, but no one else seemed to mind.

It was such a relief to get back on the ground at Port Moresby where it was hot again.

Fred and Rommy, waiting for me beside SKL at Port Moresby.

Heading home

Theo, Fred and Rommy were waiting for me when I came into the terminal.

"You took long enough," Fred said.

That didn't merit a response.

"We're leaving right now," Theo said. "SKL is fueled up and waiting."

"Okay." What else could I say?

We left Port Moresby and flew straight to Daru where we stopped for a couple of hours to refuel and visit a crocodile farm run by someone called George Craig. He took us to a huge shed where stacks of souvenirs made by the locals were stored ready for shipment to tourist shops in Port Moresby. George Craig was a crocodile hunter and had captured several monster crocks that had killed and eaten eight villagers who lived along the Fly River.

"You want to see some big crocs?" he said when we met him at the airport This time there was a fair bit of activity with a number of flights coming in and heading off into the country along the Fly River.

"We're in," Rommy said.

At his shed there were four large corrugated iron windows that opened up and outwards. He propped them all up to reveal a huge scummy pond behind each window. Each pond was fenced off from the one next to it.

I could see George was enjoying himself when he asked, "can you see anything?"

All we could see was algae covered water in a pond about 50 metres long by10 metres wide. There were reeds growing along the edges of each pond and a few patches of water lilies. The water was too dark to see whatever might be underneath it.

"These bastards are man-eaters. I was sent to catch them because a couple of villages had recently lost several people. The villagers rely on fishing in the river and the big crocks just come up and snatch them out their canoes."

I could see Fred and Rommy looking a bit skeptical.

"They're very fast," George said. "You won't believe how fast they are."

I believed him. I had seen crocodiles running across the mud flats and sliding into the water when I was in Humpty Doo just south of Darwin a few years back. But they were juveniles and not much more than a couple of metres long.

"When I tap on the side of the wall here, they'll come up out of the water because that's what I do when I feed them."

"Are you going to feed them now?" I asked.

"No. It's not the right time. Are you ready?"

The three of us leaned forward with our hands resting on the window sill.

George banged a short stick against the side of the shed. Three times he hit the wall... bang, bang, bang. And on the last bang the water in front of us exploded and a monstrous head surged towards us. The crocodile had its mouth open and a foul stench enveloped us. It made a horrible deep throated hiss. We involuntarily leaped backwards, absolutely stunned at the speed with which this monster had launched itself out of the water. In that instant it was only too easy to believe that such a monster could suddenly rear up out of the water too fast for anyone to react, and snatch a person right out of a canoe.

George laughed uproariously.

"I think I shit myself," Rommy said, and George laughed even louder.

The monster crocodile slid slowly back down into the pond and all we could see were its eyes and the tip of its nose just above the water surface. Its eyes were staring at us.

"Fuck that was fast," Fred said.

"Yes," was all George said.

"How big is it," I asked.

"This one is 18 feet long and weighs over a ton. I call him Oscar. The other two are 16 footers. I call them Annaga and Gomic, and they each weigh a ton."

Looking through the window across to the other two ponds I could see the other big crocodile heads both out of the water and looking at us. They too were waiting to be fed.

"What are you going to do with them?" Fred asked.

"That's a good question. There's not enough tourists up here to make keeping them a paying proposition. My plan is to move them to Australia when PNG becomes independent. I've got a crocodile farm being set up on Green Island not far from Cairns. That's where we'll go."

And sure enough, that's what happened. We saw in an Australian weekly magazine a couple of years later a photo of three monster crocodiles roped up on wooden pallets being lifted off the deck of a ship by a crane. George is in the picture supervising the unloading of the crocodiles. They were to join 30 other smaller crocodiles that formed part of the farm, a tourist attraction called Marineland Melanesia.

George took us back to the airport and we quickly took off as soon as Theo had filed his flight plan, flying South towards the tip of Cape York.

We could feel the difference in the air as we flew over the Australian mainland. South of the convergence zone we spotted a dirt airstrip and came down for a landing. We were all busting for a leak and were happy to piss on the ground beside the plane.

There were no buildings anywhere nearby, no fences either. It was just a bush strip in the middle of nowhere. Before getting back into the plane I noticed the ulcer on my shin was drying up. It was no longer weeping. It must have been because the air was dryer. There was none of that oppressive humidity that had enveloped low-lying islands like The Trobriands on one side of New Guinea and Daru in the Torres Straits on the other side.

We were intending to fly directly south more or less along the same route we had taken when we flew to New Guinea.

Getting back into the plane and about to take off, Theo received a radio call to inform us that we had to land at Cairns for Customs clearance, that we were not to land anywhere else until that had been done.

Theo acknowledged the call. "We expect to be there in about one hour," he told them.

We didn't tell them we had already landed.

Wash off the mud!

The moment we landed at Cairns two uniformed customs officials came up to us and spread out a damp mat on the ground beside the door of the plane.

"You have to step on that when you get out, and before you walk anywhere else," we were told.

Before we were allowed to get out of the plane one of the men sprayed the wheels with something that smelled like insecticide.

"Have you brought anything back?" we were asked as soon as we were allowed off the damp mats.

"A couple of souvenirs," I said.

"What souvenirs?"

"A native drum, a couple of teak carvings."

"We'll have to look at those," they told us.

We unloaded our meagre luggage from the compartment beneath the plane and the only things they were interested in were the carvings I had bought. One in particular immediately grabbed their attention.

"You can't bring that in," I was told.

It was a small carving of a woman wearing a grass skirt, a beautiful piece from the Sepik River area, quite different from the few carvings I got on the Trobriand Islands. It had native hair glued on top, but what bothered them was that it was painted with grey mud to give it character.

"Come on, It's only a statue."

Theo and Fred were busy putting our luggage back into the compartment.

"It's got mud on it."

"What difference does that make?"

"There could be bugs in it. Who knows what's in the mud in New Guinea? It will have to be washed off."

"That'll ruin it as a piece of art."

"It's either that, or we confiscate and destroy it." He looked defiantly at me.

"Okay," I said after a moment. "Wash it off and let's see how it looks."

They took it away and I followed them to a building where I was told to wait, while Theo, Fred and Rommy waited by the plane.

After five minutes one of the officials came back with the statue and handed it to me. I was surprised that they hadn't removed the grass skirt or the native hair glued to the top of the head. It didn't look too bad without the mud, so gratefully I took it back.

"Have a good flight South," he told me and went back inside.

"What a fucking joke," Fred said when I returned to the plane.

We immediately took off and headed south and inland to Roma where we planned to stay the night before continuing on to Melbourne.

Even with the mud washed off, it is still a good looking work of art.

Finschhafen to Madang
a cruise along the coast

An invitation to return

Colin Boreham, who was the local police chief and the first person we had met on arriving at Finschhafen, and who had kindly allowed us to stay with him and his wife, had invited me to come back at any time.

Since I wanted to see more of the place, I decided that as soon as it was practicable and I would return to Finschhafen.

I was also interested in collecting more pieces of art. The larger carvings I had seen were fantastic, but I couldn't get any because our little twin-engine *Piper Comanche* (SKL) was too small to carry anything heavy. It barely had room for our luggage let alone anything else. This time my intention would be to buy a few pieces from a reputable dealer and have them shipped back to Melbourne by sea freight.

I clearly remember Colin telling us about the trading boats that travelled along the coast from village to village. They also carried passengers.

"You should travel up to Madang that way," he told me. "You'll get to see how the locals live, and that is something a tourist never sees."

I took him at his word and wrote a brief letter after I got back to let him know I would be coming up during the dry season.

A bit over six months later (October 1971), and barely a month after I had met Monica, the beautiful woman who would change my life, I was once again on a plane flying to New Guinea, this time a commercial flight.

No roads to Finschhafen

There are no roads to Finschhafen from anywhere. If there were a road it would be cut in a thousand places by uncountable streams and rivers cascading down the mountains to the Solomon sea. (Especially during the Wet Season) The only way to get to Finschhafen is by light aircraft flying in from Lae, the nearest major town, or by sea in one of the trading boats that sail these along these tropical coral-reef studded coasts.

A tropical garden

From the air, Finschhafen seems a tropical garden.

Massive old trees festooned with brilliant red flowers, orchids, vines and other hanging plants, partly obscure the buildings and residences that make up the town. The rich scent from the flowers mingles with the fresh smell of salty sea air. The roads in the town are made from crushed coral, which glares brilliantly in the sun contrasting intensely against the deep green of tall wild grass and the jungle beyond. Coconut palms line the roads which lead nowhere once they reach the edge of town. Beyond there is only jungle that ascends up the sides of mountains which eventually disappear inside layers of clouds.

Several small islands form an archipelago a few hundred metres off the coast beyond the harbour at Finschhafen. They protect the bay from bigger waves generated in the deeper water beyond the island chain, allowing a safe passage from the sea to the harbour for a variety of boats and larger sea-craft that regularly travel along this coast.

A strategic location

Situated at the very tip of the Huon Peninsula, Finschhafen was strategically important during the Second World War. It was a bivouac and staging area through which some three million allied troops passed. More than twenty cinemas operated to entertain the troops. There were gigantic storehouses and massive tent-cities, officer's quarters, and broad double-lane highways made from crushed coral to facilitate movement of troops and equipment to and from the harbour.

Today, rotting hulks in the harbour testify to deliberate abandonment or Japanese bombardment. Massive battles were fought in the nearby mountains and thousands of Australians, Americans and Japanese lost their lives not far from Finschhafen. Today, virtually nothing remains other than what can be found salvaged for building materials.

The jungle has reclaimed everything else.

A number of barges can be found along the channel inside the island archipelago. These were deliberately sunk by the departing Americans so they could not be used by the Japanese. It was these barges we dived on during our earlier trip here.

The small plane I used to get me to Finschhafen... landing at Fanschhafen.

Early flights

Most flying in Papua New Guinea is done early because extremely unstable weather conditions develop early in the afternoon and progressively get worse as the day proceeds. There are always storms and heavy rainfall in the mountainous regions, and this country is almost all mountains, massive chains of them. Commercial flights fly pressurized planes over the tops of the clouds that obscure the peaks, but since ninety percent of the air traffic is to small towns and villages in and around the mountains, light aircraft are used and these do not have the capacity to fly at great heights, nor are they pressurized. They fly in between the mountains, along narrow passes and land and take off in the most dangerous places imaginable. The pilots need to be familiar with the terrain, and they need to see where they are going.

Every morning the warm tropical air is heated by the sun and rises. It hits the cold mountain air and forms dangerous storm clouds. By noon, most small towns and villages are cut off, and no one would dare fly a small light aircraft where they can't see the terrain they have to fly over.

It was very early, a bit after 7 am, when I landed in the small plane from Lae. Only Inspector Colin Boreham was waiting for me. There must have been ground staff somewhere; it is an airport, but the place looked deserted. There were a couple of planes chocked and tied near the terminal building. The plane I had landed in was already turning and taxiing to the end of the runway in preparation to fly back along the coast to Lae.

Colin was dressed immaculately in his police uniform standing beside his polished and shining police Range Rover. This I had not seen before since we had been there on a weekend and he was off duty.

"You're just in time," he said after we had greeted each other and shook hands, "for the weekly inspection. It's the only chance you will have to take photos of them all together."

As we drove from the airport, which like most small airports in Australia is around 10 kilometres out of town, Colin told me it was payday for the troops, and he always carries out an inspection before paying them, to make sure everything is of the highest standard.

"It keeps them on their toes," he said. "If I see something isn't good enough, then those responsible find themselves with extra duties and less time off."

We pulled up in front of his place and I could see the troops quickly lining up in front of the police station which was only a couple of hundred metres from his house.

The inspection

Walking the couple of hundred metres from his house to the police station where the unit was now lined up and standing at attention, Colin said, "This is the only way I can get them to keep their gear in order. In this climate it's too easy for things to rot or rust. If they want the respect of the locals as well as the European expatriates, they've got to look good. They have to take care of themselves as well as their gear. They used to go barefoot you know."

He smiled as he remembered how they had been when he first came here.

We stopped at the front entrance to the police station. I watched the men

— Grab that Moment —

standing in two rows shuffling slightly as they adjusted the distance between each other.

"You would have laughed your head off. They didn't know which foot to put the boots on. Even after three weeks some would still turn up with terribly pained expressions on their faces because their boots were on the wrong feet."

They now stood perfectly still, immaculate.

"Look at them now!" There was sincere pride in Colin's voice.

The toes of their boots gleamed as did the leggings. If you got down close enough you would probably see your face reflected in them. Their navy shorts and light blue shirts were pressed perfectly, and they all wore their berets at precisely the same angle. They held rifles by their side and attached to their belts were short bayonets. I had never seen policemen carrying bayonets before, so perhaps these were more a para-military force than a police force.

Colin stepped forward one pace, and they visibly stiffened. He snapped a command and in perfect unison the men placed their rifles in front of them where they could hold it with their knees while extracting the bayonet from its scabbard. The bayonet was clipped onto the rifle, which was immediately returned to its place beside them. Standing at attention the back of the bayonet rested against each policeman's right shoulder. Colin then walked along and inspected each person. Once again standing in front of them he barked an order and the rifles were raised and again placed in front when they were held by the knees while each person unclipped the bayonet and returned it to its scabbard. The rifles were then held up at an angle in front of their chests while Colin again walked along each row to carefully inspect the condition of the rifles. Having done that, he stepped back and ordered the men to be at ease.

The inspection was over. They could now collect their wages, and those not on duty were free to go.

Colin speaking with one of his off-duty officers after the inspection.

Meeting village children

" I've got to go to a village about 10 miles down the coast to sort out a small problem. Do you want to come along?" Colin said as soon as the inspection was over.

"I wouldn't miss it."

I grabbed my camera and joined Colin in his Range Rover and off we went. We parked in the middle of the village and while I waited in the car quite a few kids stood around and watched us. Eventually, curiosity got the better of them and they came closer to the vehicle which gave me the chance to shoot some close-up images of them. Colin was gone about an hour before he came back.

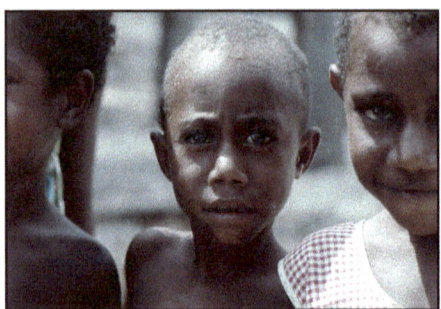
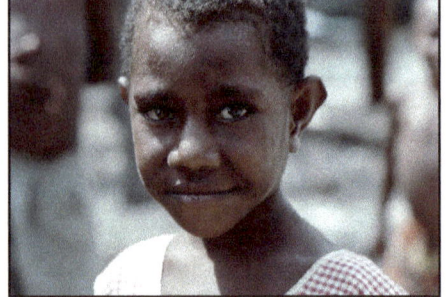

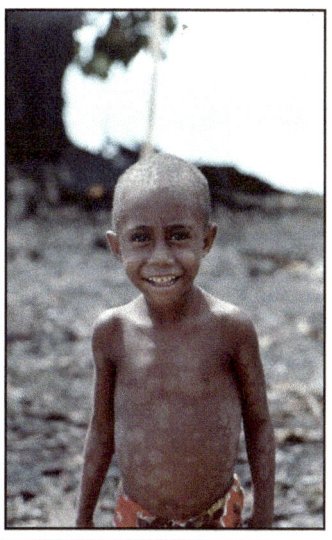

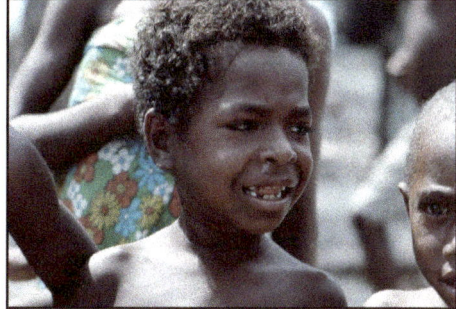

"I want to show you something else," Colin said when he came back.

I followed him to a wooden bridge that crossed a creek and we walked over to the other side. Further along we came to an old path made with crushed coral which we walked along for a couple of hundred metres.

A Stone memorial

Alongside the track, highlighted against the dense green jungle was a memorial to honour Japanese soldiers killed in the battles that took place in this part of New Guinea.

It was a simple square stone block with rounded ends that stand a bit less than a metre high with Japanese Kanji carved into the face of it, highlighted in black.

Behind it was a white wooden post also with black Kanji etched into it. In front, piled loosely against it were numerous small wooden plaques, each one with the name of a Japanese soldier who had been killed during the war in this part of the country.

"When the people who set this up here first came, they were apprehensive, really nervous about what kind of reception they would get. They thought we would be hostile towards them because of what had happened here during the War." Colin explained as we stood by the monument.

"Some of the fiercest fighting took place on the Huon Peninsula, especially around Finschhafen as the Allies were forced to abandon the town. But once they came into the club and met everyone they were stunned at the warmth of their reception. Not only that, everyone was interested in helping them set up the memorial; as well as searching for those lost and never recovered so their bones could be returned to Japan. That's really something isn't it?"

I stared at the lonely memorial. The pole and the many plaques looked brand new.

"How long has it been here?"

"For years. The village we were just in has been entrusted to look after the memorial. They always repaint the Kanji and replace the wooden name tags whenever they start to look faded or the wood begins to age. I think they've done a great job."

It was obviously more than just a shrine. It was a superb example of how the past can be forgiven, and of the respect that many Japanese and their former enemies now have for each other. It was also a reminder of the uselessness of War, and of the young lives that never needed to be lost but unfortunately were.

Seeing that small memorial standing bright and clean against the dark backdrop of the jungle made me feel quite emotional, and I was relieved when Colin said it was time to return, and we got back into his Land Rover and returned to the police station.

The Saturday Boung

I remembered the boung from my visit here with Fred and Rommy six months earlier. It was a thriving place full of gossip and happy people trading goods with each other. I wouldn't miss it for anything. I'm glad Colin reminded me it was on. It only happens once a week, on Saturday mornings from around seven until nine. I was there with my camera before hardly anyone had arrived.

Soon, people were coming from all directions, from coastal villages as well as those in the nearby mountains. Women had their bilums (a string bag woven by hand from hemp string knotted together in the way a fish net is made.) packed with whatever they wanted to sell. They often had these woven mesh bags hanging down their backs with the strap across their forehead or over the front part of their head. Others had small baskets balanced on a shoulder which they held in place with one hand. Unlike the Trobriand Islands where I saw women balancing shallow baskets on their heads, no one here seemed to do that. Using a bilum with the strap held across the forehead was the most popular and efficient way of carrying stuff.

Stalls were quickly set up and goods displayed: fish wrapped in banana leaves, breadfruit, cucumbers, peanuts, betel nuts, coconuts, plantains, tropical fruit — some of which I had not seen before and had no idea what they tasted like, large bags of what looked like kapok, sweet potatoes and yams, and stacks of other stuff.

The townsfolk came ready to buy, to trade, and to gossip, for markets are always a hive of information.

I tried to remain unobtrusive, and this wasn't hard because other Australian expatriates living in Finschhafen also turned up to buy fresh produce. Nobody took any notice of me as I happily wandered about.

— Grab that Moment —

After the market was over and people had dispersed I got to talking with one of Colin's policemen and asked how coconuts were collected.

"I'll show you," he said, and promptly took off his shirt.

He grabbed a woven coconut fibre rope and wrapping this around his ankles he proceeded to basically crawl up the trunk of big coconut palm tree.

He made it look easy. Simply wrap your arms around the trunk and hold tight, then move both feet up and use the rope to hold the feet in position.

Then reach up and wrap your arms around again. Move your feet up, move your arms up. Very quickly he got to the top. I have no idea how the rope didn't cut into his feet around his ankles. That fibre was incredibly course. But when he came down there was not a mark on his legs.

Once he reached the top he hung onto one of the fronds where it was thick and solid at the base, and using a machete, he chopped off several coconuts which he let fall to the ground. Slithering down after was much easier and quicker than climbing up.

Exploding old bombs

After the climbing demonstration I ran into a chap I had met the night before at the Club. All European residents are members of the Finschhafen Club, and any visitors, like myself, are automatically signed in as temporary members, thus obtaining the same 'drinking privileges' as regular members. Sergeant Tas Holloway was also a visitor, but unlike me, he was here on government business. He was leading a team of Army demolition experts and it was his job to see to the removal, defusing and destruction of old unexploded bombs, mortar shells, live bullets, and any other dangerous explosive material left over from The War.

"We're dumping a load today," he told me. "Do you want to come along?"

"Oh yeah," I agreed instantly.

"Follow me then."

His Land Rover was parked nearby, and moments later we were heading towards the town's wharf.

"The jungle here is full of wartime shit," he said. "Bombs dropped that didn't explode, ordnance like mortars and their ammunition abandoned and left to rot. There are thousands of unfired bullets, some still packed in boxes, rusting or rotting away and highly dangerous if touched. If anyone discovers something like that, they are not supposed to touch it, but have to report it to the local police or the District Commissioner's Office. The site is then marked and a report sent to a larger centre like Lae. When enough reports from a particular area are received, an expert is sent out to destroy them. And in this case, it's me. I've been here several days collecting the material and the team has been getting ready to dispose of it."

"And do they report it?"

"Not as often as they should. There are people here who make a living from salvaging the brass and copper from abandoned ammunition. They don't always report what they find and sometimes there are accidents and fingers or hands get blown off when they try to remove the shell casings."

About a mile out of town we pulled up beside a concrete wharf that extended a fair distance into the sea. Stacked at the beginning of the wharf were thirty or forty rusted mortar shells. Many were stuck together with rust or if they had been underwater, with coral growths. They were all too dangerous to defuse or even to try and separate them before attempting to defuse them. Beside the mortar shells were several hand grenades and a few larger bombs.

An ugly steel boat about forty feet long was moored next to the wharf. The name painted on the side by the bow was Boroko.

"It's far too dangerous to try and explode them," Tas said, "so we'll load this on board and dump it at sea where it's too deep for the locals to dive and salvage it."

I remembered a lot of brass and copper had been salvaged from the weapons and ammunition that had been on the barges sunk in the channel between Finschhafen and the row of islands that protected the harbour from the deeper water beyond. Some locals made a good living from salvaging old ammunition.

Tas Holoway carefully taking hold of an old mortar round to load onto his boat.
Setting a fuse into another larger bomb in order to explode it safeely away once out to sea.

More mortar shells being passed up to be loaded carefully on the deck of the boat (the Boroko). It took a fair while to load all the stuff that had been collected over several months.

Tamai island where the villagers wanted Tas to bring out an unexploded bomb they had found deep in the jungle.
The team climbing up to where the bomb had been found.
One of Colin's policemen watching as the team goes deeper into the underbrush in search of the unexploded bomb.

"We don't want any more locals getting their hands or feet blown off."

Once the shells, hand grenades and bombs had been carefully loaded onto the aft deck of the Boroko, we set off. It must have been a flat-bottomed boat like a barge because it rolled alarmingly even in a slight swell. Water washed over the back, splashing against the stack of mortar shells. It was worse once we got out of the channel and into the deeper water half way to a nearby island.

"It's about a thousand feet deep here," Tas told me.

The water was a deep indigo colour. Looking over the side I saw the occasional flash of light as the sun sparkled against the silvery side of a fast swimming deep water fish. There was no sign of coral reefs here. We had left them well behind us.

Tas and the few locals on board began throwing the dangerous cargo over the side.

"Leave that one," Tas told them men.

It was an unexploded hundred-pound bomb. It didn't look as bad as some of the other stuff.

To me he said, "The Tami islanders have requested I use a bomb like this to widen the entrance through the reef to the island, so we'll do that for them. But before that, we have to check a bomb found near the village. That we'll have to dispose of as well."

Half an hour later we were anchored inside an island fringing reef, went ashore and followed the well-worn path to the village where several men and some children were waiting for us. They led us along an almost invisible path through dense jungle to where a half-buried monster of a bomb sat in a bed of clay.

"Wow, that's a big one," Tas said when he saw it.

He was extremely careful as he approached it.

"You blokes better stay well back," he advised us.

No one made a sound as Tas carefully examined the visible part of the bomb. He took quite a while, but when he came back, he was all smiles.

"It's a dud," he said. "An empty casing, that's all."

But of course, no one could have known that until it had been opened up and examined.

On board the Boroko again, Sergeant Holloway set a charge in the unexploded bomb he had kept on the aft deck. It was an old-fashioned charge with a waterproof fuse. He was extremely careful about measuring the length of the fuse, and making sure the charge he set inside the casing was properly waterproof.

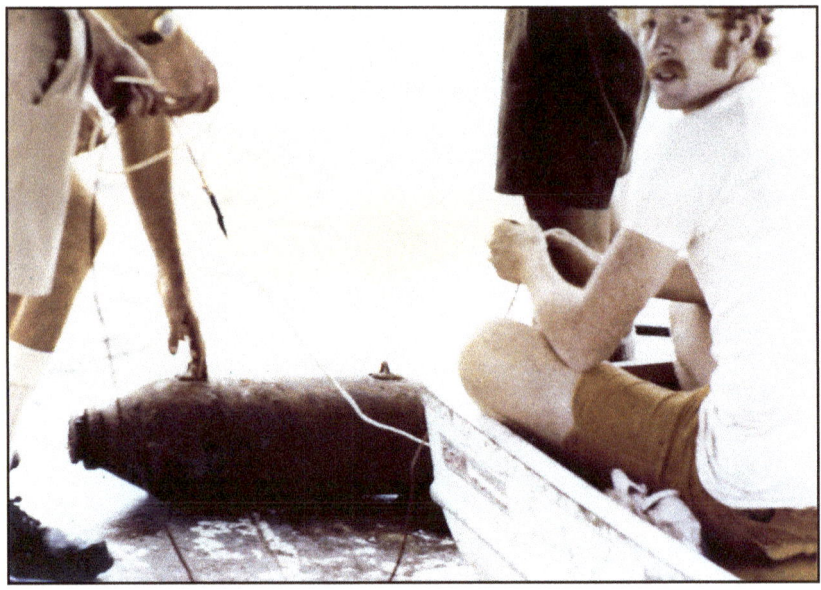

Tas and his team setting the fuse in the unexploded bomb prior to rolling it over the side to blow up the bommie blocking the entrance to the lagoon.

He got the skipper to line the Boroko up with the bommie partially blocking the entrance through the reef. "Can you pass by as close as a metre?" he asked.

"I can probably get a bit closer if you want."

"As close as possible. We'll roll the bomb off the deck into the water and hope it falls on top of the bommie."

The Boroko moved forward. Tas and one of his local helpers stood beside the bomb. As soon as they came parallel to the bommie Tas lit the fuse and two seconds later they rolled the bomb over the side.

"Go," he yelled to the skipper.

The Boroko surged ahead. Waves from its wake splashed against the bommie.

"We've got three minutes, and a few seconds," he said. "Go as fast as you can," he yelled pointlessly. The skipper was already going as fast as the boat would allow.

The Boroko rolled heavily as we continued away from the island. It seemed to smash into every wave rather than ride over the tops.

Three minutes and four seconds later there was a dull CRUMP and the water at the reef entrance surged upwards. A huge spume shot high into the air. The shock wave in the water hit us and we rolled wildly for a few moments.

It was done. Broken pieces of coral cascaded down in a two hundred metre circle. Once that had stopped the skipper turned around and we headed back towards the entrance to see how much wider it was. Dead and stunned fish floated on top of dirty coloured water. And at the site of the explosion millions of bubbles obscured any view of what lay underneath.

Several native canoes appeared as if by magic, filled with young men who scooped up the dead and dying fish. The boys on the Boroko scooped up a few as well before we headed back to the Finschhafen harbour.

The next day Sergeant Holloway and his team moved on, and the Boroko left to return to Lae.

That same morning I also accompanied Colin who was taking his wife Fran to the airport. She was flying off to Lae and on to Port Moresby where she would visit for a few days. I had no idea why she was going and didn't ask. I just went along to take a photo and to say goodbye, because when she came back I would be on the Simbang heading to Madang.

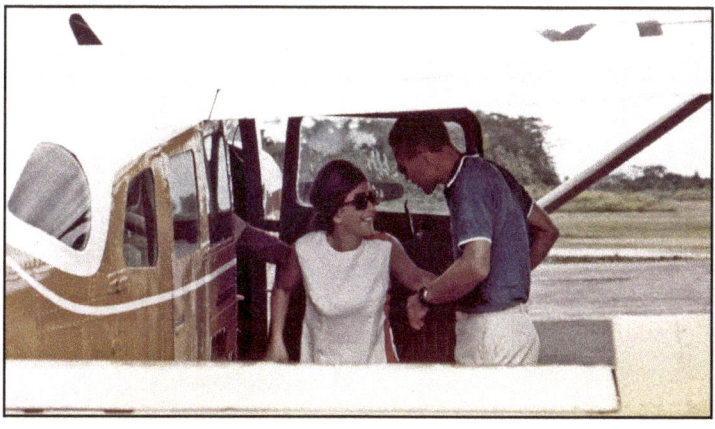

The Simbang ready to load goods and passengers.

A group of young women (Meris) waiting to board the Simbang.

The Simbang

I was due to board this coastal trading boat the next morning. Colin woke me before sunrise and we had a lovely breakfast before he drove me to the harbour. The sun was barely above the horizon and deep shadows fell across the road down to the wharf. I didn't expect to see many people this early. In fact, I didn't think the Simbang would arrive until later in the morning but it had come in overnight, and when we got there, people were unloading cargo from the boat's hold. There were hundreds of people all over the place. We left the Police vehicle parked well away and walked down to the wharf.

Stacked on the wharf were cartons of beer for the club, crates of tinned food for the general store, and fresh fruit and vegetables brought in from the market at Lae, I watched bundles of copper pipes and sheets of corrugated iron being unloaded.

A battered Land Rover with a tray back was sitting on the wharf beside the boat and a crane was in the process of lowering a car engine onto the back of the tray. Several people called out directions to the crane driver but he ignored them. The moment the engine was sitting on the tray a couple of men jumped up and released the crane, then tied down the engine so it wouldn't move about when the Land Rover drove off. The driver waved to Colin before jumping into the cabin to start the engine. The Land Rover moved slowly along the wharf, scattering people aside, then once it was clear he gunned the motor and drove off along the road back into town.

Then a whole car was lifted up, swung out until it was over the wharf. It swayed from side to side. The crane made grinding wheezing sounds as the weight of the car strained the cables holding it almost to the point of breaking. The car's owner, a young doctor from Sri Lanka who had only recently arrived, almost suffered an attack of apoplexy when he saw how quickly his car was lowered, almost dropped, onto the wharf. He rushed forward to examine it, but there had been no damage done, and as soon as it was uncoupled, he drove it off the wharf and disappeared.

"It won't stay new for long," Colin said. "He's the worst driver you've ever seen."

Passengers patiently waiting for their turn to board the Simbang.

We walked through groups of Meris (women) sitting with their children around camp fires that had been used for cooking breakfast. Others stood patiently along the wharf, women with bilums (string bags) filled to capacity, men smoking and chatting amongst themselves as they waited to board the Simbang. Children played by the water's edge or climbed exuberantly over crates stacked on the wharf. Other men were passing on board hessian bags filled with copra (dried coconut). A crewman from the Simbang was selling

— John Litchen —

Top previous page: Copra ready to be loaded for shipment to Madang. People patiently waiting pushed up tight against the side of the Simbang. Above: Men with drums waiting their turn to board. Perhaps they were off to a Sing Sing somewhere up the coast or inland from Madang.

tickets to people on the wharf. These would be deck passengers. As soon as the copra from Finschhafen was loaded on board a cover would be placed over the hold and the deck passengers would be allowed to board.

Colin and I walked through this melee to the side of the boat, which up close was much bigger than I expected. She was about 90 feet long with a beam of 22 feet and was capable of carrying 100 tonnes of cargo. It delivered goods and carried passengers along the coast from Lae to Madang, stopping at the larger but still isolated villages. There are many boats like this trading in the waters around Papua New Guinea, some of them quite disreputable, but others such as the Simbang are clean, very regular as far as trading is concerned, and excellently captained.

On board, Colin introduced me to the Captain, a Norwegian who spoke perfect English as well as fluent Pidgin, the local version of English. He informed me that he had plenty of room. There were four cabins for European passengers, and only one of them was occupied by two ladies from the Lutheran Mission in Madang. I could have a whole cabin to myself. Meals would be supplied but would cost a total of four dollars while the trip itself was to cost me eight dollars. How cheap is that?

Colin left then and I stood on the bridge with the Captain and we watched as the hold was covered over. Once the hatch was secured a large canvas sheet was dragged across and lashed tight. The winch boom swung

It seems the women were allowed to get up front of the crowd and they were the first to scramble aboard so they could find somewhere to sit on the deck.

across and lowered to form a beam along the centreline of the boat. A large awning was stretched across this and tied to the railing along each side of the boat to shade the whole deck. Colin, standing in front of the passengers waiting to board, waved to me, giving me a thumbs up, then he turned and headed back to where he'd parked his Land Rover.

The passengers were then allowed to board.

There was a mad scramble as all the waiting passengers tried to get on at the same time. Babies cried, dogs barked, women yelled, their voices seeming to harmonize antiphonally, while the men shouted at each other. They pushed, shoved, and quarreled. Everyone wanted to get a good spot where they could sit with their luggage. Those that couldn't find a spot immediately were left standing. Eventually everyone would find somewhere to sit on the deck once we were under way.

The Captain yelled orders to the crew, side ropes were released, aft lines were cast off and the Simbang drifted slightly away from the wharf.

Finally, all the deck passengers were seated and were excitedly waving to those left behind on the wharf.

Under way

The cacophony died down as the passengers realized we were under way. The Simbang drifted away from the wharf and turned slowly.

The deck vibrated as the engines revved up. Surprisingly enough, the engines were very quiet. It was only because the deck vibrated underfoot that I knew we had started to move.

The Simbang languidly moved along the channel between the mainland and the row of small islands that protected the shore from the bigger waves in the Solomon Sea. The captain was careful to stay in the middle of the narrow channel to avoid the many rusting hulks of barges sunk during the Second World War.

We very quickly passed the spot where Fred, Rommy and I had dived on a couple of these sunken barges during our previous visit six months earlier. Once we'd passed the last of the little barrier islands and we were in deeper water about a half nautical mile offshore, the captain increased our speed to roughly six or seven knots. The Simbang rolled gently in the larger swells as it traveled parallel to the coast.

I settled into a canvas chair on the deck outside the cabins behind the bridge and watched the jungle covered coastline drifting past. Our first call, Sialum, was five hours away. Most of the passengers under the canvas awning on the deck were relatively quiet once the excitement of leaving was behind us. A few of them sat on the bow, but the rest stayed under the awning to avoid getting sun burnt.

One of the crew standing outside the wheelhouse studying the coastline.

A chat with the captain

"Mind if I join you?"

The captain dragged a deck chair closer and sat down.

"You don't have to be on the bridge?"

"I leave it to the boys now. They've worked hard over the years and can run the Simbang as well as I ever could. My first officer handles all the navigation as well as the business side of running the Simbang, and he does it well, too."

"That gives you some time to relax then."

"I'm basically retired now. I just oversee them to make sure it all goes well. They do all the work. In fact, the Simbang goes to them in another year's time, after which I will step down as captain."

"How do you think they'll compete against other trading boats?"

"There's no competition. There are other boats trading up along this coast, but many of them are unreliable. When I was asked to captain the Simbang I made a point of keeping to a regular timetable. Once the people of the villages, and settlements along the coast between Lae and Madang knew the Simbang would always call into their village at set times they were able to go ahead and develop the copra industry. Without the certainty of getting their product to market, they hadn't bothered to do much, but with the regularity of the Simbang they could plan their harvest accordingly. They also travel a lot more between villages and towns along the coast as well as to Madang and back, something they rarely did before. There is a cooperative in Madang which buys their copra and markets it to international buyers. Everyone benefits."

"What will you do when you retire?"

"I think I will go back to Norway, for a little while anyway. I do miss the place, but I've grown used to climate here in New Guinea, so I don't think I will be able to stand the cold of a European winter anymore."

One thing the captain told me was that he would not permit was the consumption of alcohol on board the Simbang. He was adamant about this.

"It has brought the ruination of life and culture to many tribal groups. It should never have been introduced to Papua and New Guinea."

Unfortunately, it was something no one could have prevented.

The canvas awning covering the deck from the wheelhouse to the bow.

Sialum

Sialum is a small coastal village facing an island not far offshore. Stretching between the island and the shoreline are coral reefs that sit just below the surface to form a shallow lagoon. There is only one entrance into the lagoon with a channel that is dotted with clumps of brain coral making the passage through the reef and the lagoon a zig-zag course, which is especially dangerous at low tide. I couldn't imagine the captain getting the 90 foot Simbang into the lagoon and moored at the wharf, especially when I was told by one of the crew that most boats over 40 feet in length wouldn't even try, but the captain guided the Simbang in through the entrance and along the channel with such casual ease, it almost appeared as if he was doing nothing. My estimation of his skill went up considerably.

There were stacked bags of copra, too many to count, piled up high on the short pier.

The Simbang bumped gently against the pier, cushioned by a series of old rubber tyres. The moment the ropes were tied to secure her, the passengers surged over the deck and raced along the pier to mingle with the many people standing under the shade of coconut trees a way back from the pier.

The whole village must have been there. The Simbang calls once a fortnight and its arrival always causes excitement. Everyone comes down to hear the gossip from the passengers who all must go ashore so the hold can be opened up to unload cargo and supplies, after which the stacked bags of copra would be loaded.

The passengers joined the villagers under the coconut palms while kids ran and played along the foreshore. Fires were lit and food cooked. Old men and women sat chewing betel nut while watching the goings on. The crew heaved and sweated as they removed the canvas awning, then the canvas cover sheet, undid the bolts holding the hatch to the hold and moved it aside to expose a large dark space beneath the deck. They unloaded boxes and cartons which were stacked on the pier, after which they proceeded to load the bagged copra.

Sialum

It took several hours before the hold hatch was reattached closing the hold, the canvas cover sheet stretched across and the awning replaced. As soon as this was done there was a mad scramble as the passengers, hanging onto their kids, their bilums, and other possessions, all tried to board at the same time completely ignoring the crew who tried to get them to board in a more orderly fashion.

Once everyone was on board the captain took the Simbang back out through the channel and we continued our journey along the coast.

Passengers disembarking so the hold can be opened to load the waiting copra.

Children playing. Passing time, waiting, watching the Simbang being loaded.

Preparing to load the bags of copra waiting on the pier.

Waiting patiently before the sudden mad scramble once allowed to board

The last passengers boarding.

A small trading boat anchored near the island offshore from Sialum.

Strange flashes of light

Late afternoon and the jungle ridges along the coast were getting darker, when periodically flashes of light appeared. They were intermittent and didn't seem to have any real pattern, like Morse code would have. Several passengers jammed closely together near the bow were using small mirrors to flash sunlight back towards the darkening jungle ridges where I had seen the flashes. Whenever they received a response from the distant jungle, they would turn to each other excitedly talking and gesturing before turning once again to flash more signals towards the darkening cliffs along the shoreline.

"What are they doing?" I asked the Captain.

"Nothing. Saying hello, that's all. This goes on all along the coast. They're like children playing a game."

It stopped after a while, when the sun got too low to be reflected.

Anchoring offshore

The Simbang slowed so it barely made headway. The Captain cautiously edge the boat around a wide promontory and anchored just inside. It was too shallow to take the boat in any further, with a broad flat reef extending all the way back to the beach. This time the Captain stopped the engines and the Simbang rocked as shallow swells washed past us and over the barely submerged reef. The wind had freshened slightly and we rocked uneasily sideways. The passengers spoke quietly amongst themselves.

A dilapidated dinghy was lowered into the water and two crewmen jumped in. One was to bail out the water that leaked into it while the other steered and drove the craft with a small outboard motor. A dozen deck passengers climbed down into the dinghy. Their possessions were passed to them which they immediately clutched close to themselves. They quickly sat down so they wouldn't fall overboard once the dinghy got underway. It headed shore-ward where a bunch of people stood waiting on the beach.

Meanwhile the crew herded the remaining passengers towards the fore deck so they could open the cover to the hold. There were many bags of copra stacked on the beach and 10 of these were loaded into the dinghy and ferried back to the Simbang. They were passed up to the waiting crew who then stacked them into the hold. The dinghy returned to the beach to collect another load. It was a slow process, and after about four hours almost half of the bags stacked on the beach had been transferred to the Simbang. The Captain called a halt.

"We've been here too long," he told me.

"No more room," he told them. "The rest will have to wait for the next trip."

He ordered the crew to seal the hatch and replace the cover.

Loading bags of copra from the dinghy.

The head man from the village came out and argued with the Captain over the amount of copra still to be loaded, but the Captain was adamant that he had no more room and the rest would have to wait until the next trip. They argued for half an hour in Pidgin English which I couldn't understand. Receipts were given for what had been loaded, and that was it, there was no more room. Each village had a certain space allocated to it, and if the village produced more copra than the space allowed, the extra would have to wait until the next trip up the coast to be shipped.

The sun was setting and the Captain wanted to be in deeper water before it got dark. With the hatch sealed and the passengers back on the main deck the Captain started the motors. The anchor was hauled up and we moved away from behind the promontory and out into deeper waters.

We were a kilometre offshore when the sun dipped below the horizon. Within minutes of setting it was pitch black. There was virtually no twilight, it went from light to dark almost as if a switch had been turned off. We cruised through the darkness with only stars glittering in the sky. There was no moon yet.

The next village was Wasu, several hours away through the darkness.

I'm glad the Captain knew where he was going.

Cruising in the dark

The stars overhead were brilliant points in an infinity of blackness. All around was blackness. Even the sea we traversed was black. The only light was the wake we made as we moved forward. It sparkled with phosphorescence, momentarily marking the path behind us.

There was no moon to cast light on the water. Although I knew we were about a kilometre off the coast, it was totally invisible.

The Captain, on the bridge, stared forward into the darkness. Every few minutes he would rush back to his cabin which doubled as the navigation, communications, and radar room. He would stare at the glowing greenness of the radar screen where the position of the Simbang was abstracted to a glowing point alongside the paler shadow of the coastline. The radar didn't show the reefs, so the Simbang remained well offshore to stay clear of them. During the day the Captain would have traveled closer to the shoreline because it was easy to see the reefs, but at night, like everything else, they were invisible.

The only other person on the bridge was a crewman steering the boat and controlling the speed. They didn't mind that I stood quietly observing.

After what seemed an interminable amount of time, the Simbang began to slow.

Ahead, there were a few tiny points of light off to our port side.

"That's Wasu," the Captain said. He had his binoculars out and was looking through them towards the distant cluster of lights. "No one goes in there at night," he said. "Well, almost no one."

"Are we going to wait until light?"

"No, as soon as we line-up we're going in. They've been waiting for us for several hours. It's a calm night, not much swell, so we should be fine."

The entrance through the reef to Wasu was a small opening, the end of a channel that had been blasted through the coral from the beach to the edge of the reef. It was a straight line and to enter at even a slight angle would have meant scraping against the coral which would seriously damage the boat. Fishing boats had no trouble going in and out, but larger vessels like trading boats had to be precise with the angle they entered. They had a deeper draught and often were so wide that barely a few centimetres of clearance existed on each side. A direct line had to be steered towards two markers, always keeping the higher more distant one exactly over the top of the closer one near the beach.

The only problem was that we couldn't see the markers. The lights of the village were visible, a tiny cluster of brightness in the all-pervading blackness of the surrounding jungle covered coastline.

The Captain kept peering through his binoculars, searching for the markers. "We should have been here at sunset," he said. He said something in Pidgin to the crewman and the Simbang started to turn towards the coast instead of running parallel.

The lights had drifted much closer as we approached the coast. There was one extremely bright light right on the beach which blotted out any other light, including the one that shone on the lower marker.

"That blasted light wasn't there two weeks ago," the Captain muttered. "I can't see the other marker."

I think he was referring to the distant one higher up and further back, the one we needed to be able to see to line up correctly. The bright searchlight on the beach, no doubt meant to light up the channel had blinded us to the other more distant marker light.

We got closer and still I couldn't see the edge of the reef. There were no waves breaking against it to mark the edge. The lights of the village were much closer and brighter and I could see dark silhouettes of people walking around near the beach. There were a lot of people waiting for the boat.

"Spotlight," the Captain yelled, and immediately above the bridge a brilliant beam of light stabbed at the beach. "More to starboard," he ordered.

The Simbang shuddered slightly as its course was modified. We were now barely moving forward. I could hear the water sloshing against the reef but still couldn't see anything.

"Where the Hell's that other marker?" He peered through his binoculars again.

Suddenly he grabbed a huge torch, adding its brilliant beam of light to the spotlight above the bridge. He was looking for the darker shadow the indicated the entrance to the channel.

"There it is," came a shout from above the bridge.

"Ah Ha! I see it now," the Captain shouted.

Whether they were referring to the entrance through the reef or to the distant marker, I wasn't sure. I couldn't see anything. With all the bright lights, my night vision had vanished.

"Keep that spotlight on the markers, The Captain yelled to the men above the bridge. "We'll make another approach," he told me, then ordered the crewman to put about.

A full circle was made until once again we were heading cautiously towards the lights of the village. Finally, I managed to see the lighter colour that marked the edge of the reef. The light shining down from the bridge had traveled a bit under water and it was just enough to reflect off the pale coral immediately under the surface. I couldn't see any gap though…

"Steady there…" the voice of the Captain near the starboard side of the boat.

The reef seemed to drift apart as we got closer. There was a small gap, and suddenly we were in it. The Captain stood beside me and looked over the side. The clearance was barely a metre. "It's the same on the other side," he told me. "Now you see why you cannot come in at an angle."

Five minutes later we were inside the reef and edging towards the short pier beside which a large motor cruiser was moored. It was this vehicle that had the bright light on top of its cabin. The light that had blinded us further out hardly seemed bright at all now that we were up close to it.

"Here, take this." The Captain gave me his torch. "Shine it along the edge of the pier so the boys can see to make the lines fast."

It seemed as if the channel concentrated the height of the swells, funnelling them directly at the pier They rolled along behind us, making the boat rock up and down more than it should, so docking beside the one hundred metre pier was a bit awkward. The pier was covered with people all yelling and talking, some giving directions to the Captain, which he ignored. It's a wonder no one accidentally got pushed off or fell into the water. The Simbang heaved up and down as it neared the side of the pier.

"Spring-lines ready," the Captain yelled to the crew as they scrambled across the deck.

The passengers were calling out to people on the pier.

He yelled at the people on the pier to get back, but they ignored him. They didn't move. They didn't want to miss anything.

"They are the craziest people," he said to me. "It's no good getting angry at them. They'll just go blank and ignore you completely."

He turned and looked aft. "Those stern lines ready?"

"Yes Boss" came the answer.

The Simbang was now right against the buffers which had no problem absorbing the weight of the boat as a swell pushed us onto them then alternatively sucked us away again. One of the crew jumped onto the pier and pushed some of the people back. The spring-lines were thrown and fastened.

"Two's not enough," the Captain shouted over the noise of the people calling greetings to the deck passengers.

The Simbang heaved away from the pier and one of the spring-lines snapped.

"Get that stern line tied."

More ropes were thrown onto the pier and were immediately grabbed and wrapped around a couple of large bollards

There were more bollards along both sides of the pier, free standing about thirty centimetres from the actual pier. Each bollard had numerous old thick rubber tyres wrapped around them to protect any boat from damaging itself as it heaved against them. Since the pier faced directly towards the entrance channel any swells coming in along the channel ran the full length of the pier.

There was confusion as the crew pushed aside deck passengers to grab more ropes, only to find them tangled. It took a lot of yelling and cursing before they were untangled and could be thrown onto the pier where they were tied off.

"They're like children," the Captain said. "If something goes wrong, they get confused and only make things worse for themselves. You've got to tell them everything, or nothing gets done. Still, I do have faith in them; once they get used to running things, they'll do all right."

Finally, the untangled front lines were thrown and tied off and the Simbang stood at ease, moving up and down as the swells rolled in through the channel and along the pier.

The rest was routine

Most of the passengers disembarked by jumping onto the pier. Once they got off, the crowd on the pier wandered back into the village and the crew could get on with its work uninterrupted. They opened up the hold. Twenty tonnes of cargo and stores had to be unloaded, fifty bags of copra had to come on board and be stacked in the hold, and after that was done and the hatch sealed, new passengers for Madang were allowed to board, as well as those who were to continue on.

Two hours later, when everything was complete, the Captain ordered the crew to cast off. Ropes were untied and hauled back on board. The Simbang carefully backed away from the pier before executing a sharp turn. She headed straight towards the channel and quickly went through without any problem. About a half a kilometre off shore the Captain turned to run parallel to the coast again. He then turned the steering over to his number-one man and retired to his cabin. The deck passengers were already silent, most of them asleep. I also retired to my cabin and immediately fell asleep while the Simbang cruised on through the darkness. We had left the Solomon Sea behind and were now traversing the Bismark Sea.

Yara

The sun was just edging above the shimmering horizon when the Captain woke us up to tell us we had arrived at Yara, a small sleepy village almost hidden by thousands of coconut palms. Immediately behind Yara a four-thousand-foot jungle covered mountain was the first of a series of ever higher mountains further inland stretching up to the sky. Many of them peaked at over seven thousand feet.

The Simbang was anchored in a small bay, which, blocked by a wide circular reef, was dead calm. As I came out onto the deck, I saw a fire burning on the beach, its smoke drifting lazily up and mingling with the palm fronds. The coconut palms came right down to the water's edge. A few people stood around the fire and in the water a small dugout outrigger canoe with three people in it headed towards us. It had a platform on it loaded with billums full of fruit.

Two crewmen busied themselves lowering the Simbang's leaky excuse for a dinghy. We had nothing for Yara apart from several sleepy passengers who climbed down into the dinghy as soon as it was ready. It ferried them over to the beach beside the fire.

An outrigger canoe pulled alongside about the same time as the passengers were jumping out of the dinghy to be greeted by the people around the fire. There were two young girls and a boy in the canoe and they offered to sell us their mangoes, paw paws and melons. The ship's cook spoke to them in Pidgin for a few moments until a price was agreed and most of the fruit was passed up to him. The remaining passengers bought the rest, and the kids paddled away happy with the result.

As soon as that was done the anchor came up and the Simbang turned around and headed across the lagoon to the entrance gap, and through that into open water.

Why there are no roads

Looking at the coastline drifting past it was clear to see why there were no roads connecting these coastal villages. The immense jungle covered mountains cascaded ridge after ridge, right down to the coast. In some places there was no beach at all; just a jagged drop from the edge of a mountain straight into the water. Coral grew in reefs all along this mountainous coastline making it difficult for reasonably sized boats to come too close to the shore. Smaller trading boats like the Simbang were the only means of transport and communication, as well as the only connection those villages had with the rest of the country. The few villages that we stopped at were completely isolated from each other and from the rest of the country.

It was the same further inland where tribes lived in isolated valleys with barely any contact with anyone, even from the next valley over, let alone with someone from the other side of the mountain. Their only means of connecting with the rest of the country was by using small planes. It never ceased to amaze me how good those local pilots were when it came to landing on tiny strips cut into the side of a mountain, or hidden in a deep gully between two mountains.

No wonder thousands of dialects evolved across the whole country. Pidgin English was the only way they communicated with each other and that only evolved because Australia was given a mandate to look after the country until independence. Everyone learnt Pidgin English and thus could understand each other no matter what their local dialect was.

The end of my Journey

Biliau was the last small village stop. We had quarter of a tonne of corrugated iron sheeting and a Patrol Box to be unloaded, and that was it. The next stop would be Madang: five hours of cruising over sea as smooth as glass.

There was no wind, and the sea was glassy this early in the morning. There were no clouds on the mountain tops either, but that would change as the day warmed up. Hot air rising would suck in wet air from the ocean. Clouds would form obscuring the mountain tops making it impossible for small planes to navigate safely through the mountain passes. The sea would begin to get choppy and a swell would develop as the air being drawn in towards and up the mountains flowed over the surface. But at the moment it was as smooth as glass.

Suddenly we were surrounded by an enormous school of dolphins, leaping and cavorting as they traveled along beside us. They were chasing a school of fish, many of which leaped out of the water as individual fish tried to escape the dolphins. After about thirty minutes they veered off and quickly disappeared into the distance further out to sea.

As time moved on the sea became ruffled with the breeze flowing in towards the coastline.

It was about one o'clock when we finally moored along the quayside in Madang. All the passengers left the Simbang while others waited there until the cargo was unloaded before they boarded for their trip back down the coast to Lae.

I found a motel with reasonable accommodation. After that I went in search of shop where I could buy some quality artwork.

A fabulous art gallery

I wasn't interested in the cheap stuff made for tourists, but wanted some reasonably sized pieces that represented the different culture that existed in this part of New Guinea. I found a fantastic shop/art gallery with superb carvings and paintings on display. There were life sized pieces, many smaller works, and overall, the quality of the art, the skill of the carvers and painters was far greater than I would have thought. It wasn't all local work because the owners of the gallery had collected art from all over New Guinea.

After much consideration and discussions with the owners regarding shipping things to Australia, I bought several large pieces and some smaller items, mostly from artists that lived along the Sepik River. These people were renowned for the quality of their art.

I arranged for the seller to have it shipped to my Williamstown address, the dry-cleaning shop and factory in Douglas Parade, where there would always be someone there during working hours to receive the crate when it arrived.

After completing the paperwork for exporting, and the permissions from the PNG government for taking native art out of the country, I went out to a good restaurant to celebrate. I had a lovely dinner with some excellent wine and the next morning flew to Port Moresby where I had a one-day stopover before flying back to Melbourne.

A general store in Madang.   *A recently constructed outrigger canoe under a palm tree.*

A few extra photos

A friendly face

Wearing local attire standing beside Colin's patrol car.

With Colin Boreham

With Colin's Chief Constable

Part Two

A profound change...

An unexpected encounter

One night early in the first week in September 1971, the phone rang. Mum answered it. Suddenly excited. I heard her say, "Why don't you bring them over for dinner? John would love to practice his Spanish."

I had been home about a year a half after spending most of 1968 in Mexico. I had not spoken any Spanish since that time, so I suppose having someone to speak with in Spanish would be a good idea. If you don't use it you lose it. To maintain a language you learn late in life –I was 28 when I was in Mexico – you have to be in an environment where you can hear the language all around you, where you are obliged to use it for whatever you may need. That way you acquire the ability to think in the language rather than trying to translate internally from one to another. Thinking in the language makes speaking it easy and natural. Once away from that environment, you quickly begin to lose it. It was just over two years since I last spoke in Spanish, so I was looking forward to having a conversation with whoever Mum suggested the caller bring over.

She came into the lounge room to tell me that Mary was in Melbourne for a few days and would be coming over for a visit.

Mary was one of our Sydney cousins.

Whenever relatives from other parts of the country were in Melbourne, they always called us and came for a visit. Our house was like a hub where friends and relatives could drop in any time, often unannounced, and be welcome.

In the 1970s, Mum had a brother and sister who lived in Sydney, Bill and Betty. Bill had three children, and Betty four children, which meant we had seven cousins in Sydney. Bill's twin brother Jack (Lofty) lived in Brisbane with his family. Mum's youngest brother Eddy, lived in Melbourne for many years. He had two children our age. He later separated from his first wife and married again. His second wife had one daughter and later gave birth to another girl. In 1968 Eddy and his new family went to Germany, passing through Acapulco in Mexico where I met up with them again. I also visited them when he was working and living in Bonn, Germany, early in 1969, before I returned to Australia. It would be several years before he returned to Melbourne.

Unfortunately, at this writing, all of my uncles and aunts in Melbourne, Sydney, and Brisbane have long passed away, as have both my parents, and a few of my cousins. But in 1970, everyone was still alive.

Mary worked as a receptionist at a major Sydney hospital, and it was here she met a young lady from Chile who worked alongside her for a year. Mary told Mum that the Chilean girl whom she worked with in Sydney had recently moved to Melbourne with two of her friends who had migrated from Chile to Australia with her, and that they were going to catch up for a coffee. The girls were planning on working for a year in Melbourne – as they had in Sydney – before moving on to Adelaide or Perth where they would do the same. They wanted to see as much of Australia as possible before settling down somewhere. They arrived with visas that gave them an indefinite stay since they were migrating rather than visiting. The visas allowed them permanent residency.

Mum immediately suggested to Mary that she bring the three girls over for dinner. "…so John can practice his Spanish," was her excuse to invite them. But she didn't need an excuse, she would have invited them anyway.

Mum just loved having new people visit, giving her an excuse to cook some of her favorite foods to share. She was gregarious, a real party person jumping on any excuse to invite people over for afternoon tea (during which she would whip up a batch of scones in no time), or for dinner.

Oddly enough, it was Mary who introduced my brother Phillip to the girl who would become his wife. Nijole, of Lithuanian heritage, lived across the road from Mary in the outer Sydney suburb of Fairfield, and they had been friends for years. When Nijole and her family moved to Melbourne Mary came for a visit, and of course visited our family and was accompanied by Nijole. Phillip became the second one of us to get married. Zara had married Fred in 1963, but that had nothing to do with Mary.

I could see Mum thinking... *it's about time John met someone nice he could settle down with...*

Why are mothers always like that?

I was the oldest of her children, and at 31, still unmarried. At this point, after just coming back from a year overseas, I didn't have a girlfriend. I was quite happy as I was, but mothers are always wondering when their children are going to get married and often pester them about it with questions and statements like: "Don't you think it's time you settled down? Zara and Phillip are both married, and they're younger than you."

"I just haven't met anyone yet..." I would mumble.

"Surely there were beautiful women in Mexico."

"Of course there were, but I was having too good a time playing drums and traveling about to even think of something like– getting married. Come on Mum."

And she would give it a rest for a while...

Christine was still in England where she had met some guy. She came home later in 1971 and this guy, Morgan, followed a few months later. Paul, 16 years younger than me, and I (the oldest at 31) were still at home. Maybe Mum just wanted to get me out of the house.

My old room was not the same anymore. It seemed smaller than I remembered, and it felt empty even though it was full of books and records, a turntable an amplifier and speakers as well as my drums. There was room for a bed along the side wall, but not much else. After the excitement of living in Acapulco and traveling around parts of central and northern Mexico, with two side trips to the USA, I was ready for another trip, another adventure.

I had recently returned from a trip with Fred and Rommy, and a pilot called Theo, in plane we hired to take us to the Trobriand Islands off the coast of Southern New Guinea. The police chief we met in Finschhafen who had looked after us while we were there had invited me to return. He had suggested I take a cargo boat along the coast up to Madang before the next Wet season started. The idea sounded fabulous and I had already booked a flight to Port Moresby in anticipation.

In the last week of August, I think was a Wednesday, the weather in Melbourne was at its most miserable. Winter was finishing and Spring beginning. We had icy winds from the Great Australian Bight being funneled up Bass Strait bringing sleet and driving rain to the city; certainly not the best time to be in Melbourne. But it was cozy in the lounge room with the gas heater filling the extended space with a lovely warmth. Mum had set the big table in the back half of the Lounge room which had once been a separate dining room but was now part of a large living space since she'd had the wall dividing the rooms removed. The table was set for eight. Paul, Mum and Dad, Me, Mary and the three Chilean girls. Zara and Fred had come over from North Altona, a fifteen-minute drive away. They were not there for dinner, but they wanted to catch up with our cousin Mary to hear all the gossip about our relatives in Sydney.

I clearly remember when the girls arrived and walked into the lounge room. Mum was ebullient, Dad sat quietly in one of the lounge chairs, observing but saying little. He stood up when Mary introduced the three girls, Monica, her friend Laura, and Laura's sister Alicia.

"John, come and meet the girls from Chile," Mum called out unnecessarily, since I was already in the room.

Monica caught my eye immediately. She stood out definitely as someone from South America, whereas the two sisters could have come from anywhere in Europe rather than South America. Monica had sparkling brown eyes, a beautiful smile and gorgeous long black hair tied into a pony tail that hung down to her waist. I was immediately attracted to her. There was a kind of charm about her that captivated Mum as well. She had a good figure too. Laura was shorter and a bit overweight which contrasted with her sister Alicia's small trim figure. Neither Laura nor Alicia could speak much English, but Monica had studied English at an American Language school in Santiago before migrating to Australia and seemed to manage quite well speaking to Mum and Dad.

I only had eyes for Monica but as the dinner progressed, I found myself speaking with Laura and Alicia more or less acting as a translator so they could participate in the dinner conversation. I really wanted to speak with Monica, but hardly had a chance before dinner was over and they had to leave. They had to go to work the next morning. Apparently, they had already been in Melbourne for a couple of weeks and had found jobs as well as a small flat to rent in Elwood.

The last thing I remember about that dinner was Mum giving Monica our telephone number and telling her that if they ever needed assistance with something to call and John would be there to help. I also told her the same thing as we said goodbye.

Once they had driven off in the car with Mary, I suddenly realized I had no idea of how to contact them or where they were living. I felt like kicking myself. Why didn't I ask for their address? Mum didn't have it either. But Mary knew of course. I would ask her the next day.

As it turned out, we didn't know where Mary was staying either. No one had thought to ask. She went off and did whatever she had come to Melbourne for and then went back to Sydney. We didn't see her again after that until several years had passed.

A dinner interruption

A couple of days later, as was usual on Friday nights, Fred and Rommy and I went out for dinner. This time we went to a new restaurant in a tiny narrow street, Alfred Place, that ran between Collins Street and Little Collins Street. It was the Kai-Kai Curry House. *Kai-Kai* was Pidgin English in New Guinea for food. It was being managed by my friend from Brazil, Antonio Rodriguez. We'd had a few sips of wine, and the main course had just arrived, when a Greek gentleman came into the restaurant looking for me. I recognized him the moment he walked in the door. He was the owner and manager of a reception centre in the same street as the Kai-Kai Curry House. He was a compatriot of my father whom we had seen at many Greek functions, and his place was where we held Fred's and Zara's wedding reception eight years earlier. He also remembered Fred, but it was me he wanted.

"Your mother is on the phone," he told me. "It seems urgent. She said you would be having dinner here, and she had tried to call but they don't have a phone, and when she found out the address was in the same street, she rang me and asked if I would come here and get you."

"They don't have a phone?"

A restaurant that doesn't have a phone! I could not get my head around that.

Antonio suddenly appeared at our table, apologetic. He'd heard our conversation. "It's not connected yet. We've been waiting since we opened a week ago, but it still isn't connected."

"Unbelievable…" I stood up. "It must be urgent for Mum to call and ask someone to come and get me," I said. I usually would tell Mum where I was going for dinner in case anything urgent came up and she had to call me. I couldn't imagine what might have happened for her to actually call. She'd never done that before.

At the reception centre, I asked her "What's up?"

"It's the girls," she said. "They've been robbed."

I was trying to figure out who the girls were that she was talking about, when she went on; "They came home from work and their door was broken open. Everything they had is gone. The police are there, but no one understands them…"

And then it hit me. The girls from Chile. Mum had given Monica our phone number and said if they needed help to call us.

"Can you go over and translate for them. The police don't understand them."

"I'll go right away. What's the address?"

It was somewhere in Elwood, an area serviced by the St Kilda Police. I wrote it down. "I can probably get there in about fifteen or twenty minutes…"

I went back to the restaurant and told Fred and Rommy I had to leave. "I'll explain later."

"No worries," Fred said. "We'll take care of the bill."

A moment of chaos

It was a small block of units where the girls were living. Twelve flats, four each to a floor. The girls were on the top floor. There were a lot of people crowding the stairs, all taking in different languages.

As I neared to top floor, I saw two uniformed police officers trying to get people to move away enough so they could converse with the girls. One of them was yelling at the girls who were inside their small flat. I suppose he thought that if he yelled loudly at them, they would understand. He was looking frustrated at his lack of ability to make sense of anything the girls said. I looked past him and saw Monica was the spokesperson. Of course, she was the only one who could speak reasonable English, but no matter what she said, he couldn't understand her. Perhaps it was her accent? There are people who simply can't understand anyone whose accent might be slightly different; they hear the accent and not the words. He was trying to write something on a pad he held.

Monica saw me and she smiled with relief. I stepped forward, and the policeman turned to me.

"What do you want?" he said threateningly.

I could smell alcohol on his breath so he'd had a few drinks before getting the call to investigate a reported robbery.

"I'm a friend of the girls. I'm here to translate for them. Anything you want to know, tell me, and I'll ask them."

"Thank God for that," he yelled at me.

"I'm not deaf."

"Sorry, I couldn't get them to understand."

"And you think yelling at them helped?"

He was about to say something back but I pushed past him to speak to Monica, who was relieved to see me. She looked nervous, but suddenly she relaxed.

"*Este borracho no entiende nada.*" She said. "This drunk doesn't understand anything."

"*No te preocupes. Hablo con él.*" "Don't worry, I'll talk to him."

I found out that he was trying to make a list of what was stolen, so I asked Monica and the other two to tell me and I then told the policeman what it was. Apparently, there was nothing of real value taken, only clothes.

There was nothing the police could do about that, nor did they care, but they still had to file a report.

The owner turned up and examined the door lock which had been smashed. They could close the door but they couldn't lock it. The three of them didn't feel safe, especially when the owner said he couldn't fix it for a couple of days. I also understood that he was going to make them pay for it as well… like it was their fault the door lock was smashed! What an arsehole.

"You'll have to stay here tonight," I told them. "But first thing in the morning I will go and look for another place for you to stay."

"Not in this area," Monica said. "*No confiamos en nadie aqui.* We don't trust anyone here. I think it was someone in this building who broke in. They would know that we were out all day at work, so they had plenty of time to do it."

"Okay." There was not much I could say about that. Whoever it was must have been pretty desperate to steal clothes.

A new place

I talked to a real estate agent the next morning and they had several flats available, and one in Northcote just past the Clifton Hill overpass seemed suitable. Since it was a Saturday and the girls weren't working, I went back to Elwood and got them. We went and looked at the flat and they liked it, so they signed a year's lease right away, paid a security deposit, and we went back to the place in Elwood, got what was left of their stuff, and immediately moved to the new place. They didn't notify the owner of the flat in Elwood, they just left. They lost their security bond, but he was going to make them pay for the door anyway, so it would come out of that.

The girls didn't care about the bond. What they cared about was feeling safe and secure. They didn't have that at the place in Elwood. The place in Northcote was a larger nicer flat in a reasonably quiet area, close to the shops at the nearby Clifton Hill junction, so they were much happier.

To celebrate, I asked the three of them to come out to dinner that night at the newly opened Japanese restaurant in Melbourne, the Sukiyaki House. The Sukiyaki House was the first Japanese restaurant to open in Melbourne and it was a wonderfully different experience to eat there. It was a lovely dinner, and during that dinner I decided if I didn't do something, the girls would go on their way and I might not ever see them again. Feeling a nervous I finally asked Monica if she wanted to go on a date, just the two of us?

She didn't hesitate for a second. She said yes.

I felt a great relief. I hadn't realized how much tension had built up inside me as I considered asking her out. I relaxed completely and couldn't stop smiling. Maybe the *sake* at the restaurant had something to do with that as well, but whatever, I felt great.

Later, when we had returned to the new flat and we were alone, she said, "I didn't think you were interested in me. I thought it was Laura you wanted. You spent a lot of time talking with her."

She was referring to the dinner we'd had at my place earlier in the week when we'd first met.

"Well, she can't speak English and I didn't want her to feel left out. You seemed to manage okay with Mum and Dad."

"I liked you the moment I saw you and I was wondering when you would ask me out. Then the dinner was over and we were gone and it was too late…"

"Same for me. I never really got the chance to talk to you. I didn't know what to do and then suddenly you were on the phone about the robbery…"

If it had not been for the robbery, she wouldn't have called Mum and I would not have known how to contact her, and we would never have started going out together nor had the life we have subsequently had together. It's impossible now to imagine what kind of life I would have had if Monica wasn't a part of it.

Do we all not have moments like that, where a sudden decision changes the course of your life? That Japanese dinner after the robbery and finding a new place for them, were pivotal moments that changed the course of my life, and I do not regret it for one second.

Out and about

Fifty years later, ask me where we went on our first date, and I can't remember exactly. I do remember though, that we went to a number of places that first week or so.

We went to Williamstown where I grew up, and which is one of the most picturesque places in the city. It was the site of the original landing by the British fleet with their ships loaded with convicts, and there is much history to be seen with many buildings more than one hundred years old and protected now by the National Trust. There are huge old canons overlooking the sea-ways on both sides of the peninsula where Williamstown is located, massive anchors from historic ships displayed in the parks and gardens, a cast iron drinking fountain that was built in 1875 and is meticulously maintained in the park on Nelson Place, and being a sea port, there are innumerable piers and jetties where hundreds of small ships, tugboats, yachts, and boats of all kinds and sizes are moored or at anchor nearby.

The view from one of the oldest yacht clubs in Australia. The Melbourne skyline is vastly different now than it was in 1972

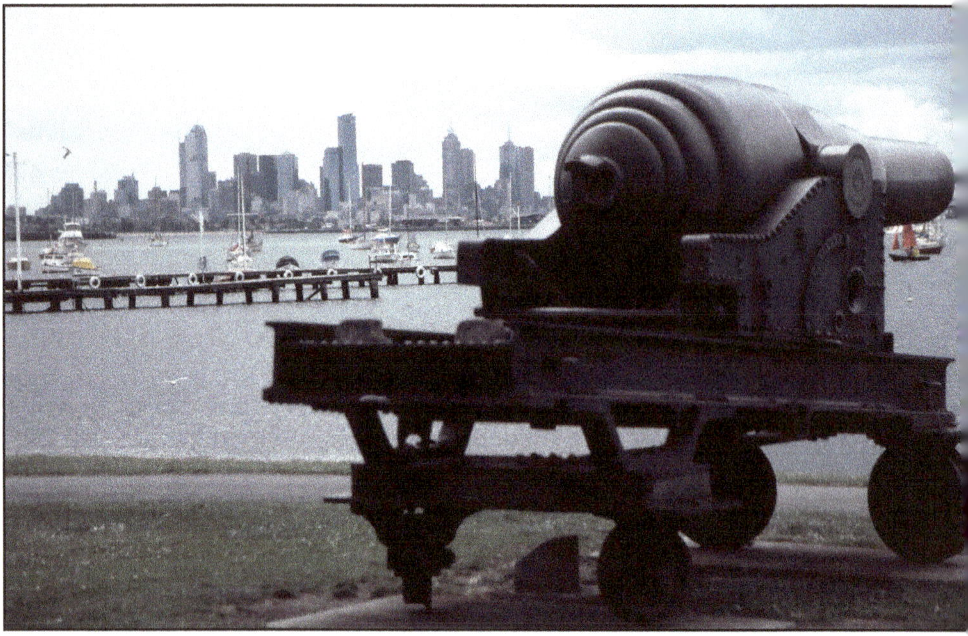

MB44 HERITAGE
BAY & RIVER CRUISES
SCENIC BOAT CRUISE

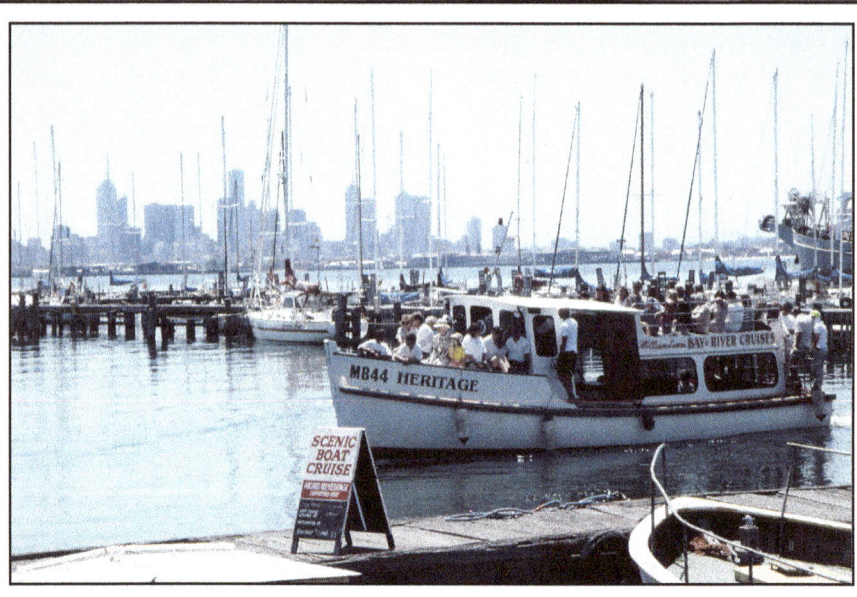

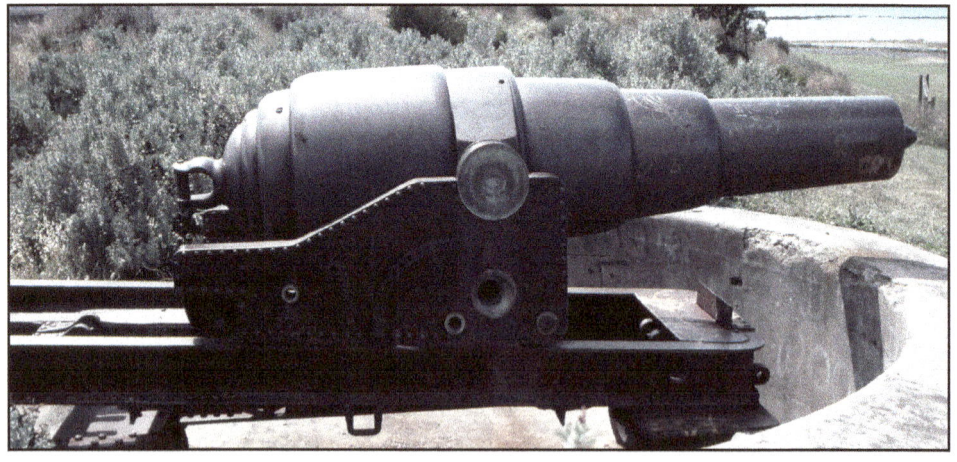

Around Williamstown: Canons, anchors, ferry boats, and yachts.

This drinking fountain was built in Scotland in 1875 and brought to Williamstown by ship and installed in 1876 in the Commonwealth Gardens in Nelson Place. It is generally well maintained but when Monica used it, it clearly needed a coat of paint.

Fresh scallops at Gem Pier. She had not seen scallops before.

We went to the National Art Gallery of Victoria in St Kilda Road, one of the best, if not the best art gallery in Australia. We went to Ackland Street in St Kilda where the best continental cakes can be found, shop after shop in the street filled with cakes so delicious and inviting it is impossible to resist buying some. We went to the beach at Seaford, far around the Bay from Williamstown where there are lovely views across to Melbourne, and at the end of the week we went to Portarlington where Mum and Dad had the family holiday house.

By the end of that first week I can truly say that we were madly in love with each other. Was it love at first sight? That's hard to say. I was certainly attracted to her the moment I saw her as she came into the lounge room for dinner that night, but if it hadn't been for the robbery, nothing may have eventuated, so love at first sight had nothing to do with it. It was how we related to each other on those first days we went out together. She was (and still is) such a beautiful person, such a caring person, and what a fantastic smile she has; it lights up the space around her. It was not conscious thought, but rather a subconscious feeling; we just knew we were right for each other. We didn't decide this, we accepted it wholeheartedly.

The inviting display in just one of the 15 or so cake shops in Ackland Street St Kilda. It's hard to resist wanting to buy something in every shop, but we managed to keep it down to six cakes from two different shops.

Top, at the Ferguson Street Pier in Williamstown.
The two of us in the Ti-trees at Seaford.

We were both 31 years old. She was born in April, the same month as me, but 8 days later. We had both traveled to different parts of the world. She had been to Brazil and Argentina before migrating to Australia. I had spent eighteen months in Europe from 1964 to the end of 1965, and then again, another eleven months in Mexico in 1968, returning to Melbourne early 1969 after visiting the USA, Canada, and Germany again on my way home.

I suspect there comes a time in your life when you feel not so much lonely but empty, even though you have family and friends around you. Something is missing, only you can't say what it is. It's a time when you feel you need to share your life and what happens with someone. It probably was that Monica felt the same and that we were both attracted to each other, so without really thinking about it we took the chance to be together, to share our lives.

Monica left Chile because she couldn't adhere to the concepts espoused by President Frei who had started nationalizing Chilean property so it could be controlled by the State. With new elections coming up, the likely successor, Salvador Allende, promised to continue the work of the previous President. He accelerated the acquisition of land holdings and nationalizing of major industries like copper and coal mining, with a policy he called '*La via chilena al socialismo*' or The Chilean way to Socialism, turning the country into a Socialist State where everything and everybody was controlled by the Government. He was an admirer of Fidel Castro, and the thought that what had happened in Cuba could very well happen in Chile spurred many people to leave. Monica was part of a wave of immigrants leaving the country at that time, many of whom came to Australia. Monica had arrived in Sydney on August 10th 1970, two months before Allende was elected as President on 4th November 1970. Having a maximum of 6 years to execute his policies he went about it with in such a way that he alienated many people as well as all the armed forces who three years later took over the country in military *coup d'état* on the 11th of September 1973. Allende was said to have committed suicide during the storming of the presidential palace 'La Moneda', but many believed he had been assassinated and that it was made to look like a suicide.

After the coup by the military junta, another wave of immigrants also left Chile for similar reasons, but this second time they were escaping from Pinochet, who had forcibly taken over the government. Pinochet turned out in many ways to be much worse than Allende, although he was quite the opposite politically. But enough… that's all I know about Chilean politics, and won't mention the subject again.

Monica moved with her two friends Laura and Alicia to Melbourne in September 1971.

September in Melbourne is the beginning of Spring and when the girls arrived the weather was beautiful; cool but sunny with a hint of warmth, and hardly a breeze to disturb the air. The water in the Bay, when they walked from their flat to the beach at Elwood, was calm, as clear as crystal.

She told me she thought this place was fabulous. But a few weeks later you would have thought it was in the middle of Winter. An icy cold wind had blasted the city for several days, bringing rain, even hail in some places. Port Phillip Bay was severely agitated, grey in colour and filled with wind-swept whitecaps that blasted the beaches with salt spray cutting into any skin you left exposed. Miserable weather to say the least. Typical Melbourne Spring. Beautiful one day, shithouse the next. In fact, it often changed from warm and beautiful to bloody cold and miserable, a couple of times a day, even in Summer with sudden cool changes coming across from the Bight dropping the temperature by as much as 20 degrees Celsius.

"You picked the worst time to come to Melbourne," I told Monica. "The best weather is at the end of Summer and early Autumn. Even early in Winter it can be beautiful. Spring is always worse than Winter."

She just wrapped her overcoat tighter around her and shrugged.

Weather is weather and there is nothing you can do about it other than to endure it, which is probably why everywhere around the world (but especially in Melbourne) people always talk and grumble about it.

A few days later when we went to Seaford and then later to Portarlington for a weekend, the weather was once again beautiful, warm, and benign. The view across Corio Bay was clear and the sea sparkled. We wandered around the pier where the fishing and scallop boats moored. The photos I took that weekend are some of my favorites. (Quite possibly because that was our first weekend away.) She was nervous about spending a weekend away with someone she had only recently met, but I assured her that nothing untoward would happen. Once we got to Portarlington and she saw the house, after we'd been down to the harbour and taken some photos she relaxed, and we had a wonderful two days.

We were together virtually every night after work was done. She had a job with a clothing manufacturer in North Melbourne, Berkley Apparel, working in the accounts' office. They made Pierre Cardin suits under license to supply leading department stores in Australia. They also made department store clothing as well as their own range, so it was quite big company. I usually finished work around 6 pm and would go over to Northcote to pick her up at the flat and we would go somewhere for dinner, or to a movie, and always came home late. Monica spent more time with me and my family than she did with her two friends, only seeing them when she went to the flat to sleep. Alicia, who was the older one of the two sisters also found a boyfriend with whom she spent a lot of time, while Laura hadn't found anyone at that point. She did get a boyfriend later, whom I never met, but that didn't work out and I suppose that was the reason she started suggesting that they move on to Perth.

Alicia with her boyfriend Allan, Myself with Monica, outside the apartment block in Northcote where the girls moved to after the robbery in Elwood.

Monica and Alicia.

Laura.

Scallop boats moored at Portarlington.
The rusty dredges on the backs of the boats are used to collect the scallops from the sandy sea bed. Unfortunately, these kinds of dredges do a lot of damage to the environment at the bottom of the sea. Nobody particularly worried about that in 1970, but these days there is a push for scallops to be hand collected by divers using scuba or hooka gear. A labor intensive but more sustainable means of collecting the shell fish. Not everyone is 'on board' yet with this method of scallop fishing.

*We had a lot of fun taking photos with Monica posing amongst the cranes and rusty equipment on the pier. It made me think of a fashion shoot where a beautiful model is posed against a run-down or worn-out urban environment, only in this case it was run-down rusty machinery on the wharf at Portarlington.
And of course, I had the most beautiful model...*

— John Litchen —

— Grab that Moment —

Relaxing on the grass in the front and the back of the house that first morning in Portarlington.

We went to Portarlington many times after that, and the photos here were taken a few weeks after I'd come back from my second trip to New Guinea. It was well into summer and much hotter. The grass had dried out.

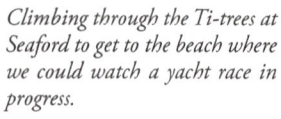

Climbing through the Ti-trees at Seaford to get to the beach where we could watch a yacht race in progress.

A better part of the sand dunes and the beach.
The Mornington Peninsula at Port Phillip Bay Heads is in the background.

— Grab that Moment —

Monica walking along the beach at Seaford with the yachts racing along on the horizon. Unfortunately, when we got to the beach the yachts were so far away we could hardly see them. Besides, they barely moved, so it wasn't as exciting as we had hoped. Far in the background is the Queenscliff side of Port Phillip Bay Heads.

Watching the yachts from the sand dunes beside the beach while Monica walked along the beach.

Back to Portarlington

In November I went back to New Guinea. I'd booked the flight to Port Moresby before I met Monica and was looking forward to catching up with Colin in Finschhafen as well as traveling up the coast to Madang on a trading boat. Although I was excited to be going, I was also concerned about not being able to see Monica. I missed her a lot while on that trip, and once I'd got to Madang and bought several spectacular carvings and a couple of snake-skinned drums, and arranged for them to be shipped back to Australia, I flew straight to Port Moresby and transferred to a flight back to Melbourne.

I had been gone only two weeks, but it seemed like two months. I couldn't wait to see her, to hold her, to hug and kiss her… I had written a letter to her from Finschhafen, telling her that I missed her, and was hoping she felt the same, but I needn't have worried; she did feel the same and couldn't wait to be with me again.

By this time, it was December, and Christmas was upon us. We had Christmas at Portarlington and Uncle Eddie came, and Mum's other brother Lofty drove down from Brisbane. It was a great time with far flung members of the family together, which was not something that happened very often. By then Monica was a part of the family, like she'd been with us for years rather than only a few months.

Even though it was early summer it was cool enough to wear jumpers.

The house was situated on the side of the land that rises behind the main part of the town which gave us a view across the town and across the water (Corio Bay) towards Avalon on the left side and on the right side when it is clear, all the way to Melbourne at the other end of Port Phillip Bay. Because we were half way up the hill behind the town we often got breezes blowing up, or rising off the water below which meant on hot days we had a cool breeze. The colder winds that blow in off the ocean in Bass Strait are forced to rise up by the hill behind us so they blow over the top without affecting us all that much. It was a good spot. If you went to the top of the hill behind us you could see across to Port Phillip Heads and Queenscliff, and beyond to Bass Strait.

Paul who was sixteen in 1971, had built an enormous radio-controlled glider. He wanted to try it out and Lofty, or Uncle Jack, and Uncle Eddie decided they would assist. Lofty being the tallest ran through the tall dry grass and launched the gliding plane, and once it was airborne, Paul controlled it so he could turn it and fly it using the thermals generated by the wind above the hill. It flew beautifully, around and around, up so high sometimes you could hardly see it, but all controlled by radio activated servo motors that moved the tail, and raised or lowered the ailerons and flaps on the wings so he could make it land near the house instead of letting the wind take it and having to chase after it. I think Lofty and Eddie were more excited than Paul. Paul was quite serious, making sure he controlled the plane, whereas Lofty and Eddy were like big happy kids running through the grass and launching the plane.

But as always, the weather varied a lot and within a day it became hot and dry and stayed that way for the rest of that summer. as the photo of Zara and her young son David clearly shows.

Lofty, Uncle Jack, had a Polaroid camera and we took these few photos, to remember his visit.
Above: On the back steps of the house: Lofty, John, Monica, Zara, Mum and Dad.
Above left: Eddie is in the picture on the front steps instead of Lofty.

John, Dad, Mum, and Eddie out front.

Above: Eddie, Mum, Lofty, Zara and Monica checking the photos taken.
Below: Inside the house checking out the Polaroid photos are Monica, Dad, Eddie, Lofty and Mum.

Also out front again, Dad, Lofty, Mum, Monica, John, Zara and her son David.

Relaxing at Portarlington with Larry Niven's 1971 Hugo Award winning novel, **Ringworld.** *I had just got it from Space Age books and could hardly wait to read it.*

Further afield

On long weekends we went further afield. The first long weekend that came up was near the end of January 1972 (Australia Day). We went to Phillip Island to watch the penguin parade, after which we drove to Wilson's Promontory, and then up to Lake's Entrance where we stayed at the motel overlooking the town as you drive in.

The penguin parade was a let-down. It was middle of summer when the sun sets very late in the southern parts of Australia and we sat there waiting to see the little penguins return after being at sea all day fishing and doing whatever they do. They return after sunset, after the long twilight has vanished and it gets dark. There were thousands of people crowding the pathways the penguins take and after putting up with the pushing and shoving of those who wanted to get closer for far too long, we were most disappointed when only a few penguins waddled back up the path to their nesting spots. It was too damned cold to sit and wait for the rest of the penguins to return. An icy wind coming up Bass Strait had dropped the temperature way down. Other people had wrapped themselves in blankets but we didn't have anything like that, so we left, pushing our way back through the masses of people waiting to see those little penguins. We drove a short distance and pulled over to the side of the road where we slept in the back of the van.

We woke up shivering the next morning. The weather had not improved, and this was supposed to be the middle of summer. We drove on to Wilson's Promontory, the southernmost point of the Australian mainland, and by the time we got there several hours later the day had improved. The air temperature was still cold but at least out of the wind it was warm enough. Wilson's Promontory pushes into Bass Strait with a number of rocky islands further out pointing the direction to Tasmania. The wind and the storms funneled through Bass Strait push out into the Tasman Sea and always cause problems for the yachts in the Sydney to Hobart Yacht Race as they sail past on their way to Hobart. The weather that year was reasonably benign and the race had gone smoothly without too many mishaps.

The drive through Gippsland to Lakes Entrance was wet. It rained all the way up from Wilson's Promontory until just before we got to Lakes Entrance. It was almost like we were underwater. Things in the distance were hazy, the grass on either side of the road was tall and thick, replete with moisture, and the trees that overhung the road seemed to droop alarmingly low. It was dark and gloomy all the way through this part of East Gippsland and as evening approached it was almost as if we were driving through a long, wet tunnel. Finally, we got out of the wet as we approached Lakes Entrance, and even though by this time it was evening, the sky was lighter because we had left the rain behind us. We booked the last room available at the motel on the hill overlooking the town and the harbour, and enjoyed a good hot meal while listening to a quartet of old guys playing New Orleans jazz. They were good musos having a great time playing, and their enthusiasm made everyone cheerful and happy enough to entice a few couples to get up and dance.

The next morning, Lakes Entrance was beautiful, sunny, warm, with not a cloud in the sky. Someone knocked on the door early to announce breakfast and I staggered out of bed to open the door. It was 7 am. Breakfast was handed to me on a tray, and a good filling breakfast it was too. After that we spent a relaxing day wandering about the town and the port full of fishing boats; a really interesting place. Unfortunately, after that we had to drive back to Melbourne because the long weekend was over.

— Grab that Moment —

I am always fascinated by fishing ports and all the activities that go on in and around them. And Lakes Entrance was one of the more interesting places along the Eastern Victorian Coast. It seems the local climate is more benign than what is found further south or more inland, which makes it a very popular place for visitors all year around. This was out first trip there, but certainly not the only one. We passed through Lakes Entrance and stayed there on several occasions when we had traveled inland up to Queensland and returned back down the coast, or when we went to Sydney a few times, we usually came back along the coast so we could stay at Lakes Entrance. The highway along the coast is always more interesting than the highways inland.

Then there was the Chinese New Year with crowds filling Little Bourke and Lonsdale Streets with drummers pounding gigantic drums and smashing symbols creating a cacophony that followed a massive dragon cavorting along the street. Exploding firecrackers scattered ahead of it announced its imminent arrival. People were pushed back by police to make room for the dragon. Shortly after that we mingled with the crowds during the Moomba Weekend and as the weather cooled, we went to Healesville wildlife sanctuary and further up into the Victorian ranges to see the changing autumn colours. The first few months of the year in Melbourne are always full of activities and excitement. These were things that I had taken for granted, growing up in Melbourne, but in the company of Monica I experienced them in a new light. It was wonderful to share the excitement of these events with someone who had never seen them before.

Monica and my young brother Paul waiting for the dragon, the dancers and the Chinese drums.
The weather wasn't the best, but who cared with all the excitement and fireworks involved with the Chinese New Year celebrations.

Monica and big birds

I rarely go to a zoo because I don't like to see animals in cages. Monkeys and gorillas look so sad and depressed in these enclosures. It's just not natural to imprison them, or any other animal. I could not remember the last time I went to the Melbourne Zoo, but it must have been when I was younger than ten. But trying to think of places to take Monica —and this is what you do when you have visitors or friends come over to see you— you take them to all the tourist spots you would never consider going to because you live there. So we went to the Zoo, and it was an eye-opener.

Sure, there were enclosures for such animals as the big cats, but there were no cages like I remembered from when I was a kid. There was a moat separating the animal's open space from a very high fence to keep people visiting well away from any possible contact with the animals. The giraffes and the elephants also had enormous open enclosures as well, where they could gain a semblance of freedom to wander about. And Australian animals like kangaroos and wallabies seemed to be free to hop about where ever they wanted. Emus too!

These big kangaroos were inside a large enclosure, but their smaller cousins wandered freely about. This was the first time Monica had seen a live kangaroo.

Monica had a bag of potato chips in her hand and was nibbling on them when she came face to face with an emu. It stared right at her. She didn't know what to do and stood there a moment, but suddenly the emu lunged down and snatched some ships from out of her hand.

She let out a squawk, Monica that is, turned and ran. The emu followed a couple of steps, but then stopped and wandered off in search of someone else more willing to hand feed it.

— Grab that Moment —

Monica walking towards me with the bag of potato chips.

The emu stared at her with eyes that seemed so intelligent.

To me the expression on its face seemed to say, "well, what have you got for me?"

It was used to people feeding it and didn't expect the reaction it got from Monica.

It seemed puzzled when she let out a strangled scream and ran away. It watched her for a few moments before turning and walking off to look for someone else to offer it some food.

I'm sure Monica was relieved to see the back of it.

Something similar happened five years later when we went to Ballarat with our friends Wally and Betty. We had just pulled up beside the lake Wendouree in the centre of town and had barely got out of the Camper Van when we were surrounded by a gaggle of enormous black swans looking for food.

Lake Wendouree was created from swamplands in 1851 during the Gold Rush, and has been a recreational lake ever since. It is about 2 kilometres long by 1.4 kilometres wide with 6 kilometres of shoreline. It is a popular spot for locals as well as tourists and is home to a variety of water birds. It's just that the black swans are the most notable.

People shouldn't feed these birds food scraps or pieces of bread because that is not what they would naturally eat. But they have become so accus-

tomed to being fed that the moment someone emerges from a vehicle parked near the lake's edge, they swarm around honking and flapping their wings to attract attention. If it looks like you have anything in your hands they will try to snatch from you. After her initial scare Monica relaxed and enjoyed watching Wally, holding our son Brian, feed the birds.

The two of us during Moomba, March 1972. One of my favourite Photos!

A Freezing night at Loch Ard Gorge

The next long weekend we could get away was The Queen's Birthday weekend in June, the beginning of winter. We went to Port Campbell and the twelve Apostles, a long drive from Melbourne. We took The Great Ocean Road which runs along the coastline from Torquay all the way to Peterborough before it turns more inland and zig-zags through rugged mountainous country to finish at Warrnambool. Before The Great Ocean Road was constructed, the only way to get to the several small towns along this coast was to use roads that ran from the Princes Highway, quite a distance inland, down through the Otway Ranges to each individual town on the coast. Going to any one of these towns was a long torturous drive at the best of times and in bad weather generally impassable. In 1919, as a tribute to the soldiers who took part in the First World War, the government got thousands of workers together and they literally dug the road out of the cliff-sides using picks and shovels. It was later widened and surfaced in the 1940s and has more or less remained the same since.

It's a spectacular drive, and rivals anything similar anywhere else in the world. Typical of the many who take this drive, we stopped along the way to look at the views and on arriving in Apollo Bay we also stopped for something to eat, and spent time watching a yacht that had been in trouble being towed back into port.

By then it was late afternoon and the light was fading. A short walk around the harbour was all we could do before having to push on. The fishermen had come in and unloaded their catches, hundreds of Cray pots were stacked up ready to be taken out the next day, and apart from the yacht that had been towed in there was not much other activity.

As always, I underestimated the time taken to get to the twelve Apostles and Port Campbell.

As we approached the area where the twelve Apostles were located it was too dark to see anything.

We drove the extra ten or so kilometres to Port Campbell, the only safe port along this wildest part of the coast. Every motel was booked out for the weekend.

"We have two choices," I said. "Drive on to Peterborough where the Great Ocean Road ends, or further on to Warrnambool if Peterborough is booked out as well. It's a lot more driving which I don't really feel like doing."

"I don't want to drive anymore," Monica said. "What's the second choice?"

"We could backtrack the ten kilometres to the Twelve Apostles and sleep in the van."

"Let's do that."

I had a mattress in the back and plenty of blankets to keep us warm.

"We should get something to eat first though."

We went into the motel dining room of the last place we had checked which was lovely and warm and packed with people, and very noisy. There was a jukebox playing but the music was mostly drowned out by the people talking and laughing loudly. Most of them had obviously had a few too many drinks, but the atmosphere was good. It was a holiday weekend and everybody there wanted to have a good time.

As soon as we had finished eating, we went back outside to the van and it was freezing.

A strong wind was blowing in off the ocean and it cut through whatever we were wearing. We got into the van and drove back along the Great Ocean road until we came to the signs that told us we were at the Loch Ard Gorge. Stepping out of the van the wind buffeting me as it blew up off the ocean and over the tops of the cliffs which we couldn't see in the dark. There was no Moon, and it was pitch black. Waves pounded and smashed onto the rocks below with a continuous roar. Even the van shuddered as the wind hit it. Jumping back in I drove a few hundred metres away from the road to a flat spot well away from the cliff edge and that's where we parked. Away from the edge of the cliffs it wasn't so windy, but it was still cold. There were no other cars around.

The area is part of the Port Campbell National Park, and these days you would be forbidden to sleep beside the road in that area, but in 1971, they weren't so strict. I knew if we had driven the extra 20 kilometres to Peterborough and another 65 from there to Warrnambool, I wouldn't have wanted to drive back and we would have missed seeing the Twelve Apostles altogether.

We discovered early the next morning that we had been parked beside the cemetery where the victims of the shipwrecks in the Loch Ard Gorge were buried. There were still no other vehicles around so we moved back to the public parking area, and I set up my movie camera on a tripod to take some film of the waves smashing into the gorge and the base of the cliffs. The wind had died down and although it was cold, the air didn't have the same bite it had the night before. By the time the camera was set up the sky had brightened, the clouds started to clear and the morning sun turned the sandstone cliffs a beautiful warm shade against the stark whiteness of the breaking waves.

Early morning, walking along the cliff-top looking for a spot to set up the camera.

The gorge is named after the iron clipper, Loch Ard, which was wrecked here on the 31st of May 1878. A thick haze had obscured the Cape Otway light and the clipper ploughed straight into the gorge and was smashed to pieces by the pounding waves. There was no way anyone could climb up the cliffs and 50 people lost their lives. There were two young survivors. An apprentice called Tom Pearce who managed to swim out of the gorge and around to a beach. He also dragged ashore a teenage passenger called Eva Carmichael who had drifted away clinging to a hen coop.

With some reluctance, Monica emerged from the van and followed me along the cliff top. Apart from the two of us, there was no one else around this early in the morning.

— Grab that Moment —

Sailors and skippers feared this wild stretch of coast but they had no choice if they wanted to get to Port Phillip Bay and Melbourne. They were safe if they stayed well offshore, but with powerful winds blowing up from the south, and sometimes thick fogs which obscured the coast and blocked the Light houses, many ships came too close and inevitably they were wrecked. There are probably more shipwrecks along this stretch of coast than anywhere else in Australia.

As the sky lightened, I shot some film of spectacular wild waves smashing into the Gorges while Monica stood there shivering wrapped in her hand knitted poncho. Even though the sun later managed to peek through the overcast sky it was very cold.

Surging water in the Loch Ard Gorge.

After that we moved along to the Twelve Apostles and a bit further along the coast to the spectacular rock formation extending out into the ocean, called London Bridge. By that time there were other people about, and a group had even walked across the arch forming London Bridge to stand on the very end of the cliff to see the waves smashing into the rocks below. I thought that was crazy because the wind pushing the massive waves onto the coastline could easily have blown them off the edge. If they fell into that wild water they would never have survived.

Wild and beautiful. This coast is without a doubt, one of the most spectacular places in the whole country. It's always different every time you come and see it. Coming here with Monica was the first time I had been here. This was in 1972, Since then we have been here quite a few more times, and each time it seems to be more spectacular, and more beautiful.

Monica, walking back across the bridge can barely be seen. Our white van is parked on the cliff top with several other cars. By this time there were quite a few visitors about.

Monica decided that she wanted to walk across the bridge which surprised me.

"While you do that, I'll go around the edge of the cliff to here so I can get picture, a view of the structure with you walking across it."

"You're not coming with me?"

"I'd rather stay over here and take a photo…"

She looked at me for a moment, uncertain perhaps about whether she should walk across it alone, but then she shrugged, and said, "okay." And off she went.

In the photo she seems so small she can hardly be recognized.

That middle part – the arch – that she walked across, in later years suddenly collapsed into the ocean in the middle of the day. Several people who had moments earlier walked across it were trapped on what became a rock pinnacle after the connecting arch collapsed. We weren't there when that happened but it was all over the news. The people could not get off and the only way to rescue them was with a helicopter. It was sheer luck that no one was actually walking across the arch when it crashed into the sea beneath.

We finished up in Warrnambool for afternoon tea and then drove back along the main highway to Geelong and Melbourne which was a straighter run and much quicker than coming back along the Great Ocean Road.

London Bridge seen from the other side. The part in the middle where the tiny figure is walking across collapsed and fell into the ocean a few years later so it no longer looks the same.
Below: part of the Great Ocean Road.

Extraordinary coincidences

Sometime around mid-April Monica showed me a book she had been reading that had been sent to her from Chile while she was still in Sydney, but having received it just before leaving for Melbourne she hadn't had the chance to read it. And now, finally, she found the time.

"What's it about?" I asked her.

"It's a collection of science fiction stories."

"Really!" I was surprised. She knew I had plenty of SF books. She had seen them in my room, but she wasn't particularly interested in them, even though she was always reading books in English to help improve her speaking of the language.

"These are stories my brother Hugo wrote. He sent me a signed copy. He knows I don't normally read SF stories, so it was a surprise to get this. It's his first collection of short stories"

She showed me two other books of his that she had. They were both novels.

Wow... I didn't know what to say. She hadn't mentioned before that her oldest brother was a writer of science fiction. She had told me he was a journalist and worked independently for a number of magazines and a newspaper where he had regular columns, but I couldn't recall her mentioning that he wrote science fiction.

So, she enlightened me. Her brother Hugo (Correa) was a co-founder of the Chilean SF Club, *Club de Sciencia Ficción de Chile*, as well as President of a club called UFO Chile dedicated to the study of unidentified flying objects (*OVNI- objetos volando non-identificados*), and he had published in 1959 a novel called **Los Altísimos**, which many consider to be an extremely important novel in the field of science fiction in South America. It is the only novel among half a dozen that he wrote which has been reprinted several times since its initial publication.

Hugo along with another young Chilean SF writer had been invited by Ray Bradbury in 1961 to participate in writers' workshops at the University of Iowa. Bradbury was also instrumental in sending three of Hugo's short stories to editors of Magazines in the USA and they were subsequently published in English. **Element Z** published in *The Magazine of Science Fiction and Fantasy* (1962), **Meccano**, a robot story, published in *International Science Fiction* (1968) and **Alter Ego** published first in *F&SF* (1967), then again in a college textbook on psychology (1974), and once more in *The Penguin World Omnibus of Science Fiction* edited by Brian Aldiss and Sam J Lundwall (1986).

I had no idea he had written so many stories. In fact, I had no idea at all that he was a writer of science fiction and one of the seminal writers in that field in South America until Monica told me.

But that's not the only coincidence. Shortly after Monica and I had Married (May 19th 1973) and after we'd been to Canberra, and shot some film with John Bangsund, we were back at his house when I happened to mention that Monica was the sister of a Chilean writer of science fiction.

"You never told me that before."

"I only recently found out. His name is Hugo Correa."

He looked at me in astonishment, and said, "hang on a minute," and promptly disappeared. He returned a moment later with a very professional looking magazine.

"This," he said as he handed it to me, "is a special edition dedicated to the work of Hugo Correa."

It was issue number 33 of *Nueva Dimensíon,* (1972) a bi-monthly Spanish science fiction magazine.

He could have knocked me over with the magazine.

How often does a coincidence like that occur?

How on earth did he happen to have that magazine? I didn't think he could read Spanish. I flipped through the pages, and each story had an illustration accompanying it, old fashioned black and white ink drawings like the early pulps had. And it all looked as professional as any other major SF magazine of that time, only it was all in Spanish.

"It's a prozine," he said. "Most of it contains stories by Spanish speaking writers from Spain as well as Latin America. It also contains stories by well-known science fiction writers translated from English as well as other European languages. The last third of the magazine is like a fanzine with letters of comment, and articles by fans."

"And you can read this?"

"No, I can't really, but they send it to me. I get lots of fanzines and magazines from around the world. You can have this one. I've got earlier issues if you want to read some. This is the latest one."

"I don't think Monica has any idea that this exists. She'll be over the moon when she sees it."

"Maybe," John said, "you can write something about Hugo for me. Something I can put into an issue of Philosophical Gas?"

"I've never met him, I'm not sure I can write about him."

"Of course you can."

And he said that with such confidence I felt I had no option but to do it.

Monica had several clippings of articles Hugo had written for *Ercilla,* a popular magazine in Chile. Her mother had sent them to her in various letters. They were always writing to each other.

I read these articles as well as the stories in the collection Monica had, (*Cuando Pilato Se Opuso*) and talked to her about her brother and his writing and eventually came up with an article that I presented to John. I can't remember what I called it but John immediately changed the title to *The Other Hugo*. He also retitled *Philosophical Gas* to *Gas Filosófico* for that issue (published in 1975 before Aussiecon took place) and drew a delightful cartoon for the cover that was a gentle dig at the prolificity of Isaac Asimov who wrote hundreds of books about all kinds of subjects apart from his SF stories and novels.

Note: *Nueva Dimensíon was published from 1968 until 1982 and there were 148 editions before it ceased publication. Another 12 special issues were published a few years later in an attempt to revive the magazine but eventually it folded. Copies of most of the issues can be found on Spanish websites that specialize in selling books etc but the prices being asked are phenomenal with each issue going for somewhere between $240 to $500 (US) per copy. At the time it was being published, it was probably the best SF magazine in Europe. For some reason, it reminded me of the British magazine New Worlds, though there was nothing in common between them. I liked New Worlds and preferred it over the contemporary American Magazines. I also liked Nueva Dimension.*

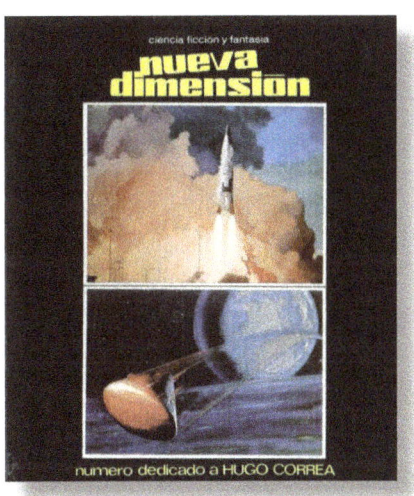

Most of the stories printed in **Cuando Pilato Se Opuso** *have been reprinted in this special edition of* **Nueva Dimension**. *Hugo sent this book to Monica in 1971 just before she moved from Sydney to Melbourne.*

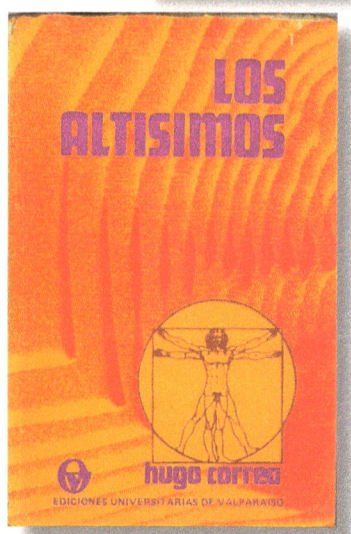

The 2nd edition -1973- Hugo sent to Monica on her birthday. It has a message inside hoping that she would remember Chile while experiencing all the adventures that he himself imagined having during his childhood.

This 3rd edition -1983, is a reprint of the 1973 2nd edition which is why it says on the cover **segundo edicion**. It was given to me by Hugo when we met in 1991. The message inscribed was to my brother in law John, with much respect and hopes that this first visit to Chile would not be the last. It was reprinted again in 2000 and remains his most popular book.

Part three
What was the name of that film?

*The author, filming a scene for **The Antifan Film** in Melbourne 1972.*

The possibility of a WorldCon in Australia

John Bangsund changed houses, or at least places where he lived in Melbourne, several times in the 1970s, before he moved to Canberra. I remember going to a gathering at his place in Bundalohn Court, St Kilda where he was then living. This may have been a few weeks before I met Monica which would place it mid-1971. Everyone there was talking about bidding for a 'WorldCon' to be held in Australia, more specifically in Melbourne.

There was a lot of excitement in the air once the idea of holding a WorldCon became a firm resolve. We were going to bid for it to be held in Australia in 1975 and all of Melbourne SF fandom worked towards achieving that goal. A WorldCon had never been held in Australia before, and those who became the bidding committee were determined that they would succeed.

Merv Binns and Space Age Books

Merv Binns with Ron Graham had started Space Age Books, I think in 1969, operating from a small office on the sixth floor of a building in Elizabeth Street (the Beehive building?) a block away from McGills News Agency where he had worked and had helped establish their line of science fiction books. Space Age Books was the very first specialist science fiction bookshop in Australia, although operating from an office on the sixth floor wasn't good for passing trade. Only the dedicated fans who used to buy from him when he worked at McGills took the trouble to find where he was to buy their indispensable books.

Fortunately, he moved not long after to a location in Swanston Street opposite the public Library which was a far better location being at street level and visible to passers-by, and business started to boom. And when that shop got too small for the amount of stock carried, Merv moved a few doors down to a bigger and brighter shop where he re-established the SF Club's library upstairs. Club members and any other dedicated fan would turn up on Friday nights to chat, browse the books and generally do what fans did.

But it was in that first smaller shop where the original ideas for the unnamed movie to publicize the bid for the 1975 SF Worldcon, to be known as *Aussiecon*, were planned, and some pivotal scenes were shot. Interiors and exteriors featured the shop along with Merv and other staff members. In my view, without Merv's input, his enthusiasm for the idea of a film, for allowing his shop to be used and his financing with Ron Graham of the production of the release print, the film would never have been completed, and *Aussiecon* would never have eventuated. The film and its showing in America tipped the votes in our favor.

The wonderful Paul Stevens in character as he prepares to shoot a scene in the film.

The film

The film never had a name or a title.

It was sometimes called *The Aussiefan Film*, *The Aussiecon Film*, *The Antifan Film*, or even *The Australia in 75 Promotional Film*.

The only title that appears on the film simply denotes the place where the action happens, **Melbourne**, but for me it was always *The Antifan Film*.

Antifan was the star, and Paul Stevens was Antifan. Paul will forever be remembered for his role in the film. He dominated every scene and he outshone every character with his dastardly enigmatic smile while rubbing his hands together.

On one particular night in 1971 a small group gathered at John Bangssund's place in Bundalohn Court, St Kilda, to discuss to the bidding for a WorldCon in 1975, while others there continued to party elsewhere in the house. In that room where the discussion took place were John Foyster, Lee Harding, Leigh Edmonds, David Grigg, Paul Stevens, Merv Binns, among others including me. It was a serious affair, so I stayed quietly in the background. Most of that discussion concerned fanzines and how they could use them to publicize our bid for Australia in 75. We were competing against San Francisco who were bidding for the same 1975 WorldCon,

John Bangsund wanted more people to write about Australia to publish in his fanzines which he would post to people over in America. He suggested other fanzine editors who were there promote the idea as well. He was hoping that collectively they could build a picture of a fantastic country full of interesting people who did fascinating things that would induce North American fans and writers to come to Australia.

In 1964 I went by ship to Europe where I stayed for 18 months, visiting and working in a number of countries. After a short time back in Australia I went to Mexico where I lived in Acapulco for eleven months before again going to Europe briefly before returning home via East Africa as well as South Africa. After telling John Bangsund about this he said that I was the most-traveled person he had met, and suggested I should write something for one of his fanzines. I had just come back from a trip to New Guinea and the Trobriand Islands. I told him I would write about that.

"That's exactly what I'm after," he said.

I promptly forgot about that when another idea came up later in the evening after a few too many glasses of wine. I suggested to John Bangsund that we should make a film as part of our bidding presentation. I had plenty of film left over from an underwater project that didn't get done... twenty-five 100-foot rolls of black and white 16mm film. At four minutes for each roll of film, that was a good amount of film.

"If you guys are interested, I'm happy to donate the film, as long as I get to shoot it. The only thing you would have to pay for would be processing and the final release print once the filming and editing was done."

It was discussed briefly, but I got the impression they thought it would be too expensive, or too difficult to do. No one had shot a film and used it as part of a bidding process before. Maybe it was a bit too far out of the box to what they were accustomed to? I didn't think they had taken the idea seriously. Paul Stevens however looked thoughtful. He and Merv were the ones who organized the films shown at the recent convention in the theatre that I had attended.

Weeks went by, and I heard nothing. The end of the year arrived and a new year had started. I had met Monica by then and wasn't even thinking about anything other than her. I still went to Space Age Books on Friday nights to see what new books Merv had imported, and more often than not would buy at least one or two of them. Then one Friday night at Space Age Books everyone was talking about the film we were going to make and coming up with ideas about what should be in it. That surprised me because I had totally forgotten about it. Few of the ideas mentioned would have worked, but at least they were thinking about it.

A few days after hearing everyone talking about it, John Bangsund contacted me and asked if I was still interested in making the film.

"I am…" I told him, "but to make it work someone will have to come up with a script."

"Paul Stevens is already working on it," he said.

So, we were off and running.

I got together with Paul and a few other enthusiastic fans who had come up with a working story. Paul was a big fan of early silent films with their melodrama as well as the Saturday movie serials full of cliffhangers that as kids we loved to watch. What he hoped we could do was something that would generate in the minds of the overseas fans that same excitement and feelings we used to get as kids when we saw those early films.

Some of the main characters in our film.

Merv Binns

Bill Wright

John Foyster

Robin Johnson

Malcolm Hunt as Aussiefan

David Grigg and Peter House

...and of course, the star of the film, Paul Stevens as Antifan.

The story was: another country was bidding for the Worldcon in 1975, and this country, fearing that Australia's bid would beat theirs, decided they would infiltrate Space Age Books (then the centre of SF activity in Australia) with a nasty character who would set out to destroy our bid. He was to do this by eliminating members of the bidding committee one by one until there was no one left to put in a bid. This super nasty character, Antifan, would almost succeed with this dastardly deed, only to be foiled at the end by an Aussie superhero, Aussiefan, who manages to get Antifan blown up by his own horrible bomb. Aussiefan, played by Malcolm Hunt, would of course be rewarded for his valiant efforts and presented with a gold medallion from his grateful fans.

The idea was to use as many famous locations around Melbourne as possible so potential visitors could see what Melbourne was like. Thus, the Art Gallery became the palatial home of John Foyster. Space Age Books, always a hub of SF activity was prominently featured. Our beautiful parks and gardens were used, the city square in its early manifestation was seen, our tree-lined streets, and trams were all featured. Committee members used them to go in search of a suitable location for the convention.

Entrance to the palatial home of John Foyster, The National Gallery of Victoria. Waiting for filming to begin are John Breden, Merv Binns, Robin Johnson, Bill Wright, and with their backs towards us, John Foyster, Peter House, and Leigh Edmonds.

With the scene of John Foyster entering his home while Antifan sneaks in behind him over and done, everyone relaxed with a gelati bought from the street vendor out front, before heading back to the main part of town and **Space Age Books** for the next scene to be shot: John Foyster being pulped.

Paul Stevens, Robin Johnson and Peter House, Leigh Edmonds, Merv Binns, John Breden, and Bill Wright.

Back in town, in a small plaza in front of the GPO, setting up to shoot the scene where Peter House is given a mysterious message that will lure him away, the promise of an assignation with a mysterious lady, only for him to be hit by a car and eliminated, thus generating the newspaper headline; Car Hits House.
I am giving directions while John Breden looks on. David Grigg and Peter House are facing us ready to begin the scene.   Bottom: David Grigg and my young brother Paul watching me film Peter House heading off for his assignation and eventual demise.

— Grab that Moment —

Paul Stevens and me, working out what scene to shoot next with the rest of the cast.

For some reason Peter is feeling dejected as he walks slowly along Elizabeth Street, but on being given a mysterious message by a stranger (my brother Paul), he brightens up, and together he and David head off with a bounce in their step. The message was purportedly from Rachel Welch.

Malcolm Hunt's first appearance in the film: He is relaxing inside a sculpture in the plaza by the GPO while Peter House and David Grigg receive the mysterious message that lures Peter away.

The Peter House stunt team creating the fight scene that looked great but had no relevance to the story, apart from Peter winning the fight after being set upon, only to be run down by a car immediately afterwards.

This is one of my favourite scenes in the film. It was done slowly, with the car traveling at about 15 kilometres per hour so Peter could have enough time to leap onto the bonnet and roll across it. Once he came over and back onto the ground, the car sped away. We shot this at 18 frames per second instead of 24 fps to give the impression that it was done at a higher speed.

Malclm Hunt in costume and Merv Binns in front of Space Age Books before shooting the scene where Antifan leaves a bomb at the front door.

— Grab that Moment —

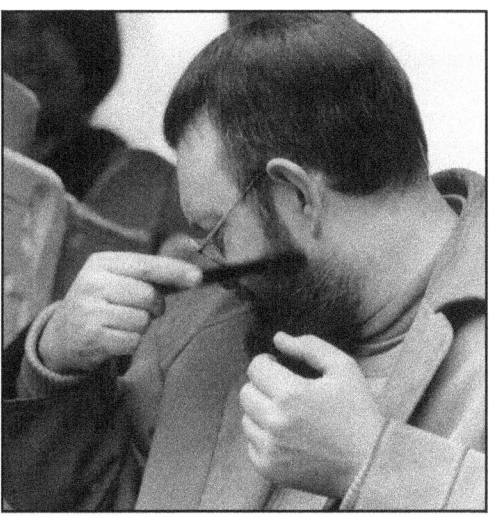

Bill Wright, Leigh Edmonds, and Antifan discussing the scene in a back alley where Bill Wright is disguised as the strange foreigner who hires Antifan to eliminate the bidding committee.

Robin Johnson combing his hairpiece which he wears throughout the film. Being bald was supposed to be a secret and no one knew until Antifan reveals the truth to all and sundry resulting in Robin committing suicide in shame.
This scene was shot in the gardens opposite the site of the Hilton Hotel, under construction when the film took place.
Antifan uses a fishing reel and line to hook the hairpiece, ripping it off Robin's head. He reels it in and sets fire to it in a drinking fountain, then hands Robin a pistol which he uses to shoot himself in the head. All done with absolute glee.

— John Litchen —

How could you not love a character like Antifan?

After the scene had been shot: Robin mucking about with the burnt hairpiece.

If the finished film had a lot of spontaneity, it was because none of us knew exactly what we would film. We followed the rough plot, but generally invented a scene when we found an appropriate location. The result was as delightfully surprising to both Paul Stevens and myself as it was to the audience who first saw it at The Australian National Convention in Sydney in August 1972.

The real star of the film was undoubtedly Paul Stevens. Most of the ideas were his, and he inhabited the role with glee. He did it so well, being the dastardly Antifan that he completely convinced a bunch of kids in the park when we filmed the chase scene. In this scene Robin Johnson, with a handgun given to him by Antifan, shoots himself in shame after Antifan using a fishing line reveals that Robin is actually bald and has been wearing a hairpiece. Antifan takes off into the park with the remaining bidding committee chasing him. Out of nowhere half a dozen kids (who we had to keep out of the shot) also joined in to chase after Antifan, who runs behind several trees to elude the chasers until he finally runs behind a big tree and disappears, only to reappear much further away from behind another tree to run off and

Aussifan makes his first appearance at the Golden Globe Hotel, where a phone call alerts him to the danger of Antifan. He immediately slips into a small room only to emerge seconds later as the super hero who will save the convention bid. In Melbourne's city square, he encounters John Breden in one of his magnificent costumes and is given a message.

The amount of detail that went into the costumes was remarkable, and although John Breden's character has little to do with the storyline, it was too good a costume not have it in the film, hence the scene in the city square where a message warning Aussifan that Space Age Books was about to be blown up with a bomb as included. This scene isn't actually in the film, but it was too good not to photograph. Aussifan of course saves the day by getting the bomb and racing down Swanston Street to the bridge that crosses the Yarra River, he throws the bomb over the side. Unfortunately for Antifan who was hiding under the bridge, the bomb falls in front of him and explodes. The final scene in the film has Antifan staggering along a deserted beach (St KIlda) where he collapses while holding up a sign saying he will be back...

escape while the committee run in puzzled circles around the first tree. The kids however spotted him, and yelling and screaming they gave chase and caught up with him. Paul was forced to remove his hat and evil cape and his black gloves to show them he was an ordinary person like the rest of us. He wouldn't take off his black leather jacket, which he always wore no matter what, leaving them still doubtful. It was only when we showed them the movie camera that they let Paul go.

Paul was a natural as Antifan. In the scene in which he leaves a bomb at the front door of Space Age Books before running away up the street, on impulse, he raised his hat to salute a passerby who stared at him in astonishment. Then he did that little jump he always did before turning a corner, and disappeared.

Paul Stevens, Antifan, being prepared for the final shot at St Kilda Beach.

The very final scene, improvised as most of them were while filming, was to have Antifan survive vowing revenge. The idea was that Antifan couldn't be destroyed. Somewhere, in some future time, he would reappear to once again foil whatever plans Australians would have for holding a world convention. This allowed Antifan to be revived when a group of Sydney fans decided they would bid for another Worldcon to be held in Sydney in 1983.

At the scene where he changes into his Antifan costume, we were going to do it in a phone booth, but considering the nature of Antifan, one of Melbourne's iconic pissoirs was selected. This is near the start of the film.

There was actually someone in there taking a leak when he ran in to change, so we incorporated that into the scene, and had a gentleman come out after Paul's quick change, shaking and scratching his head.

For the crowd scene we only had six people. When Aussiefan steps up to receive his award for saving the Worldcon bid, the crowd of six was to applaud and cheer and try to look like six hundred. We did it as a tight shot to create the impression it was more crowded than it was. One of those six was Bill Wright who was the only committee member not killed by Antifan.

Filming was rushed, chaotic at times, but it was a lot of fun. Peter House, one of the members of the committee was also doing work as a stunt man on a TV show. He got several of his friends together and staged a spectacular fight scene. He is tricked outside of the central post office on the corner of Elizabeth and Bourke Streets into a rendezvous with a mysterious woman at a remote location. Once at the location, House is set upon by a bunch of ruffians whom he fights off before being run over by the car. The fight scene was in the first version of the film shown at the convention in Sydney, but was later removed before the release print was made. We kept the scene of Peter being run over by the car. The headline in the paper was Car Hits House.

We used an old heritage listed cemetery at St Kilda for the burial scenes. We never actually showed a coffin or a burial, but each time a committee member was eliminated the other members would solemnly walk through the cemetery implying that there had just been a funeral. And as each committee member was eliminated the people waking in the cemetery became less. All the cemetery shots were done in one afternoon, which typical for Melbourne in the Winter, was overcast and grey, cold, with a drizzle of icy rain. Exactly what you need for a funeral…

— Grab that Moment —

John Litchen with camera discussing the scene to be shot with Antifan.

Below: The funeral for Leigh Edmonds.
Valma is inconsolable as she holds onto Merv.
Bill Wright looks suitably solemn.
Mostly hidden is John Breden who is holding the umbrella.
By this time there were very few committee members left.

Antifan at the cemetery reading the news of Foyster's death reported as a freak accident. John Foyster was the first person eliminated by Antifan after a committee meeting at his palatial home. He is killed when Antifan causes a huge set of bookshelves filled with pulp magazines to collapse on top of him.

Robin Johnson and Paul Stevens in between shoots. At this stage Robin had not been eliminated and so he is wearing the hairpiece that is later, the cause of his demise.

It was a cold wet day and everyone wore coats and jackets to keep warm.

Paul Stevens, John Breden and Malcolm Hunt having some fun at Space Age Books once the city square scenes had been shot. We still had one scene to go, the crowd scene where Aussiefan is rewarded for having saved the bid for the Worldcon, now being called Aussiecon.

— Grab that Moment —

Always having fun. That was what was great about the making of this film.

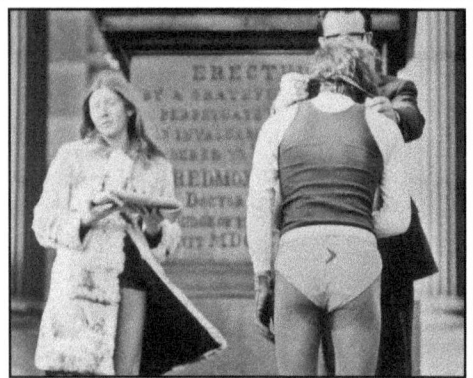
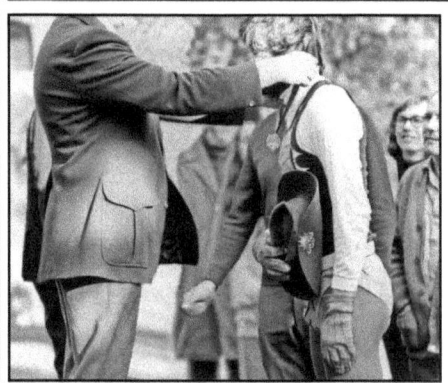

The infamous crowd scene where Aussifan receives his award from the grateful fans. The award is presented by Merv Binns while the crowd of grateful fans smile and clap and cheer him for his success in vanquishing the dastardly Antifan.

...and outside Space Age Books, Aussiefan with two appreciative fans.

Paul and I spent two weeks editing the film, and he came with me when I took it around to the news room at Chanel 9 studios in Richmond where I knew Peter Smith who was the warm-up man who got the audience primed before the Don Lane Show aired. I had sold some footage to the news room and asked him if we could use one of their editing benches to look at the finished film. He joined us and was surprised at how good the 'special effects' were, namely the disappearing act of Antifan behind the tree only to reappear from behind another much further away tree when the committee members chasing him discovered he wasn't behind the first tree. The film looked much better than we had expected.

We took this first version to Sydney to present it at Syncon 72, the National Convention in August 1972. The music had been selected — I can't remember who did that — and taped. The tape was played a bit out of sync while the film was projected. We received a standing ovation, and we knew then that what we had done would be successful.

The Worldcon in Los Angeles where the bid was to be officially launched would occur in three weeks' time, so there was a huge rush to get our film finished to be taken over to the US in time for that convention.

We only had a week to make the release print. It was during this week that we decided the fight scene was not needed and removed it. The whole film was tightened up so it flowed better making the final edited film about four minutes shorter that the version showed in Sydney. I recorded Lee Harding at Space Age Books making the narration. I had previously created the bomb sound effects by pinching an explosion scene from an old movie I had a copy of and splicing it into the film. I also mixed the narration, music and the explosion onto a tape that matched the film scenes.

The final edited film and the sound tape were taken to a film lab in South Melbourne where the release print was produced. They had to work backwards from the scene of the explosion because the tape we recorded on had stretched slightly throwing the explosion out of sync if we had started from the beginning. They made a magnetic 16 mm film soundtrack, then winding back from the explosion to the beginning they transferred the sound optically as the images were copied to make the release print. This resulted, because they worked backwards from the explosion, with Lee's narration being out of sync by one second. This print and the work in the film lab was paid for by Space Age Books, that is Merv Binns and Ron Graham.

None of us saw the release print. It went straight to America to be shown at the 1972 Worldcon in Los Angeles. During the next three years Jack Chalker and others showed it at hundreds of conventions throughout America.

The film was only a part of the bid. The credit should go to all those people who worked behind the scenes both in Australia and North America who went about talking to people, promoting Australia, and our bid, and writing about it in fanzines.

It wasn't until Aussiecon, our first Worldcon in Melbourne in 1975 that we finally saw the film, shown on the opening night. It was as good as everyone kept telling us.

That was our reward. To see a Worldcon in Melbourne Australia for the first time, to meet our favorite authors and actually speak to them, to know that what we had done was instrumental in achieving a dream. That week you would not have found two happier people than Paul Stevens and I. Except perhaps for the late John Bangsund, who was toastmaster for the convention and who I believe was instrumental in originating the idea that we should bid for this wonderful convention.

What strikes me as odd now, is that John Bangsund never appeared in the film. After calling me to see if I was interested in doing it, he virtually disappeared.

He wasn't in the planning or the scripting of the film. This might have been the time when he moved to Canberra to work for *Hansard* as an editor, which in retrospect would explain why he wasn't around for the filming and why he doesn't appear in it, because if he had been in Melbourne at the time, he certainly would have been included.

Sadly, John died of Covid 19 on Saturday 22 August 2020.
Merv Binns also passed away a few months earlier, 7th April 2020, from heart problems.
They will both be missed.
I personally feel that without either of these two gentlemen, Aussicon in 1975 would never have happened.

There was a cartoon strip about Aussiefan and Antifan, drawn and scripted by Greg and Grae (I don't know their family names) who were guests of honor at a local convention held in the Golden Age Hotel in Melbourne in 1972, where in the film the beer drinking scene takes place with the first appearance of Aussiefan.

As discussions were going on at that time regarding the bid for the Worldcon in 1975, the characters who appeared in the comic strip may have been the catalyst for the characters who appeared in the film. It could have been the other way around, but… One thing is certain, the comic strip appeared in a fanzine before the film was commenced, or near enough to the initial filming as to be simultaneous. I think the comic strip and the film concept both evolved through the discussions held over several months prior regarding how to publicize our bid and what we could do to make it stand out from the bid San Francisco was making. *A frame from the comic strip appeared in an article written by Keith Dunstan to promote Aussiecon a week or so before the commencement of the event in 1975.*

Over the six months after the film had been sent to America, many discussions were held regarding continuing promotion for the Worldcon and my suggestion was to do a short film, like a TV advert, that we could send over to the USA to assist and remind people that we were bidding, that we were still there and were waiting for them to come and visit.

This short film was around 8 minutes long, and in color.

I didn't take part in much of the discussion because I was spending a lot of time with Monica and as we got into 1973 we decided to get married.

I shot the first part of this short film very quickly just before we got married. It consisted of many very short 2 second shots of faces of Australian Fans and a few of the odd things that they do. I also slipped in a shot of a naked lady standing in a window, which I don't think anyone noticed. But this time I wanted to include John Bangsund who was then living in Canberra. I contacted him to see if he would be interested in appearing in the film and he was all for it. So, on the first long weekend that came up after our wedding, The Queen's Birthday (in June 1973), we drove up to Canberra in our van.

That weekend was officially our honeymoon. We got married on May 19th, 1973 and three weeks later were in Canberra for that long weekend. We weren't able to go anywhere immediately after the wedding and the Queen's birthday weekend was the first opportunity. We drove up on the

Having a late lunch at a famous wayside stop before driving the rest of the way into Canberra. From here, looking down into the valley beneath is the scene depicted in a famous painting by Sir Arthur Streeton, possibly his most famous pastoral scene. It was very cold on top of that lookout.

Saturday, arriving quite late in the day.

We parked our camper van in front of John's place or in the driveway and were prepared to sleep in it overnight, but John kindly offered us his double bed when we told him that this trip was our 'official' honeymoon.

In fact he insisted that we use his bed. "I'll sleep somewhere else," he said, and pretty soon after that he disappeared. I'm glad we didn't sleep outside in the van because the temperature went below freezing during the night and everything was covered in a heavy thick frost. When I went outside in the morning I had to scrape the frost off the windscreen with a knife.

Back inside I had a look in the fridge to see if there was any milk to use for a cup of coffee, but all that was in it were a few eggs and a half empty flagon of wine. It surprised me that someone could have such a large fridge and have nothing in it. I guess John wasn't much into cooking.

John Bangssund and Sally Yeoland.

When John did come back, he introduced us to a lovely lady called Sally.

Now whether he brought breakfast back or whether we all together went somewhere for breakfast, I can't quite remember. We spent some time wandering about after that, Monica and me, John and Sally, and Robin Johnson, who was also there that weekend. He always seemed to turn up whenever anything interesting was happening. We discussed what we would film and went back to John's place so he could change into the clothes he wanted to wear for the filming, as well as to gather a couple of props. He put on his favourite t-shirt of the moment, a Michael Leunig *Nation Review* t-shirt, grabbed a half bottle of port wine and his favourite book **Here's Luck**, and off we went to the National Library of Canberra, which of course was appropriate for someone who loved books as much as John did.

I think we had fish and chips for lunch.

— Grab that Moment —

John Bangsund, Robin Johnson, Sally Yeoland and Monica Litchen

After buying 5 copies each of the weekly National Times newspaper specifically for the colour supplement, Robin and John dumped the rest of the papers in a rubbish bin, John made sure afterwards that we hadn't missed any copies of the supplement which contained an article on SF Fandom by Tony Maiden featuring many of our friends.

Monica, soaking up the cool Canberra sunshine while we went looking for something to eat.

By the time we got back to John's place and he could change for the shoot it was mid afternoon and already the light was fading. The temperature had also dropped and was starting to get cold.

Somewhere along the way to the library we collected Leigh and Helen Hyde and their children who accompanied us and appear in some of the photos but I don't think they are in the film we shot. The kids helped carry my tripod in between running about and having a good time.

— Grab that Moment —

John playing with Helen's kids while I get the camera ready. Robin and Sally chatting off to the side. Above: One of Helen's kids carrying my tripod.
By the time we started filming the sun had gone behind the hills and it was getting dark.

— John Litchen —

We spent an hour or so in front of the library shooting a couple of scenes with John and that was it. Again we stayed at John's place on the Sunday night, and I think Robin Johnson slept on the couch. John stayed at Sally's place. I don't recall now what happened early in the morning but it probably was the same as on the Sunday morning. John and Sally came back, we went somewhere for breakfast and after that Monica and I would have started the drive back to Melbourne.

It was a delightful long weekend not only because it was our official; honeymoon, but because of the wonderful people we spent time with while there.

This short film shot during the Queen's Birthday weekend in June 1973, and was not long after sent over to America to help boost our bid for the 1975 Worldcon. Whether it had any effect, I have no idea.

I suspect the original film had done its job and those who were coming had already been convinced, and our little color short was a bit of overkill.

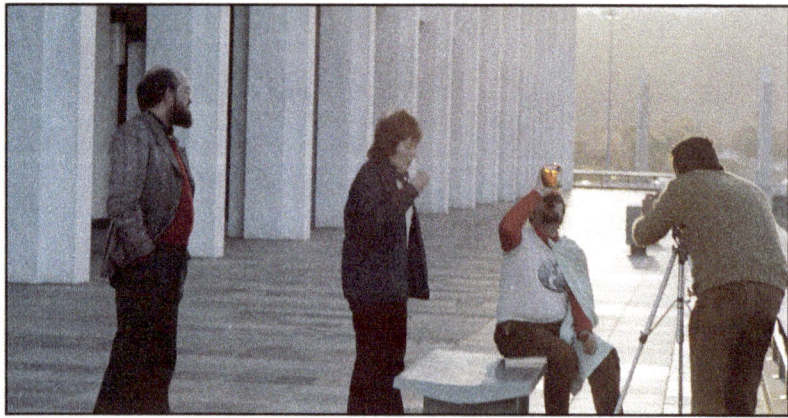

— Grab that Moment —

John, contemplating the sunset...
Below: Robin enjoying the filming before it got too dark and cold.

Above: John holding one of his favourite books.
Monica watching as we filmed.

It was also very cold by the time we finished the shoot since the sun had set and the light was fading. It was just a bit after four o'clock in the afternoon.

Why would anyone want to live in Canberra?

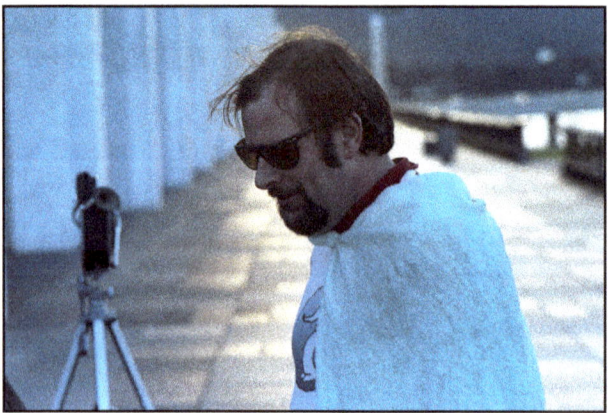

A football game at Foyster's farm

After we finished filming the first 'Antifan' film, we premiered it at a convention in Sydney (*Syncon 72* in August 1972). It was received with great enthusiasm, after which we had two weeks to make the final edit and a release print to be sent to the US. In September 1973, John and Elizabeth Foyster threw a party at what I always thought of as Foyster's Farm.

The Victorian countryside near Blackwood, between Kyneton and Ballarat, along the road that separates the Wombat State Forest from the Lederderg State Park is a beautiful wild area. The farm was along this road. It was owned by Elizabeth's parents, Mr and Mrs Pike, and John and Elizabeth merely visited there regularly at weekends. There was often some fannish activity there at these weekends, but I only ever went there once, and that was after the film we'd made had started doing the rounds of American conventions to publicize our bid for a world convention in 1975.

The reason for the party at the farm was to celebrate both the successful completing of the publicity film for 'Australia in 75'. and the announcement that we had won the bid, confirmed at ***Torcon*** in Toronto in September 1973. Most of the people involved with this film celebrated that day; Paul Stevens (Antifan), Merv Binns, Robin Johnson, Bill Wright, Leigh Edmonds and Valma and of course John Foyster all of whom appeared in the film. Lee Harding who did the voice-over for the film was also there as were other active fans who were involved in promoting Australia in 75 through their fanzines and other publications.

I don't remember seeing any chickens or other farm animals. I don't even remember what the house looked like, since most of the time we were outdoors.

Near the farmhouse, fenced off, was a large paddock where John decided a game of football would be played. John, who acted as referee, divided most of those present into two teams which then proceeded to play the game, whatever it was. I stood to one side and shot some memorable photos. Lee Harding and Merv Binns also stayed out of the game and took photos of the activities. The game seemed to be a mixture of AFL and a form of Rugby, and whatever rules there were, they were dictated by John who was all over the field while the game was in progress. It was fun to watch, but not being a football fan, I had no idea of what was going on. It just seemed utterly chaotic to me.

What stayed in my mind though, was that we had a fantastic time, that we were living in a year full of promise, and were enthusiastic for a future we could hardly wait to experience.

Before the game, while some were already in the paddock... Others were getting ready, changing into something more appropriate for a football game which included their Australia in 75 t-shirts Watching on are: partially obscured Robin Johnson, Carey Handfield, Lee Harding, while Leigh Edmonds and Paul Stevens are engrossed in their own discussion.
Below: Merv Binns uncertain about what is in his cup, Monica Litchen enjoying a snack, and Irene Pagram looking at who is already on the field.

Below: Robin Johnson and Merv Binns before the game started.

— Grab that Moment —

Bill Wright warming up for the game while Paul Stevens looks on amused.

Bill wright heading into the field with one of the players while Lee Harding readies his camera.

Uncertain about the rules, a discussion takes place, while others wander about the field, John Foyster finally explains the rules with graphic emphasis.

Robin Johnson, on the field, ready for the game.

Get the ball and run seemed to be the only rule.

Bill, about to be sent off by John for breaking an obscure rule.

— Grab that Moment —

Discussing the fine points of the game. Lee Harding and Robin Johnson. Below: looking for the ball which they don't know Valma is holding.

Bill gets a free kick while Robin watches.

Finally, Ken Ford gets a chance to grab the ball, while John Foyster and Valma look on amused and Lee Harding takes a classic photo.

— Grab that Moment —

*Merv Binns and his winning team.
Stephen Campbell, Michael Creaney Standing, Peter millar sitting,
Ken Ford leanaing on Merv Binns, and Tony Thomas.*

Lee Harding about to take their picture.

— John Litchen —

Robin Johnson checking his camera, while the photographer and editor John Litchen, and the director and star of the film, Paul Stevens celebrate the moment.

The lake at the bottom of the paddock.

Jumping ahead...

Jumping ahead eight years, Sydney fans decided they wanted to bid for another Worldcon which of course they wanted to hold in Sydney in 1983. Even though there is some rivalry between Sydney and Melbourne fans everyone decided that a group effort would be the way to achieve it.

At Space Age Books on Friday night (early in 1980) Paul Stevens told me Carey Handfield had contacted him to see if he would be willing to appear in another Antifan film. Carey was the 'chair' of the Sydney in 83 bidding committee.

"They want to make an Antifan film?" It was a surprise to me.

"Carey and I have already done a script..."

"And?"

"They want us to fly up there and do it. They want Antifan, and they want you to film it."

"Are they going to pay for the flights up and back?"

"And the accommodation overnight. It's all planned. We fly up on a Saturday afternoon, stay overnight in a hotel, shoot the Sydney scenes on the Sunday, and we fly back that night. Carey Handfield has organized it."

I'm always willing to go off and do something unexpected, something that crops up on the spur of the moment. It's what makes life interesting.

"Okay, I'll go along with it."

After looking at the script that Paul had, it occurred to me that we would need some linking shots, some way getting Antifan after he is revived to Sydney. Reviving him would be easy. In the final shot of the original film, Antifan, his clothes ripped and torn from the explosion, staggers along a deserted beach where he finally collapses. The unstated implication was that the wind would blow enough sand over him to eventually bury him. To revive him the plan was to have some fans relaxing on the beach, and one of them is reading a copy of Bruce Gillespie's **Science Fiction Review**, while another accidentally knocks over a fizzy drink which boils into the sand and wakes up Antifan who emerges, resplendent in his black cape and hat, in front of the startled fan. Antifan then calls on his assistant, also buried, a giant zombie, who emerges from the sand and promptly does away with the startled fan. And then Antifan finally gets to blow up Merv Binns who is manning a news stand on the beach.

"How are we going to explain your arrival in Sydney?"

"There is no mention of how they want Antifan to get there in the script. It's just about what he does when he gets there. I guess its up to us to figure that out."

On going through the script again I saw there was a scene in which Antifan is supposed to go into Sydney Harbour near the Opera House, swim along underwater and pull out a giant plug that would drain the harbour.

"We can shoot the underwater scenes at Williamstown. There is easy access by the Lifesaving Club, and there is a huge concrete drain pipe just offshore there. We could make it look as if you pulled the plug out there."

Paul was wary about doing stuff underwater. He'd not been scuba diving or skindiving as far as I knew, but he was willing to give it a go.

"I've got a spare wetsuit you can wear, extra masks and snorkels, flippers, but more importantly, the water where we'll shoot the film in not much deeper than a metre, so you can actually stand up and walk out over the rocks. It's probably easier to swim over them though."

"All right." He said it reluctantly, no doubt wondering about how he was going to pull a giant plug out of an underwater drainpipe.

"And once we've shot that scene we can get you in full costume to run up and jump on the giant anchor on the foreshore of The Strand where you can see Melbourne in the background. We can do a short in-camera dissolve that makes you disappear, and then when we're in Sydney we can have you appear in front of the Opera House, after which you get up to whatever they have scripted for you to do." And that was to immediately go down to the water's edge and look for a way into the water in order to pull out the plug and drain the harbour.

Paul spoke to Carey about that and he was in favor of it so we went ahead and got ready. Carey came with us as we did the filming at Williamstown and St Kilda. The actual disappearing happens so fast it's barely noticeable in the film I watched on YouTube. My memory is that it was better than that, but I can't deny what I saw; it's a very short shot.

Once the filming in Melbourne was finished Paul and I flew up to Sydney where the rest of the film was shot.

The second film, *Antifan Strikes Back* was shot around 1980 and was entirely financed by the fans in Sydney. They wrote the script, paid for Paul and I to fly up there one weekend over which most of the film was shot.

The idea and the funding for the *Antifan Strikes Back* film came from the Australia in 83 committee which was bidding to hold the 1983 Worldcon in Sydney. Carey Handfield was chair of the bidding committee and helped organize the film project. He wasn't in Sydney when Paul and I flew up to do the film, but he was in Melbourne and was with us as we shot some of the initial scenes in Melbourne at St Kilda Beach, Williamstown, and once again inside Space Age Books where Antifan gets some assistance from the resident zombie with boxes full of explosives used to blow up the Sydney Headquarters.

John Litchen and Carey Handfield, making sure Antifan, is properly covered with sand before we film him emerging. This was filmed at St Kilda where he collapses in the final scene of the first film. He is woken by a fan accidentally spilling a drink on the sand where he is buried.

Completely buried, only the edge of his hat and the top of his cape kept the sand out of his face.

— John Litchen —

Enlisting the help of a zombie posing at Space Age Books, Antifan begins his campaign to destroy the Sydney bid for the 1983 World con.

Andrew Brown is the zombie in the Melbourne scenes, here with myself and Paul Stevens having some fun in front of Space Age Books. (May or June 1980.)

— Grab that Moment —

With Andrew Brown in front of Space Age Books. He really was very tall which probably explains why he wears that t-shirt emphasizing how much he hates Basketball.

At Williamstown, Carey is standing beside me as I shoot a scene with Paul.

At Williamstown for the scene where Antifan disappears. Paul getting ready while I wait.

Paul Stevens — the one and only Antifan.

Shooting the disappearing scene on The Strand with the city of Melbourne in the far background, Antifan runs along the water's edge and leaps onto the anchor and while spreading his cape he dissolves into thin air.

— Grab that Moment —

Paul, getting into the wetsuit for the underwater sequence.

The underwater sequence was shot before the disappearing scene. It was early in the morning before there were any crowds to get in the way. Not that there would have been too many people considering that it was the beginning of winter. Even though the weather was good, the fact that it was winter is enough to keep people away. The water was like glass, beautifully clear and very calm, perfect for someone who was nervous about being underwater.

The water was also quite warm, having had all summer to heat up, but Paul just wasn't comfortable doing these shots.
He was 'Out of his depth' as the saying goes.

Relieved that it was finally over, Paul is much happier as he chats with my young brother Paul. We then went around to The Strand where we shot the scene with the anchor.

Above: *Ready to start filming... Antifan waiting for us to bury him in the sand for the opening scene. Carey Handfield and John Litchen checking the script.*

— Grab that Moment —

John Foyster with his two cameras looks on while a scene is being set up. Andrew Brown, the zombie actually can smile...

Launching the dinghy for the final scene. They had to drag it out into water deep enough for Antifan and his zombie to start rowing.

There are a couple of delightful moments in the second film, that were not scripted but just happened. The first is near the beginning when Antifan after emerging from his coma under the sand, and after getting his zombie assistant to kill an annoying fan, runs off across the sand, and just before he exists the frame in the distance he accidentally falls over, flat onto his face.
Instead of cutting before the fall and going to the next scene where he runs up to Merv Binns reading in his news kiosk on the beach and gives him a bomb, which then blows up destroying Merv and the kiosk, they left the fall in the film.
The other unplanned bits are near the end in the rowing boat. Antifan and his Zombie are rowing out to sea, (also filmed at St KIlda). The boat just doesn't go where they want it to go, since neither of the occupants had any idea of how to row a boat. It goes off in wrong directions or partially turns around in a circle, but it makes an hilarious end to the film. The sheer ineptitude of these two characters is mind-blowing.

John Breden adjusts the bolts in the zombie's neck while Paul Stevens looks on.

Paul Stevens in costume holding the bomb used to blow up Merv Binns and his beach-side news stand.
John Litchen filming the scene.

The weekend after the Melbourne sequences were shot, Paul and I flew to Sydney where the rest of the film was shot at various locations around the city.

The first shoot of the day. It was a foggy morning to start with, but it soon cleared, although it remained overcast for most of the day. The first shots we did were Antifan arriving in Sydney, the scene where he climbs up and undoes the giant bolts that hold up the bridge, as well as where he enters the water to pull out the plug and drain the harbour, and the scenes of the desperate Sydney fans attempting to refill the harbour with buckets of water.

— Grab that Moment —

Paul Stevens, Antifan, preparing for a scene to be shot under or near the Sydney Harbour Bridge. This was probably the scene where he undoes the bolts that hold up the bridge as well as where he enters the water to pull the plug and drain the harbour. The actual underwater shot of him pulling the giant plug out was done days earlier at Williamstown. We also shot him apparently appearing out of nowhere nearby. Then after those shots we did the scenes of the Sydney fans desperately trying to refill the harbour with buckets of water. It was a lot of fun shooting these scenes. Behind Paul is one of the ladies who later seduce him.
Robin Johnson as usual was there. He doesn't appear in the film because he was eliminated in the first film, but he was most likely involved in some way with the bidding committee.

— John Litchen —

The bucket brigade in action

The view of Sydney from my hotel room.

— Grab that Moment —

Finally with the harbour refilled the team could relax. The water on the road was from rain, and not spilled from the buckets.
Setting up for Antifan to climb up onto the bridge where he would undo the bolts holding it up, thus causing it to fall into the now re-filled harbour.

Outside Galaxy bookshop before the riot which destroys the premises.

The Sydney bidding committee planing on how they are going to subvert Antifan since each plan to stop him backfired on them.

Unhappy that things are not going as planned Antifan encounters a seductive young lady who convinces him to come with her.

Lured by this beautiful lady, Antifan is enticed to enter her apartment where several others are waiting to add their charms to his seduction.
It all goes according to plan and Antifan ends up deliriously happy and agrees to work for the Australian Bidding Committee and to travel overseas to destroy rival bids for the Worldccon in 83.
In the final scene he leaves for Rotterdam in a rowing boat with his zombie assistant.

It was Carey Handfield who organized the finance for the film and supplied me with the film stock. Paul and I had nothing to do with the editing this time around. Paul Stevens and Carey Handfield produced the script together and probably directed the scenes as they were shot. Carey Handfield and Don Ashby spent endless hours watching the rough cuts and selecting suitable music to accompany it. It was Don Ashby who did the final editing. It's unclear who did the initial editing before the rough cuts were sent to Don and Carey. Someone had made a rough cut and had shown the film at Syncon 80 in Sydney before this rough cut was sent to Carey and Don. They had barely a week to do the final edit so it was a mad rush to get the film ready. After the final editing was finished, they took the film to the Lab for a release print to be made. This print arrived at the very last moment and they had to race out to the airport and give the film to Robin Johnson who was preparing to board a flight to the USA. He took the film to America where it did the rounds of conventions.

The committee hoped that this new film would replicate the success of the first film in gaining them the Worldcon in 1983.

The photos on pages 248 to 251, as well as pages 256, to 259, were kindly supplied by Carey Handfield, and were scanned with the assistance of Richard Hryckiewicz.

Now, 40 years later, I had another look at the two films where they can be found together on YouTube, and my personal feeling is that ***Antifan Strikes Back*** lacked the spontaneity the original film had, in part because it seemed predictable. But I think the main reason is there is no narration to explain what is happening, as there was in the first film, and instead, it has been presented as a silent film (only with music) with titles in between scenes to explain what is happening. This slows the film down between each scene by stopping for several seconds to give a viewer time to read the words on the screen. If the film had been presented without these interruptions the flow of action would have been much snappier, and the audience would still would have been able to understand what was going on.

With the first film, no one knew what the hell was going on. It had tension. The audience were kept wondering: would Antifan succeed or would Aussiefan win the day? And the tension built as each new victim appeared until the final climactic scene where we all thought Antifan had been destroyed. The film finished on a high, but the final scene revealed that Antifan had somehow survived and the implied promise was that much more nefarious events would follow. It left in the audience's mind a feeling of anticipation.

The second film didn't do that. The twist here is that the bidding committee knows what Antifan is like and they try individually to stop him from doing what he does, only for it to backfire on them each time they try. Finally they contrive, with the help of some beautiful women to seduce Antifan into working for them, and they dispatch him off to destroy the Copenhagen bid as well as the Boston Bid. The final scene has Antifan and his Zombie ineptly rowing a boat out to sea to destroy all foreign bids.

The effort and time spent producing the film has to be commended. It was done with as much enthusiasm by those involved as had been the first film. They were competing against Boston fans in the USA who were also bidding for the same convention.

Merv Binns, among other Australian fans, tried to promote Australia in 83 to be held in Sydney, and he told me later that the American fans at the conventions they attended in the USA and in England indicated they would vote for Boston and not Sydney in 83. Boston had such a strong bid the Australian delegation withdrew their bid.

As soon as the Australian team dropped out of the bidding John Foyster, not wanting Australia to miss out on another Worldcon, instigated a new bid for Australia in 1985 which did have support from the American convention goers who indicated they would vote for that. The result was we won another Worldcon for Australia in Melbourne in 1985, Aussiecon 2.

And they did that without making a film.

— Grab that Moment —

Part Four
Moments to remember

Gunnamatta Beach 3rd February 1972

The surf was red with blood that morning.
It trickled slowly across wet sand and was
greedily sucked away by huge waves as the tide receded.
There were thirty six whales on the beach,
and all but two of them were dead.

The day of the whales

Gunnamatta beach, which is on the ocean side of the Mornington Peninsula and these days is part of the Mornington National Park, is a good surfing beach as it faces into Bass Strait, but in 1972 it was only known to the locals who lived on the Mornington Peninsula or to the holidaymakers who went there during the summer holidays or other long weekends. It was not a patrolled beach in 1972. It is located between the Heads and Cape Schanck. It is a wild beach with pounding surf and gutters between rocky reefs that make it a superb location for ocean fishing as well as surfing. In fact, it's not far from Cheviot beach where Prime Minister Harold Holt disappeared while swimming in the surf.

On the morning of February 3rd, 1972, I had just arrived at the dry-cleaning factory to start work, and Phillip was already there. He had switched on the boiler and was getting ready to clean the first batch of clothing for the day. It promised to be very hot day, and at this time of year, the middle of summer, we usually weren't too busy. As was his custom, he put the radio on to listen to the news, and the talk-back program on station 3AW. I'd made a coffee and was sipping it when the news started and the announcer was excitedly talking about a pod of whales that had become stranded on Gunnamatta Beach. There were a lot of whales. Early morning beach walkers had seen them coming in and getting stranded and had called in the news to the radio station. It was the first time a large number of whales had been stranded on this beach, and if I remember right, it was probably the first time a pod of whales had been stranded anywhere on a mainland Australian beach. There had been strandings in more remote areas, especially at the bottom of Tasmania, but not on a beach in Victoria, one so close to a heavily populated area.

"I've got to go and have a look at that," I said to Phillip.

He gave me a pissed off look for a moment as he sipped his coffee, then just shrugged. He was used to me taking off on a good day to do some diving with Fred in his abalone boat, or to go to a daytime rehearsal for a show later that evening. He just shrugged and said "okay."

I rang Fred and as soon as he answered I said "grab your camera and come here and get me."

"What's going on?"

"There's a pod of whales stranded on the beach at Gunnamatta. We should go and have a look at them."

"I haven't had breakfast yet."

"Forget breakfast. We can get something on the way. It's already been on the morning news. If we don't leave now there'll be a million people there by lunchtime and no one will get near the place."

"I'm on my way."

He turned up 20 minutes later and we were off. We stopped at my place first so I could grab my Bolex movie camera and my Nikon still camera and then we drove out along the Nepean Highway. We had a good run to Mornington Peninsula because all the traffic was heading into town, people going to work. Hardly anyone was heading out of town and our side of the highway was empty.

It was probably a bit after 9 am when we got to Gunnamatta and already it was crowded.

"Shit," Fred said when he saw all the people along the beach.

"It's a good thing we got here early," I said. "Can you imagine what it's going to be like in another couple of hours?"

"There must be a couple of hundred people here already."

I set up the Bolex movie camera on a tripod close to the whales that were completely dry and out of the water. It was obvious that the tide had gone out because most of the whales were well out of the water. Only a few smaller ones were half in and half out as the waves lapped around them. The water surrounding them was full of blood. That bloody water was being sucked out by the outgoing tide and somewhere beyond where the waves were breaking there would no doubt be a lot of hungry sharks attracted by the blood. No one in their right mind would even consider swimming or surfing anywhere on this beach today.

I shot some film of people climbing on top of the largest whale which must have been around 40 feet long. Except for a couple of the smaller whales which were feebly thrashing in the shallow blood-filled water, all the others were dead. A few people were trying to push these two smaller whales out into deeper water but it was a hopeless task. Even the smallest whales would have weighed a ton or more, and their lungs had already been crushed by their body weight (not being suspended in water) and were bleeding out. No amount of pushing was going to get them back into the water, and by the time the tide would come in later in the afternoon they would already be dead.

I said in an article I later wrote for **Skin Diving in Australia.*** *It was unfortunate that this mass stranding had occurred so close to Melbourne. Many thousands of people went to see them, but there were amongst these people many of whom no one could be proud. They hacked pieces off the whales, they chopped teeth out, and one man had even sawn off a complete jaw. He walked along the beach holding it against his chest, blood dribbling down his naked torso. A lot of people had carved their initials into the whale's skin (cracked and drying in the sun) even though the whales might still have been alive.*

It was sad enough to see so many dead and dying whales on a beach, but what was even sadder was to see people showing such a lack of respect that they turned what was a tragedy into a macabre carnival.

Why whales beach themselves, no one really knows. There are many theories and those interested can research them from many different sources, but it does seem that whales beaching themselves is becoming more common than it once was.

At first it was thought that these particular whales were pilot whales; they have a reputation for beaching. But Pilot whales have a dorsal fin on top much like a dolphin or a killer whale, and Sperm whales don't. It was determined later in the day that this stranded pod was of Sperm whales, which made this stranding a rare occurrence. Sperm whales don't generally get themselves stranded on a beach. These were fairly young whales with the biggest barely 40 feet long. A senior research officer for the Victorian Fisheries and Wildlife Department said it was unusual for Sperm Whales to be stranded, and as far as he knew it had never happened before. The odd one had been found stranded occasionally, but never had there been a Sperm Whale stranding with these numbers.

"I never imagined there'd be so much blood?" Fred said as we slowly walked along the beach.

It didn't smell though, mixed in with sea water as it soaked into wet sand or was sucked back out by retreating waves. A cold breeze off Bass Strait kept the air clean and fresh, with the tang of the sea giving it a salty flavor.

"Whales are mammals and air-breathers," I said as we stopped to look at the smallest ones still partially floating. Several people who had been trying to push them back out into deeper water had given up, and just stood there staring disconsolately at them.

"In the water, they're weightless. The water supports them. But once on land their body weight is so much it crushes and ruptures their lungs as well as other organs. There is a limit to how big a land animal can get before its own body weight crushes it. Whales are just too big and heavy to be on land. The more they struggle to breathe, the more their blood get pushed into their lungs. They spurt it out trying to take a breath which is why the water around them is so bloody… They literally drowned in their own blood."

"That's horrible," Fred muttered.

"It's an agonizing death. But what makes it worse is that they are intelligent animals and they probably knew that they were dying and that there was nothing they could do about it. They can't fight gravity when there is no water to support them."

Having walked past the last of the stranded whales we turned around to see that there were many more people on the beach than before. We hadn't noticed them arriving.

"I think it's time we went home," Fred said.

The next day the local council dug a mass grave behind the sand dunes and buried almost all the whales. A pet food company came and took the two biggest ones away on a low loader to turn them into pet food. After that, the beach was back to normal, surf crashing, wind-blown salty air, and the odd person walking along the edge where the sand was a bit firmer. It was as if nothing had ever happened.

*I didn't write the article, called The Day of The Whales, until several years later. It was published in Skindiving in Australia and New Zealand, October 1978, Volume 7 #4.

It looked like a bomb hit it

Sometime in 1972 Dad and Mum decided to brick veneer the house. The cladding that had been used to cover the original weather boards had cracked and looked dilapidated. They hired a building company based in Footscray that not only did renovations and extensions but also built new houses.

Some of the trees along the side of the garage were removed, since their roots went where the foundation for the brick wall needed to go. They were replaced with new bushes. Other trees, further out from the wall were left alone.

They came and in no time the old windows were pulled out and stacked in the back yard. Sections of walls came down, also dumped in the yard. Foundation trenches were dug all along the walls around the house, concrete was poured and a huge truckload of bricks arrived. Scaffolding went up and very quickly the house was brick-veneered. It looked fantastic except for the back yard which looked like a bomb had blown up a building. Even the garage was brick-veneered.

Putting the brick walls around made the house wider, and the driveway was no longer wide enough for Dad to drive his car up into the garage. He had to leave it in the front driveway. The garage eventually became a giant storeroom.

It didn't take long for the back yard to recover once the rubble was taken away and as Autumn approached Monica felt cold even though the weather was fine and sunny. The best time of year. We took some photos beside the newly refurbished garage.

A bold move

It was Laura who later pushed to move to Perth. I don't think Alicia wanted to go, she was happy with her situation, but out of familial loyalty, she decided she would accompany her sister to Perth. And that was the last we saw of them until the mid-1980s when we went to Perth to visit Monica's friend Sonia (whom she knew from her first year in Sydney). Sonia, originally from Peru, had moved from Sydney to Perth and had married there. She had a daughter, Fiona, who was born the same year our son Brian was born, 1976. Laura joined us for afternoon tea and that was the last time we saw her.

Monica definitely didn't want to go to Perth with the other two. So, the week before they left I went looking for a place where she could stay. We found a one bedroom flat in a building of ten in North Richmond, one block away from the railway station as well as a huge park that extended all the way back to the edge of the city. We leased it for 6 months. The flat was on the upper floor and was the second one back from the front. The first flat was occupied by a Spanish couple from Cordoba and they were delighted to have next door to them, someone who could speak Spanish. They took it upon themselves to look out for Monica. Manuel and Magdalena were their names. Magdalena was about the same age as Monica, and Manuel was a few years older. I had no trouble understanding Magdalena but as for Manuel, I found him to be incomprehensible most of the time. Whether it was his accent, or that he spoke very rapidly, I don't know; I just couldn't understand him. I thought it was me, but Monica also had difficulty understanding him, and Spanish was her language. I suspected that he used a dialect local to Cordoba and Andalucía, which would have many words Spanish speaking people from other countries would never have heard before. Apart from that, they were a good couple and we often went for a walk in the park with them.

With Manuel and Magdalena in Melbourne's Botanical Gardens.

Monica and Magdalena and a grass tree

Monica on another occasion, wearing a floral dress trying to hide amongst flowers.

I spent as many nights with Monica in her little flat as I did at home. We talked about moving in together but I didn't think Mum and Dad would approve if we both lived together at the family home in Benbow street, even though Monica spent more time there than anywhere else. And for the two of us to live in her tiny flat would not have worked out. The flat was a temporary solution which is why we only took a six month's lease. Monica brought up the idea of getting married, which to me seemed so natural I hardly had to think about it before agreeing. It was time. I wonder if I would have suggested it if it had been up to me, but once she brought it up I knew it was the right decision. We were both ready for this next step, well at least I knew I was ready, and since Monica had suggested it, I knew she was.

"Mum will love this," I said.

Our most important decision

"We've decided we want to get married," I said to Mum in the kitchen the next day.

Her eyes sparkled. I think she was going to say *Finally… or about bloody time…* but before she could say anything I said, "How would you like to arrange it?"

She stared at me with her mouth open.

"You could call the priest at the local church in Spotswood, you know, where Phillip and Nijole were married and where they had the girls christened. It's a Catholic Church and as you know Monica is Catholic. It would be the right place."

"Of course, I would love to do it."

And before she could start thinking of elaborate plans for a huge wedding, I told her, "We don't want a big wedding like Zara had, just something small. We could have the reception here at home. What do you think?"

"What reception?" Dad had just walked into the kitchen and heard the word reception.

"For John and Monica. They've decided to get married."

He looked at me and smiled. "Good for you. We should celebrate with a coffee."

He immediately went and got his little copper *cafechi* from the cupboard and put two teaspoons of finely ground Turkish coffee, two teaspoons of sugar, and filled it with water. It was on the gas stove and within a minute I could smell the rich aroma wafting through the kitchen. He poured two small cups and sat down at the table opposite me. We sipped the very strong coffee while he started reminiscing about his own wedding in Epirus, Northern Greece (the part that had been annexed by Albania) which happened around 1920 or thereabouts. Mum got up and went into the hallway where the phone was. No doubt she was going to ring everyone to tell them the news.

And that was it. I let Mum organize the date which turned out to be a couple of months away (May 19th 1973), and also to notify whatever relatives she thought should be there. She was in her element.

The first thing I did, once the idea of marrying Monica had settled, was to write a letter Monica's mother telling her what we had decided and in fact asking her for permission to marry her daughter. Her father had long since passed away when she was a teenager so I couldn't ask him. But Monica was always writing to her Mum and since she couldn't be here in Australia, I wanted her to know from me first that we were getting married, rather than to hear it from Monica. She wrote me a beautiful letter in response, giving both of us her blessings.

None of Monica's immediate family were able to come to Australia, but she did have a cousin (Minke) who had recently moved to Sydney from Chile, and he was there with his wife and two daughters. He was working as a mechanic. Naturally we invited them and he came down to Melbourne with his older daughter (Irene) the day before the wedding. They stayed in Monica's flat in North Richmond while she stayed at Benbow street where she got dressed and ready for the wedding. I went and stayed at Fred's and Zara's place in North Altona where I got ready for the wedding.

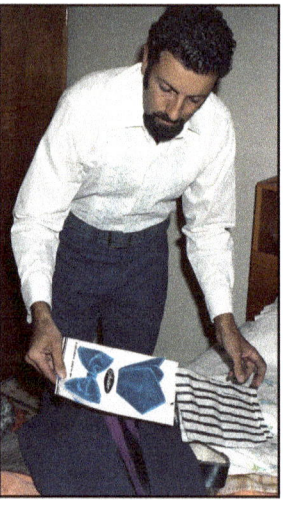

Getting dressed at Fred and Zara's place. The bow tie was tight fit. The suit was a blue pinstripe, and I wore a suede blue leather belt to match my blue suede shoes.

— Grab that Moment —

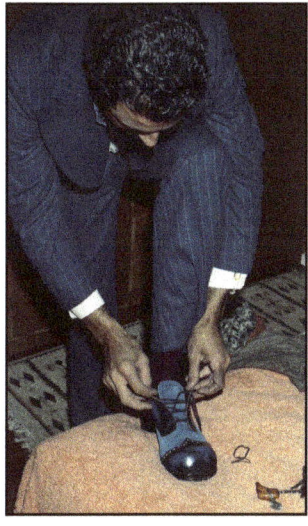

Dressed to kill! In Fred's Back yard before leaving for the church. Wearing platform shoes which were all the rage in 1973.

Monica, getting ready at home, Benbow Street Yarraville with the help of my sister Christine. Also with her was her niece, Irene, the daughter of her cousin Minke, both of whom came down from Sydney for the wedding.

Ready to leave for the church.

— Grab that Moment —

Dad was roped in to officially give away the bride. He was delighted. He also used his Ford Fairlane as a wedding limousine to take Monica to the church. After the wedding, we both came back in a hired limo. I don't know why we didn't use the Fairlane. Perhaps there wasn't enough room in the back. The reception was held at home.

Arriving at St Margaret Mary's Church in Spotswood. Greeting family and friends waiting outside.

Melbourne's weather can be notoriously bad in May but this time it was beautiful. It was a lovely sunny afternoon with hardly a breath of air moving so it was perfect. It was quite warm, autumnal without the feeling of Autumn; it was more like a not-so-hot summer's day. I got to the church with Fred and everyone who was coming was already seated inside. Fred and I walked along the aisle and stood at the front where the Priest, Father Brian Murray, was also waiting. Wally (Walter Shaw) was my best man, and he was standing by the altar waiting for me to arrive. Fred sat down and then we waited for Monica to arrive.

That's the worst part of getting married; waiting at the altar for the bride to appear. It can be quite nerve wracking, but before I had a chance to get too nervous, I heard a commotion behind us. Everybody stirred, turned to watch the bride being walked along the aisle.

And there she was. Radiant, with a gorgeous smile, being led along the aisle by Dad who looked serious. He was trying not to smile because giving away the bride was a serious affair. He of course was standing in for Monica's father, who had long ago died, and her mother, who was unable to travel from Chile to Australia for the wedding.

Father Brian T Murray was the priest, Walter Shaw (Wally) was our best man, and Zara was our bridesmaid. Phillip can be seen standing behind Zara.

And then she was standing next to me and we turned to face each other. She was nervous too, which strangely, made me feel more comfortable. Then Father Murray started talking but we hardly took any notice of what he was saying. Suddenly I had to repeat whatever he said about looking after Monica in sickness and in health and all that stuff that you traditionally vow, and then it was Monica's turn to repeat the same vow. The wedding ring went onto her finger and suddenly it was all over. It had hardly taken any time at all. He led us into a room behind the Altar where we signed a registry, he presented us with a Certificate of Marriage, which I held up to show everyone as we came back into the main part of the church.

As we walked out, a married couple, everyone stood and clapped and started throwing confetti and rice at us.

Signing the wedding registry and receiving the marriage certificate to make it official.

*Finally emerging as husband and wife.
Holding on to the wedding certificate.*

— John Litchen —

I sent a number of photos to Monica's mother in Chile, and of all of them, she chose the one above to put in the local newspaper with the inscription: El 19 de Marzo de este año se efectuó en la ciudad de Melbourne el matrimonio de la señorita Mónica Correa Márquez con el señor John Litchen Curteis.

Below: with Monica's friend Kathy and her husband Jock.

Alexandra, my elder sister, Verga's daughter.

Unfortunately, the photographer missed on two occasions to include Verga in the photos. All we got was the side of her face in profile. I don't think he knew she was my older sister.

There are no other photos of her at the wedding.

Above: with Brian Mealey my oldest and best friend, and with Carl Curtis, also a long time friend. Just behind Monica and me is Christine, my youngest sister.

Mum, me, Monica, Minke and Irene, Zara, Wally, and Dad.

Outside the church we greeted and talked with friends who had come, and with other family members. Paul used my Bolex to take some movie footage during and after the ceremony, Rommy took photos of us and our friends outside the church. I had asked him to take photos of Monica getting ready, while Fred took some of me at his house. Unfortunately, Rommy was one of those photographers who never looked at what was in the background, and sometimes what was in the background spoiled what could have been a fabulous photo. He also, like many people, tended to place the face of who he was photographing in the upper third or the centre of the image in the viewfinder, which resulted in cutting off the subject's legs at the knee or between the knee and the feet. Perhaps I should have asked Paul to take the photos; he had a good eye regarding framing of an image. It's not the camera that takes the photo, it's the person using it. But in saying that, I am happy that Rommy did take photos and most of them are pretty good especially the head shots of Monica.

The wedding was low-key, a small family affair, and the reception we had at home in Benbow street, where Mum and Dad had at various times hosted some quite lavish parties. This would be no exception. The only difference this time was it had a wedding cake which Monica and I had to cut, speeches were made by Wally, the best man, and myself, after which we ate and drank and made merry on into the night.

Apart from Minke, Monica's cousin, who had traveled down from Sydney with his daughter Irene, none of Monica's family were in a position to travel from Chile to Australia for a wedding. It was unlikely, due to the political situation at that time, that they would have been given permission to travel anyway.

There was a lot of laughter, many jokes, and a bit too much food and alcohol consumed, but we had a great time. It was a day I will never forget.

In the limousine on the way home from the church.

— John Litchen —

*A toast to the future,
cake cutting,
raunchy telegrams, lots of laughter, speeches from the best man...
it was a memorable night.*

We got up late the next morning. I was feeling the effects of too much alcohol consumed and was somewhat seedy. I'm glad it was a Sunday and I didn't have to go to work. Monica seemed okay. Mum was already cleaning the house and in no time at all you would never have known a party had been held there the night before.

Monica had nor been working at Berkley Apparel for long enough to have accrued annual holidays and didn't feel comfortable asking for some time off, and although I could have got a week off, it was our busiest time at the dry cleaners, so we delayed what most newly married couples do, that is go on a honeymoon. We did however, take the opportunity to go away on the Queen's Birthday long weekend three weeks later (in June). We went to Canberra and that short trip was, you could say, our honeymoon.

Paul was still a teenager, 17 years old, and the only other one of us still living at home. Paul used Phillip's old bedroom, while the sleep-out which was once my bedroom became a sun-room, or a small lounge room. The extra bedroom at the back which was originally built for Zara and Christine became our new bedroom.

The bedroom at the back was cozy at first, but we really wanted to be on our own. Sharing a house with my parents and younger brother was fine for a while, but the sooner we could get a place of our own the better it would be. The upside of living at home was it gave us a chance to save money towards what we eventually decided, which was to build our own house.

Time seemed to race by after the Queen's Birthday long weekend Canberra trip, and before we knew it the end of the year was upon us. We had made short trips on weekends to places within Victoria, like Healesville Sanctuary, the mountain country near Bright where we could see the changing colours of the trees in Autumn, and other places. As the end of the year rapidly approached, I suggested we should take a trip to Queensland. We wanted to be on our own for a while, to get away from living in the house at Benbow street.

"We could go up through the centre of NSW, through Cobar, up to Toowoomba and from there, further north."

"Sounds good to me," Monica said.

"Then that's what we'll do."

The place where Monica worked, Berkley Apparel, closed down for three weeks over the Christmas and New year period so that was a good time. We also were not very busy at the dry cleaning factory because of the hotter weather and the holiday period even though we stayed open apart from the public holidays which everyone took so I organized with Phillip to take a few weeks off.

Life moves on.

I wanted to go through Cobar because this city in central New South Wales held a particular interest for our family. Mum lived there as child from the age of five until about fifteen. He father was a mining engineer and he managed a copper mine in Cobar after moving from Kalgoorlie where he had worked in the gold mines, and where Mum, her sister Betty, and brothers Bill and Jack were born. Eddie was the only one born in Cobar.

My grandfather had also leased the mines after they closed down when the price of copper became too low for the mines to be economical, and the slag dumps along with the old buildings effectively belonged to him. He paid rates for years to the Cobar City Council, even after he had moved to Melbourne. After he died (in 1956) Mum looked after his estate, and managed to sell some of the slag to be crushed and used for road building.

— *Grab that Moment* —

Enough royalties were earned to pay the rates to maintain ownership of the abandoned mines and surrounds.

Although Mum managed the affairs, Eddie and Bill were recognized as executors of the estate and they did a deal with Broken Hill Mines which allowed BHM to take over the mining rights, and using new automated equipment they started mining for copper again. They also re-crushed the slag and extracted copper and other minerals which could not be done before.

Mum was pissed off that Bill and Eddie had sold the mining rights to Broken Hill Mines, after their father (my grandfather) had struggled for years to keep those rights. He knew what value was there, and that one day it would pay off. Eddie thought the money offered to them by Broken Hill was a lot and accepted their offer. He and Bill signed the documents without consulting Mum or Aunty Betty. He had no idea of the real value of that property or the ownership of those mining rights. He thought there was nothing there but wasteland and old slag dumps, and that it was relatively worthless, even though a small royalty was paid for the use of the slag for local road building. But with new technology, and a rapidly increasing demand and price for copper, they were worth a fortune. The small amount of money the five siblings received was nothing in comparison to what Broken Hill Mines would generate over the coming years.

But That's Life! People do things they later regret, but can't be changed, and life moves on.

I remember going to Cobar several times earlier with Mum when she had to sort out problems with the local council and one time, there was a circus in town and to promote their arrival, they held an elephant race along the main street.

We just happened to be there that day, and I never went anywhere without taking my Bolex 16mm Movie camera and film. I was an unofficial stringer for the channel 9 news which is why I always took my Bolex no matter where I went.

I shot two reels of the elephants gently running down the main street with a big crowd following and sent the film by plane straight back to Melbourne. Being such big animals, I was amazed to see how smoothly and quietly they trundled along. The crowd watching made more noise. I raced out to the local airport to catch the last flight to Melbourne. I called the news room at channel 9 and told them the film was on its way, and they sent someone out to Moorabbin airport to collect it. It was processed and on the news with Eric Pearce that same night. Mum and I didn't get to see it on TV but the rest of the family in Melbourne did, and they thought it was great.

Setting off...

We chucked a double mattress, pillows, blankets and sleeping bags into the back of the white van, a box of books, a small fold up table, and two folding beach chairs, whatever clothes we thought we'd need, and we were good to go. We took some food and a small gas camp stove. We weren't going to cook a lot, but sometimes you had no choice. Most of the time we would stop in the towns we passed through for meals, or afternoon tea or other refreshments. The plan was to drive directly north; through Whittlesea, Heathcote, Echuca, cross the border and on to Deniliquin, Hay, and Hillston, which is where the bitumen road finished. The next stretch from Hillston to Cobar, 178 kilometres, was an unmade road, with only the last 20 kilometres into Cobar, bitumen surfaced. I don't mind unmade roads and this stretch was the shortest way to Cobar from where we were. To stay on the bitumen would entail and very long roundabout detour to get there. I'd done this stretch many times before and thought nothing of it.

The weather was beautiful as we drove north and when we got close to Echuca we stopped for a meal beside a beautiful still river. We set up the card table and while Monica wrote a letter to her Mum, I read one of the books I brought along. We weren't in a hurry, and this was part of the pleasure of making a long trip. Stopping somewhere that took our fancy and relaxing for a while, reading, writing, just enjoying the solitude, and the beautiful countryside.

— John Litchen —

— Grab that Moment —

Leaving Victoria we soon encountered dirt roads and dry country. We found a nice tree to park under and set up for the night. The scrub-land here was so different from the lushness of Victoria's river country it was hard to believe it was only a few hundred kilometres further north.

Under a tree near Deniliquin, preparing to cook something on our little camp stove. It was a wonderful sense of freedom to be able to stop anywhere, set up the table and chairs, cook something, relax, read a bit, before sleeping in the van. I'm not so sure you can do that these days. Times have changed, and doing stuff like that is probably not as safe as it once was.

Between Deniliquin and Hay, along the Cobb Highway there is a famous place called The Black Swamp. It was said that in the late 1800s, a headless horseman terrorized the drovers bringing cattle south to market places in Victoria; that if drovers saw this apparition (at night) they felt they were doomed. It was said a local butcher used to dress up in a headless costume and would appear at night to frighten the drovers and their cattle into stampeding. He would then catch a couple of steers and butcher them in his shop. Whether he did this to take advantage of the legend, or whether him doing this created the legend is a point of contention. But whatever the truth or the origin of the headless horseman in the Black Swamp story, it does make an interesting place to stop for a break. The Cobb Highway is named after the route the Cobb and Co coaches took traveling north and south across this part of Australia, which was also part of the stock route known as The Long Paddock.

After driving through Hay, we took a minor road through a tiny place called One Tree, then Goolgowi and on up the Hillston. From Hillston to Cobar, the road was no longer bitumen, it was a graded gravel road.

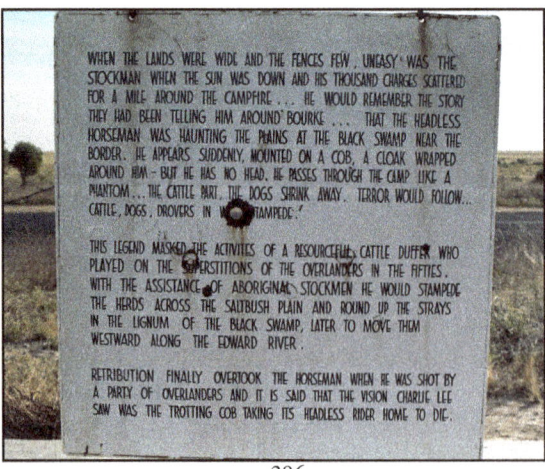

An incident along the way.

At the Black Swamp it had been hot and sunny, but only a few hours later, as we left Hillston and headed north along the gravel road the weather became atrocious. Wind made the van rock and drift to the side, apart from the shuddering created by driving on corrugated gravel and dirt. Huge rain drops splattered down from an ominously black sky. The sun had set, even though we couldn't see it, and darkness descended rapidly with no Moon and no stars visible. And bugger me, a tyre blew out. There was a sharp bang, like a gunshot, and instantly the van slewed sideways as the left front tyre ripped itself to ribbons. It shook like it was falling apart and the noise the rim made on the hard gravel was ear piercing.

No sooner had I stopped and exited the van, ready to open up the back and find the spare wheel, a Holden ute pulled up behind us. Three guys got out, and walked towards me. The lead guy said; "do you need any help?"

"It's just a blown tyre. I'll have it changed in no time." I was used to changing wheels on the van, a result of many punctures over the years of driving the delivery van past Sims Metal Works in North Altona, where I used to take a short cut to get across to the road going to Sunshine. There were always pieces of metal on the road beside the metalworks and I had to stop and change a wheel at least a couple of times a month.

"We can help," one of the other guys insisted.

"I'll be fine," I said. I had taken the wheel brace from the van and stood there looking at the guys. It was probably a touch of paranoia brought on by having seen too many films where a stranger traveling along a lonely country road comes into dire circumstances as a result of an encounter with a seemingly helpful local. These guys were scruffy, wearing stained jeans and dirty t-shirts, heavy mud-covered boots. I didn't trust them. They looked jumpy as they stood there with the headlights from their Ute partially silhouetting them. I wondered for a moment if they had put something on the road to cause the blow-out. They had appeared very suddenly the moment it had happened. I didn't recall seeing their headlights in the rear-view mirror as we drove along, so they must have emerged from a side track.

I shifted the wheel brace from one hand to the other and took a step towards them. They looked at each other for a moment then back to me.

"I've done this before," I said.

Suddenly they backed off a step. "Okay," the one in front said. "Just thought we could help."

They turned and went back to their Ute, and a moment later they roared past me going in the same direction we would have to take.

Once they had gone, I walked back along the road to see if there was anything that they may have put there which would cause a tyre to blow out. There was nothing obvious; just a lot of jagged pieces of stone sticking up through the road surface, more than likely the reason for the blowout. I quickly got out the spare wheel and changed it. We would have to buy a new tyre in Cobar once we got there in the morning.

"I was very nervous," Monica said as I got back into the driver's seat.

"Me too, but they're gone now."

A few minutes later we were back on the rough road and rain started pounding down. The road became slippery as rain runoff washed mud across the surface. We saw no sign of the guys and their Ute. I couldn't even see their tail lights ahead of us, so they must have turned off somewhere.

We drove for an hour but the rain got worse making driving difficult. When we got to Mount Hope, about a third of the way to Cobar from Hillston, we pulled over to a parking spot off the road and slept in the van.

It rained heavily and continuously all night. It was hard to sleep because we had to keep the windows shut and the van became very humid and stuffy. Condensation dribbled down the insides of the windows, and everything was damp. I was glad when it cleared up early in the morning and we could open the windows and doors to air off the van. It was still overcast with the odd shower, but actually wasn't too bad. I was wondering whether we should make some breakfast or just keep driving until we got to Cobar which was roughly 130 kilometres further north when a large truck drove into the park.

I asked the driver what the road was like and he said "It's bad mate, but not impassable."

He looked at our VW van and shook his head. "I think you'd need a 4-wheel drive, or a truck like mine to get through. There's a lot of water over the road. It's up to you mate."

He wandered around behind his truck to check something. A few minutes later he returned and climbed back up into the cabin. The engine started with a hiss and a roar and as the truck moved out, he waved to us.

We decided we would go on. Actually, I decided. I was confident that the height of the van with its larger wheels compared to a normal car would be enough to allow us to drive through the flooded parts of the road if the water wasn't rushing across or if it wasn't too deep.

What's that saying? Fools rush in where angels fear to tread…

In retrospect it would have been better to turn around, go back to Hillston and take the bitumen highway further east and drive up the New England Highway to Queensland. But we didn't. We got back into the van and drove onto the unsurfaced road heading north to Cobar.

For the first 30 or so kilometres it was fine. The surface was graded gravel and firm, easy to drive on. The sky seemed lighter although it was still overcast and it had not yet started to rain.

"Maybe it's clearing up," I said as we made good speed.

But that all changed fifteen minutes later when we stopped to look at water lying across the road.

I wasn't sure if the road had been washed away or if it was simply a lower section that was covered with water. I got out of the van and walked up to water. It was the colour of brown mud. I waded into it and the depth didn't come up to my knees all the way across. The surface hidden underfoot was solid enough, so I decided we could drive slowly through it.

Slipping and sliding

On the other side we only went half a kilometre when we encountered more water across the road. Again, I waded through it to determine the depth and we safely crossed it. But by then the sky was darkening and it began a light drizzle of rain. The road surface became more slippery with mud across it or with the gravel washed away. The road, nothing more than a muddy track now, undulated and every 100 metres or so we had to drive through water covering it. The van started skidding and sliding and I had to turn into the slide to gain steerage. I couldn't use the brakes or the wheels would lock and we would slide sideways along the track, or off it altogether. I was using only first and second gear to maintain some control and kept the speed to less than 10 KPH. It was very slow going. As soon as I felt the wheels grip, I could steer back to the centre of the track and move forward, but almost immediately the wheels would start to spin and the van would begin another slide to one side or the other. I would have to repeat the process, over and over, for several hours.

With rain drizzling down the surface of the track became semi-liquid with the consistency of thick tomato sauce. Though the underlying part was solid, if I went too fast, the wheels wouldn't grip the solid part underneath and would slide over the slippery muddy surface. I was constantly turning into the direction of the slide in order to gain traction, and to make matters worse, the drizzle of rain became more of a downpour. It lasted enough to make the road worse. Even more mud was thrown up onto the back of the van by the spinning wheels as we slithered along.

After hours of slipping and sliding between short stretches of controllable driving we stopped when we came to a construction site. It was where they were building a new all-weather road. It had been built up and graded and was about three metres higher than the surrounding surface. A barrier had been placed across the road in front of the new section (which was finished and waiting to be surfaced with bitumen) with a detour arrow indicating that we should continue driving along the undulating original track. I looked at the track and knew there was no way we could continue driving along that. It looked even worse than what we had been traveling on so far.

"We're going to have to get up onto the new road and drive along there," I told Monica.

I removed part of the barrier to allow us access, but didn't think we could just drive up the slope onto the new road; it was steep.

"How are we going to get up there?" Monica asked.

I looked at it. It was wet, but not slippery. If we had enough momentum…

The track immediately in front of the new road seemed solid so we backed the van back about two hundred metres. Driving forward at around 40 kilometres an hour we hit the rise and started up. The van went up but started to slow as we neared the top. I revved the engine and felt the wheels begin to slip, however, the forward momentum kept us going and we slid over the edge and onto the hard-new surface. The wheels gripped without slipping the moment we were onto the new road. I drove forward several metres to clear the edge and then stopped. The van was covered with mud sprayed up by the spinning wheels so I grabbed a small container, filled it with water and washed off the worst of the mud.

As we drove along started to rain again which washed off whatever mud was still over the van. We could see that the track along the side of the newly constructed road was awash with rivulets of water, and in parts glistening with slippery looking mud. We would never have been able to drive along that section, which made me wonder, how the hell did the truck get through?

The driver had been right to look at our VW with concern. I suspect he had driven along this new section, just as we were doing. He could never have gotten through if he used the old track, not in the truck he was driving.

Totally exhausted after battling the slippery track, it was relief to finally hit the bitumen surface and drive the last few kilometres into Cobar. The roads in town were awash, deep gutters flooded, and not too many people out in the wet weather. It hadn't rained for a long time and all of a sudden, the area was so wet it flooded everywhere. We stayed in a motel for one night. With rain continuously pounding down there was nothing to do in Cobar anyway so we moved on early the next morning.

— Grab that Moment —

Thinking to cross the street, Monica had second thoughts when she saw how deep the water was and much it rushed along the gutters. It didn't help that passing cars splashed up huge amounts of water. She changed her mind and came back.
Except for a few cars pushing through the flooded streets, the town was deserted with everyone staying indoors.

You can see how the water has spilled out from the gutters which were all at least 40 centimetres deep. Wooden bridges were used for pedestrians to step across the gutters but the water extended way beyond the bridges making crossing the street an unpleasant experience.

Water everywhere

Driving along the Barrier Highway East of Cobar the signs with the flood markings of up to two metres had clearly been partially submerged. Even the highway was still flooded in places. I used to wonder about those flood markings along the road where there was obviously no creeks or rivers and the land was flat and undulating grain country. I was difficult to image so much rain falling that such a large area could be flooded to a depth of two metres, but it does happen, and we just happened to be there when it was about to. It got worse after we left Cobar. We saw on the news (in a motel) that a number of highways had been closed, cut off, and Cobar and other towns in the area were isolated by large areas of flood waters. We were lucky we got through before the worst of it happened. This wet weather had been drifting down from Central and Northern Queensland and had now reached central NSW.

Heading north-east out of Cobar it was still raining the next day. Water lay across the road in places and was certainly obvious along the roadside, but at least this was a drivable road.

We turned onto the Mitchell Highway and travelled south-east until the turn off for Warren which was on the Oxley Highway going to Gilgandra, then we headed north on the Newell highway to Coonabarabran, up to Narrabri, Moree and on to the border where we crossed into Queensland at Goondiwindi.

We had left the rain behind us and the closer we got to the Qld border, the dryer it became. From Goondiwindi we continued east towards Toowoomba where I stopped to take a series of images to stitch into a panorama shot. There are minor roads criss-crossing the country everywhere in these hinterlands behind the coast. We took one that went diagonally from Toowoomba north east where it joined a secondary highway going from Brisbane and paralleling Highway One but on the inland side of the dividing range running down the east coast of Queensland. It went from Brisbane (Ipswich) to Rockhampton, but we only traveled a short distance along it before cutting across over the mountains to just north of Gympie where we joined Highway One to drive to Maryborough.

Ready to do some washing in a creek near a rest spot.

Not far past Toowoomba the weather turned tropical, hot and steamy. Coming down over the mountains to the coast the humidity hit us. The coastal country was quite wet. Rains had come down from the north and much of the Highway One, which parallels the coastline was cut in many places by flooding. The wet season had begun and was working its way south. The flooding we'd encountered inland was also caused by the wet season rains further north which run down massive river systems that barely hold a trickle in dry seasons but produce massive flooding when the wet season hits hard. We couldn't get further north than Bundaberg, just a bit north of Maryborough. To get there we drove north along Highway One and turned right at Childers to take a minor road to Bundaberg.

Bundaberg is famous for its distillery that makes the best rum in Australia (and some would say, the best in the world). There are tours one can take to see how the distillery works, but it never occurred to us to do that. It is also the place where the main part of the Great Barrier Reef begins. However, since the wet season was beginning, the river through the town was well above its normal height and was very muddy. I imagined that the water in the ocean around where the river enters would also lack visibility, making skindiving a waste of time. We went down to the river mouth and all we got to see were thousands of small crabs scuttling about on the mud flats left exposed as the tide retreated. We could have taken a ferry across to Fraser Island, one of the largest sand islands in the world, or checked out the turtle habitats where they come to lay eggs, but it was not the right time of year to see them come ashore. With more storm weather and rain on the way, a trip out to the reef was not a good idea either. It was just the wrong time of year to be in Bundaberg, or anywhere further north. We had wanted to go as far as Townsville, but the roads immediately north of Bundaberg were cut off by floodwaters which didn't look like dissipating anytime soon, So, we turned south and went back to Maryborough and down to Brisbane, stopping only to look at the rich and lush green of the cane fields that dominated agriculture in this area and to take a photo of the giant pineapple.

— Grab that Moment —

Almost every time we stopped somewhere for a rest, Monica would take the opportunity to do some exercises...

...muck about with old farm equipment set up for kids to play on...

or take some time out to catch up with reading a book. We both made sure we had enough time to read out books. After all, a holiday is not just traveling and looking at stuff, it's also about making sure we had enough time to do the things we enjoy, and reading books was one of those things.

— Grab that Moment —

Since the wet season had started, everywhere we went was wet, humid, and stuffy. Roads and streets in towns were often awash, park-lands were flooded. The highway going north along the coast was also flooded in many places and traffic had come to a standstill, with many travelers cut off and stranded between towns. We couldn't get any further north than Bundaberg, and the only thing we managed to do there was to visit the river mouth and see mud flats, Mangroves, and thousands of tiny soldier crabs that inhabited the river banks.

And while Monica was wandering about along the mud flats of Hervey Bay, I took time to catch up on another book.

An abandoned boat with mangroves starting to grow around it.

— Grab that Moment —

This is sugar cane growing country, and even though the cane was not fully grown or ready for harvesting, we couldn't miss the opportunity to have a close look at it. It was quite impressive, up close. As always, my favourite model gives us an idea of how tall this cane, which is really a variety of grass, can grow. Further inland it is cattle country and they also grow sunflowers, for seed and oil. But close to the coast, sugar cane dominates. But a bit further south towards Gympie, we find pineapples, especially one gigantic one that stands out for miles. You can't miss it as you drive through Nambour.

— John Litchen —

— Grab that Moment —

Gympie's twisting main street just after a rainstsorm had passed.
The street followed what was originally a wagon track that meandered between the thousands of tents set up on the sloping hills where prospectors lived while they searched for gold. Gold had been discovered by James Nash in 1867, and this sparked a gold rush. The settlement wasn't called Gympie to begin with, it was called Nashville. Once the settlement became established and was more like a town, it was renamed Gympie, from an aboriginal word that meant stinging nettles, a plant which abounded in this area. We drove through this town and did not see a single person out and about.

Because of the continuous rain, everywhere we went seemed deserted, as most people stayed inside. There were a few tourists around at places like the Big Pineapple, but in the towns we drove through like Gympie, the streets were empty with no one to be seen.

But the scenery was magnificent. The rain had made everything green and lush, and it intensified the colours of the earth, especially the deep red soils. It gave a misty appearance to the mountains and hillsides that gave us the impression we were driving along underwater.

What could be more tropical than clumps of Pandanus palms growing along the foreshore? They were everywhere.

The rugged mountains along this hinterland stretch were often the remains of ancient volcanoes from which the softer surrounding rock and pumice had been eroded leaving the hard basaltic core thrusting upwards. Surrounded by lush sub-tropical rain forest and often covered with clouds and misty rain, their appearance is constantly changing. We were at the start of the wet season and everything was very green and shrouded with low-lying misty clouds when it wasn't raining. We didn't see the sun shine during the time we passed through here.

I don't know how many times I have been to local art shows where there are always several paintings of farmhouses or barns and other farm sheds partially hidden by trees and long grass or bushes. It seems every amateur artist paints one, or a pair of them, as part of their evolution as an artist.

On seeing the typical Queensland farmhouse above with a car parked inside the yard, and the sheds almost lost in the tall grass below, I couldn't resist taking a photo of them. It had just stopped raining. The house appears deserted because the occupants are still inside and the threat of more rain was likely to keep them there.

Old buildings, or dilapidated buildings always make good subjects for a photograph, or as often seen, paintings of rural settings.

We only spent a few hours in Brisbane, and that was at a park with a children's playground. Monica decided she wanted a swing, while I caught up with the news via the newspaper.

Moving on

We found Brisbane too humid and enervating for our liking, so we pushed on to the Gold Coast, equally as humid, where we visited the famous Marineland of Australia and the Currumbin Wildlife Park, and try as she might, Monica could not get the lorikeets to land on her head and shoulders like they did for other people.

Monica in line to feed something to the dolphins.

Marineland of Australia no longer exists, having long been superseded by the much larger and more expansive *SeaWorld*, located on The Spit on the northern side of Surfers Paradise. But in 1973, *Marineland of Australia* was the place to go if you wanted to see dolphins, water skiing and other related stuff.

What I found depressing was the small size of the pools or enclosures in which the dolphins were kept. These magnificent sea mammals hardly had room to swim around, yet they managed high leaps, synchronized swimming and diving, which requires enormous strength to get their entire body high out of the water, often as much as three or four times their body length.

If only people training them had realized how intelligent these animals were, they would have thought twice about keeping them in such small enclosures, which only fostered discontent, and boredom. I felt sad seeing them made to perform tricks like jumping through a burning hoop, or leaping high to get a tiny piece of fish held out over the water by a trainer or a visiting tourist.

I have seen dolphins in the wild, while diving, or traveling by ship, and they are truly magnificent. To keep some in captivity and to use them to make a profit by entertaining visitors seems to me to be a tragedy. But that was in 1973. I'm sure things have changed for the better these days and *SeaWorld* does a magnificent job in rescuing injured dolphins and other sea creatures which they rehabilitate and release back into the wild, especially the whales that get caught in the shark nets along the coast during their annual migration from Antarctica to the warm tropical waters of Queensland during their breeding season.

— John Litchen —

The power and speed needed to leap out of the water, three to four metres high is amazing. How the dolphins manage to generate the speed and power in such a small space is difficult to comprehend.

— Grab that Moment —

The dolphins always came to the water's edge with smiling faces and nodding heads to greet visitors and children. Sometimes they would slap the water with their tails to splash the children. I think they got a lot of fun doing that, listening to the kids squeal with delight as they got wet.

Over the edge.

One moment I'll never forget; we'd driven south along the coast to Byron Bay and got there late in the afternoon. We drove up the winding road to the lighthouse on top of Cape Byron and parked in the parking space where people would come early in the morning to watch the sun rise. Cape Byron is the easternmost point in Australia and it is the point where sunlight first touches the land. Today, it is extraordinarily popular with visitors and locals who must see the sunrise, who want to be the first person the sun touches, but although popular in 1973 it was nowhere near as busy as it is today.

We looked out over the ocean as the stars appeared. The sea air wafted up and that particular salty smell brought back memories of the time I travelled by ship (the Elenis) across the Pacific to go through the Panama Canal on my way to Europe.

"It's a long way to South America from here," I said to Monica. "With nothing but a few Pacific islands in between Us and Chile."

She didn't say anything, but I could see there were tears in her eyes as she no doubt thought of Chile, of what she had left behind in order to come to Australia and make a new life.

Instead of going down to look for a motel we decided to stay up near the lighthouse and sleep in the van. You couldn't do that today, but in 1973, no one thought twice about it. We drove out of the car park and a short distance back along the road down into town where we pulled over to the side. There was plenty of room for other cars to go up or down the road from the top where the light house stood. We had a snack and as darkness settled, we went to sleep on the mattress in the back. It started raining after a while and got windy as a small storm blew in from the ocean.

We must have been asleep for a couple of hours when there was a loud banging on the window of the driver's side. We woke up startled. A woman banging on the window. She looked terrible. Her hair was hanging limp because it was wet. There was mud all over her face. And blood; her forehead had a scratch from one side to the other.

"I need help," she said when she saw me looking at her.
I wound the window down. "What's wrong."
"Can you drive me into town please?"
I wasn't sure if she was drunk or not, but she was definitely upset.
"My car ran off the road."
"Are you okay?"
"I don't know… yes, I'm okay, but my car isn't."
"What happened?"
"I drove up to have a look from over there just past the lighthouse. I

At the foot of the lighthouse. You can walk down to the area as can be seen with the four people very close to the water's edge. It is most dangerous because at any time, a big wave, or several big

— Grab that Moment —

waves, could smash into the rocks and suck out anyone foolish enough to be down there so close to the edge... it's much safer on the beach to the left of the rocks which can be accessed more easily.

thought the road continued on around the lighthouse, only when I started to go, I realized there was nothing there. The car started sliding over the edge."

"Shit."

"I couldn't stop it. The brakes wouldn't work."

I jumped out of the van and pulled on a t-shirt. It was drizzling rain, and had been since we had decided to stay up on the hill. The grass along the top of the cape would be wet and slippery.

"I need a ride into town so I can report it to the police."

"Of course. Can you show me where you went over?"

She led me over the other side past the lighthouse and we walked to the edge. The slope here was about 45 degrees down to a ridge after which there was a precipitous drop into the ocean where massive waves smashed into the rocks at the base of the cliff. The slope was grassy and slick from the rain. Her car looked so small it was barely visible in the darkness, wedged against the edge of the ridge before the drop into the ocean. There were muddy skid marks all the way from the top down to the car. There was no way she could have stopped it once it went over the edge.

"I thought the road went down there and started to drive, but there was nothing… The car kept sliding down. I couldn't stop it. When it hit the ridge and stopped moving, I got out as quickly as I could and climbed back up. I thought it would keep sliding."

"If you'd gone over the edge…"

"I know. It was just luck that I went over where that ridge is or I'd be …" She trailed off not wanting to say 'dead'. Her car would have been pounded to pieces by the waves hitting the rocks at the bottom and she certainly would not have survived that, or the fall down.

We went back to the van and she got in, said hello to Monica in the back. We drove down into town and dropped her off at the police station, which appeared to be unmanned at this time of the morning. It would have been about 4 am by then.

We watched her wander off, weaving slightly as she made her way along the footpath.

"Is she drunk?" Monica asked.

"She's probably suffering from shock. I don't know. She might have a concussion. It looks like she hit her head when the car smacked into the ridge and stopped. Shit, going over the edge like that would be a shock for anyone."

We parked in a different car park near the beach for what was left of the night, and the sun came up not half an hour later. Being the easternmost point, it rises very early, almost two hours before it does in Melbourne, and it was January and summer which means the sun comes up early anyway.

— Grab that Moment —

It wasn't long before we drove back up to the Cape Byron Lighthouse and there was a flurry of activity. A police car stood at the edge of the cliff where the car had driven over. A 4-wheel drive with a winch was reversed onto the edge of the slope and a cable was already connected to the car stuck on the ridge. A group of people there to watch the sunrise stayed to watch the car being towed back up the slope. The driver of the 4-wheel drive started to tighten the cable connected to the abandoned car, and while attempting to winch it up he also started to drive forward to add to the pulling effect. It took a while, but once the car came unstuck it was relatively easy to haul it back up over the edge and onto the car park. The woman driver was there beside the police but she didn't see us with all the other people crowding the space watching. Once the car was winched into a towing position behind the 4-wheel drive vehicle, people started to disperse. The excitement was over. The sun had risen and the sea sparkled.

Monica didn't go all the way down. She stopped at the point where it got suddenly steeper and more dangerous. But because there is a path down, the woman the night before drove her car down thinking initially it was a road, only to realize her error as her car kept sliding down until it crashed into a rocky ridge before the steep drop.

We drove back down into town and bought some take-away breakfast, drove south. We wanted to take the coastal highway to Sydney, but we were in no hurry and decided, wherever possible, we would divert from the highway and take the small side roads to the various coastal towns and villages along the way. Most of these had been bypassed when the highway was upgraded and reconstructed, so they no longer had passing traffic. We went to Evans Head, and Yamba, after which we had to go inland through Grafton before coming back to the coast to Coffs Harbour and Sawtell.

Shipwrecks and surf

Taking a break. Monica took time to write a letter to her Mum using the portable Olivetti typewriter we had in the van. We were parked on a rise overlooking the beach and river country south of Sawtell. The view below is looking north.

We then stopped at Nambucca Heads and after another short stretch and a detour, South West Rocks. Somewhere along this coastal stretch we encountered a shipwreck, sitting on the beach half in and half out of the water. There were lots of kids climbing on it. At another place we saw surfers in the water passing the flimsy remains of a ship right wrecked right where the waves start breaking. The water was brown with runoff from all the recent rains drifting down the coast from Queensland, which wasn't all that enticing to anyone other than surfers. The sea water was warm, about 23 degrees, but being muddy with who knows what debris floating in it after the rains, swimming was not really an option.

Shipwrecks are irresistible. Who doesn't want to climb over them or walk inside? Imagine what could have happened? And being right on the beach, how good was that?

— Grab that Moment —

The last stretch

We stopped overnight at Port Macquarie, and then headed for Newcastle and on to Sydney. In Sydney we visited the Opera House, as you do, and Kings Cross, as well as my friend George Olah, who had moved from Melbourne to Sydney at the end of the 1960s. He made a beautiful gold ring with a large opal embedded in it as a gift for Monica. Opal is both hers and my birthstone.

Seeing two icons at the same time; Sydney Harbour Bridge and the Opera House.

It's only when you get up close that you realize how huge and how magnificent the Opera House is.

The fountain in the middle of Kings Cross.

Whenever I was in Sydney, I used to buy shirts from Rogers Mens Wear shop in Kings Cross. They made and sold high quality shirts. The shop can be seen behind me.

Synonymous with Sydney: The Harbour Bridge, and ferries, old and new.

Leaving Sydney, we stopped at Bermagui, a fishing town famous for catching huge marlin. The western writer Zane Gray regularly came to Bermagui to fish for Marlin. Monica attempted to have a swim where George and Fred and I went diving some years back, but although it was beautiful and clear it was very cold.

A street in Bermagui's town centre

— Grab that Moment —

The sign says that this black Marlin weighed 202 lbs and was caught by A Taylor on a 5lb line. There have been much bigger fish caught here, but this was the only one we saw while we were in town.
Below: the road down to one of Bermagui's superb beaches about 4 km out of town. The coastline in this part of NSW is spectacular and rugged.

A bit further along a more open section of bea Monica tentatively checks the water temperat with her feet. She looks back nervously, unc tain about whether to step further out. She c swim, so there was no way she would get i

— Grab that Moment —

Not sure about whether to go in or not. Monica tentatively ventured out into the water to see how cold it was. Here in this shallow section it seemed warm, so she changed into one of her bikinis and stepped out, but when a wave splashed her it brought icy water from deeper out and she quickly got back out of the water.

er too deep, but when that wave came in splashed her, it was too cold and that was ugh! She quickly retreated back onto the ch.

She stared at me as if to say, "Why didn't you tell me how cold the water was?"

Most of the coastline near the town was sandstone. The sandstone wears away rapidly exposing fossilized roots and shells.

Before leaving, we spent time just sitting on a massive sandstone outcrop and watching the waves smashing the coastline. If you fell in there, it would be unlikely that you would survive, a risk rock fishermen take all the time. We didn't see anyone fishing from these rocks.

Leaving Bermagui we drove south along the coastal highway to Eden, almost on the Victoria border. Eden used to be a whaling town, famous for its killer whales that helped one particular whaling family by herding in humpback whales for them to slaughter. Their reward: left over parts from the slaughtered humpbacks. Whaling doesn't occur here anymore.

Eden was also touted as the likely place for the new capitol, situated almost exactly half way between Melbourne and Sydney, and with a deep water port, but that never happened and the nation's capitol Canberra, an entirely artificial city, was constructed inland closer to the Hume Highway between Sydney and Melbourne.

Late afternoon at a roadside stop. I am cooking something to eat while another family waits by the boot of their car for their turn to use the fireplace.

We enjoyed stopping at these spots where there were always tables, fireplaces, toilets, and rainwater tanks for travelers to fill their water bags.

Late afternoon in Eden: Fishing fleet moored and families fishing from the pier. Other boats at rest beside a small beach overlooked by residences.

Part Five

Our very own place

Deciding to build…

Thinking at first it would be nice to live in Williamstown, that idea was soon eliminated when we found out how much a house would cost. Not only was it too expensive, most places we saw were built anywhere up to 100 years before, and would require high maintenance costs. On top of that, almost every place we looked at had some kind of preservation order over it from the city council regarding the preservation of its heritage. They were still talking about releasing land along the railway corridor from Newport to North Williamstown, as well as opening the rifle range to housing. That wouldn't happen for some time so we decided we had to look further afield. Altona wasn't particularly attractive, so we looked further afield thinking we would build a new house with everything inside new instead of buying an old house where everything inside would eventually have to be replaced.

Being on the western side of the city we naturally went along Geelong Road towards Werribee where much land between Werribee and the western edge of Melbourne at Laverton was opening up for sale. We decided to look at Hoppers Crossing, four kilometres before Werribee, and only a fifteen-to-twenty-minute drive from Williamstown along Geelong Road and Koroit Creek Road. Hoppers Crossing was also serviced by the Geelong-Melbourne train if we needed public transport.

In February, a few weeks after we'd got back from our Queensland trip, we bought a block of land in Woodville Park Drive, a short street divided by a central nature strip, that led to a new Coles Supermarket and several other shops like a chemist and a newsagent within walking distance. It was about a kilometre from the railway station where you drove into the suburb after exiting Geelong Road and crossing the railway line. The land cost $6000, which was reasonable for a quarter acre traditional block.

Once we had the land, we started to visit building display centres where all the building companies had constructed samples of their houses. Visiting these display centres was a great pastime for Melbournians, where people could look and dream and spend a pleasant day out over a weekend. The companies sold package deals where you bought the land and the house they would construct on it, or you could have them build a house you liked on your own land. Most of them told us it would take eleven months to get it all done. That seemed a very long time. Eventually, we decided to use the company that had renovated 36 Benbow Street the year before because they promised it would be built within five months (which meant we could be in the house sometime in July), and also because they were local, their head office being in Footscray on the corner of Barclay Street and Geelong Road, where they had much material stored as well. We had seen what kind of work they could do and thought they could build us a beautiful house. And being local, I could easily pop in and discuss any matters concerning us with them. I drove past their place every day while doing pick up and delivery of dry cleaning.

I organized a loan with the ANZ bank in Williamstown, and the interest on the loan was 10%, which at the time was reasonable. We finalized the deal with the construction company and made the initial payment — it would cost us $24, 000 to build the four-bedroom house we had chosen — and construction began. We would pay a quarter of the cost up front at each stage during construction.

The foundations went in almost straight away, and floor joists were laid, then that team moved off to another site and started something else.

Monica examining the concrete foundation. They left all that dirt piled up when they laid the brick base, so it ended up under the floor instead of putting it somewhere in the yard so I could use it in the garden.

— John Litchen —

It stayed like this for three months. The site was a shambles, with rubble and cut timber everywhere. It had rained a lot as we entered winter and the grass on the site was lush. The water filled ditch is where the wall of the carport would be built. Sometimes Paul came with us to have look, at other times, Mum and Day came. After three months of nothing happening, bricks were delivered and the chippies came back and built the frame and the roof.

The timber had been lying there for a while so it was well seasoned. Offcuts were piled up all over the place which made walking around to look at the progress quite dangerous.

I thought they would have built the frames for the rooms at their factory as they usually did for package deal homes. They then transport them to the building site and erect them very quickly. Buy not this time, or with this builder. Everything was done on site, measured, cut, nailed together and then lifted into place, which made the whole process longer than it needed to be.

Mum and Dad making their way carefully onto the site to how it was progressing.

Finally the house took shape. With the framework and the windows in, it was finally becoming a reality. But it had been left like this for a few months, which why the timber lying around is covered with grass.

The bricks arrived but again nothing much happened before we left on our trip. When we came back at the end of November it was still the same, and after complaining to the head office they immediately got a team of brickies in to finish the walls.

It turned out the bricks, although the same, had been manufactured differently. They were slightly shorter than the original bricks used up to the floor line, and they had holes in them to make them lighter, whereas the first bricks used were solid. They had to allow a slightly wider gap between the bricks to keep them in line with the lower foundation part. Something I didn't notice at first, but which became obvious once we were aware of it. They also forgot that we wanted raked joints and the first lot of bricks laid were flat instead of raked. They had to send someone in with a drill to cut into the cement, and grind it out to depth of one centimetre. The second lot of brickies didn't make that same mistake.

We were told it would be a few weeks before the framework and roof went up, after which they would start the external brickwork. We were all excited about how rapidly it was progressing. We paid the next installment, and nothing happened. We went down to the site every weekend and nothing had changed. Querying the head office, we were told it would take seven months rather than five because they had so many jobs on the go and so few workers to do it all, projected completion dates had been extended.

Nothing much we could do about that. We just had to wait. But having decided to build and having started, we became impatient for it to be done. Every weekend we would go and look only to be disappointed once again by the lack of progress. I went to the Head Office and again told them I would pay a further installment to encourage them to get to work on it, and they readily agreed. Next time went down to the site we saw stacks of timber piled up everywhere. And the floor joists had be put in. There were cut pieces scattered about and tons of sawdust. I wondered why they didn't prefabricate the frames for the various rooms at their factory and then deliver and erect as most package deal companies do. It appeared that this company did it all on site. The next weekend we went there the framework was up and stacks of bricks had been delivered. There were tiles piled up as well but the roof had not yet gone on. And there it stopped again. Week after week, nothing changed. We were well past July and the five-month period they originally told us it would take. It was now September, and the house was not even half finished.

At the head office we were once again re-assured that lock-up stage would be reached as soon as the roof tiles went on, and they were on schedule to complete the house in December. Eleven months!

We were pissed off.

Unfortunately, there was nothing we could do.

They asked for another installment and I paid it. I told them that we had planned a trip to Darwin in November and we would be away for that month. They assured us that work would be continued and that we could take our holiday as planned. I wasn't sure I believed them, but I also didn't want to annoy them by continuing to remind them that nothing had progressed at anywhere near the pace they originally claimed it would.

We had been told when we came back, we would find the house at lock-up stage ready for internal fitting. Everything would be finished by mid-December.

With that in mind, we packed our gear into the new campervan and started our trip to Darwin.

Part Six
To the Northern Territory and Darwin

New Campervans

Fred had recently bought an orange *VW Campervan* and it looked great, so I decided, almost instantly, that I would buy one as well.

I thought a campervan would be much better than the van with a makeshift frame I had built inside on which I could throw a mattress, blankets and pillows. I didn't care what the colour was except that I didn't want the same colour as Fred's. What the dealer had available at that moment in July (1974) was a green one, almost khaki green, one of their four standard colours, and not my favorite.

When I asked for something different, the dealer said "there's nothing else available for at least a month. We can order any colour you want, but there are so many pre-orders, you'll have to wait."

"On second thought, green's not too bad after all."

I didn't want to wait, having decided to buy a campervan, I wanted to get it organized as soon as possible. And they did have the green van in the yard, ready to go.

We did the paperwork, I went to the bank and got a cheque, paid in full, and drove out of the dealership in the new campervan an hour or so later. This would have been the fourth VW van I had bought from them. Phillip had also bought a van from them as well, so we were known to them and never had any problems. Fred also bought his campervan from the same place. At that time there were not too many VW dealerships in Melbourne. This one was in Footscray, just up the road from us in Williamstown, and they were always busy and could hardly get stock in quick enough to satisfy demand. VW Beatles and Vans (Kombivans, Campervans) were extremely popular in the 1960s and 70s.

After taking one last look at the house construction, (nothing had changed) we packed out gear into the new campervan. I had parked on the front lawn to make it easier to load. Dad was fascinated and just had to climb in and have a look. He watched us load up and when it was all done, we took off. I don't remember saying goodbye to Mum and Dad, but I suppose we did.

— Grab that Moment —

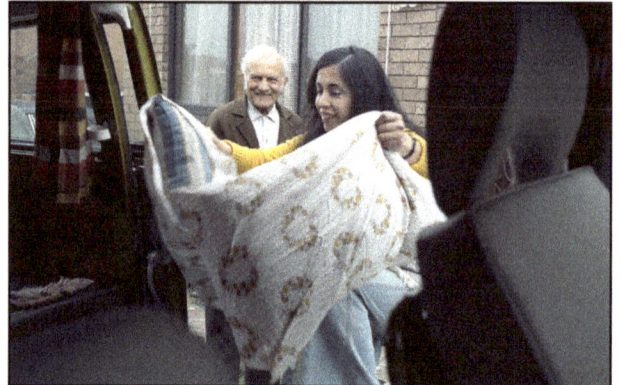

On the road again

It was the afternoon and we drove along the Western Highway towards the South Australian border. It was the end of October and the days were already beginning to lengthen as Spring started to take hold, but even so, by the time we got to *The Sister's Rocks*, just before Stawall, it was already into twilight so we decided to stop for the night. These rocks, massive granite boulders, can be seen from the highway, which is probably why so many people have decided to paint their names all over them. Why would they want to do that? I thought as I drove in and parked under a large tree.

Is painting names on rocks so everyone can see them any better than scrawling or scratching names on the walls of public toilets?

Do they feel so insecure about their existence that they need to confirm it for all to see by painting their names on these rocks?

This is the worst kind of graffiti, spray painting tags or names. It's not art. Good graffiti can be real art and is appreciated these days by much of the population. There are now places in the major cities that encourages graffiti or street art, but spray-painting names on rocks along the highway is not art, it is simply defacement of something that has a natural beauty. It has been going on for years, as names and tags are over-painted continuously. We stopped there in 1974, which was the last time I had passed by these rocks, and the most recent efforts then included the date.

The names and the date 6-9-74 had been painted a couple of weeks before we stopped there on our way to Darwin. As can be clearly seen in the photo on the previous page, a shallow depression high up has been used to dump rubbish left by visitors. Nobody cared much where they dumped their rubbish in 1974. I suspect it's still much the same today.

— Grab that Moment —

Not even time and the slow weathering of the rocks is enough to eliminate the graffiti.

People keep coming and painting their names among other slogans and comments, continuously covering over what had previously been painted.

I didn't feel like staying there, but it was getting late so we decided to stop overnight parked under a tree off to one side of the graveled area.

We woke early, and didn't even bother to make breakfast. We would do that further along the road. We just pulled the roof down, folded back the blankets, and off we went, leaving those desecrated rocks behind us.

Bad news at Port Augusta

Leaving the Sister's Rocks early the next morning we drove to Bordertown and from there we headed diagonally through the wine growing district towards Port Augusta. We didn't stop at any of the famous wineries since that was not the reason for the trip. We just wanted to get to Port Augusta the shortest way possible.

Port Augusta is the terminus for the Ghan, the train that goes to Alice Springs. It is also the end of a bitumen surfaced road if you are driving north, and the place where you need to visit the Police station in order to find out the condition of the road ahead.

Has it been raining?

Are there sections that are impassable?

What is the general condition of the road?

Do we need a 4-wheel drive, or can we manage in a campervan?

It's also where you tell the police you are driving to The Alice, and when you expect to get there.

If you don't get there because you become stuck or bogged or have car trouble, someone will come looking for you. But only if they know you are out there. If you don't tell anyone and just drive off, no one knows and no one will come looking for you.

At the police station we were told it had been raining a lot across the centre and many kilometres of the road were flooded. The Wet Season had started early this year and was already sending flood waters down the rivers and creeks through the centre.

"You can't drive there," we were told emphatically. "Beyond Coober Pedy the road's a real mess. You'll have to put your vehicle on the Ghan."

We had no choice, we had to book a spot on the train, The Ghan, which I had traveled on to Alice Springs back in 1957.

"You'd better be quick, because there are a lot of other people like you who won't be able to drive north, not for a few weeks yet, maybe not for a couple of months."

We drove around to the railway terminus and found a queue of people waiting to book a space on the Ghan for their vehicle. We were lucky, and got a spot, along with a double cabin to travel and sleep in. If we'd missed out we would have had to wait a week for the next trip to Alice Springs. The train takes two and a half days to get there, and after unloading and loading up for the return trip, it would take another two and a half days to get back to Port Augusta where it would be prepared for the next trip to Alice Springs.

The campervan would be loaded, along with 20 or 30 other vehicles, onto a long line of flatbed cars. We booked a sleeping compartment for two. Sixteen years before, I traveled sitting on hard wooden seats in what would be classed 3rd class. I didn't care. I was young and could sleep on anything. At 34 years of age this time, I wasn't prepared to rough it that much, and I'm sure Monica would not want to spend two and a half days sitting on hard wooden seats. Although I didn't ask, I don't think they had those kind of carriages anymore in 1974. Traveling on the Ghan was a lot more comfortable.

We spent several hours watching the cars being loaded onto the flatbeds, and how they shackled them with chains and blocks so they wouldn't move.

This Ghan was a lot better than the old rattle-trap I had previously traveled on. It still traveled on the same standard gauge railway line to Marree where once the passengers would switch trains. The line from Marree to Alice Springs was rebuilt from the earlier narrow gauge that the train had used when I went to Alice Springs in 1957. I wondered how they would transfer the goods carried and all the flatbed cars with people's vehicles chained to them. They certainly wouldn't be unloading them and reloading them onto the other train. Perhaps the bogeys had a double sets of wheels and they simply shunted them onto the narrower track and connected them to the two diesel engines that would haul us all the way to Alice Springs. I don't actually remember changing trains at Marree this time so maybe the sleeper carriages also had double sets of bogeys with the inner set running on the narrow gauge after Marree.

The older Ghan followed the track that the explorer Stuart had used so he could make use of creeks, water holes and lakes that the original inhabitants of the area used. It was a low-lying country where water could generally be found. It was also the way, years later when European people began to settle this remote area, that the Afghan cameleers used for their camel trains to supply goods and deliver mail to remote settlements. The narrow gauge line followed the camel route because water was needed for the steam engines. The train used to stop overnight at various places, but when a sleeping car was added so passengers could sleep while on the way, the journey became a couple of days shorter.

Most people assume that the name given to the train that replaced the camels and their handlers, **The Ghan**, was named after them, or in honour of them and their camels. The line didn't go all the way to Alice Springs until 1929. Before that, the last stages of the journey still had to made by camel train. The original line used to run through Quorn and when the first sleeping car and a new train was introduced, everyone living there went to the station to watch it arrive in the evening of 30th of August 1923 expecting loads of passengers, but the car was empty except for one lone Afghan man who got off and immediately went to the end of the station. He ignored everyone, and proceeded to recite his prayers on his knees as he bowed towards Mecca. Some wag jokingly called this new train '*The Afghan Express*', and that's the name that stuck for a while, eventually being shortened to *The Ghan*.

The Ghan ran from Port Augusta to Alice Springs via Quorn until 1956, the year before I first traveled on it. After that a new line was built and the train then ran from Port Augusta to Marree, where passengers had to change to the narrow gauge train to continue on to Alice Springs via Oodndatta and Finke.

This is also the way we had to go when we booked the sleeper and put the campervan on board.

They were at that time constructing a new standard gauge line 160 kilometres west of the this line so that no one would have to change trains again, but that wouldn't be finished until 1980, after which the old lines would be abandoned. This new line would be the first step in building a standard gauge line all the way to Darwin.

But in 1974 when we were there, the line had not been completed to Alice Springs let alone on to Darwin. We would still have to drive the rest of the way once we reached Alice Springs, which was fine, because that had been our intention in the first place.

"It's a good road from the Alice, with a proper bitumen, all-weather surface," we were told many times. "Don't go off the highway though, or you could be stuck for weeks, or maybe never found."

"If you break down, stay with your vehicle," was another one; which made sense because it was easier to spot a vehicle from the air than a person wandering about in the bush. And if you were in desert country, you could become dehydrated much quicker than you imagine, and this would kill you.

I'd heard all this before and wasn't concerned, but it did worry Monica. She didn't like desert country because she was from Chile and had lived in Iquique, which is in the far north of the country smack in the middle of the Atacama Desert, one of the driest, most inhospitable deserts in the world. It hadn't rained there for over 500 years. At least in Australia, it does sometimes rain in the desert country. It's not like the empty quarter in Arabia, or parts of the Sahara. Australia's deserts are mostly classified as semi-arid, rather than true desert, but that doesn't mean it isn't inhospitable or dangerous. There are places like the Simpson's Desert that is shattered rock as far as you can see, and sandy deserts in the far north-west bordering the Indian Ocean that are truly inhospitable and would rival any other desert in the world.

— Grab that Moment —

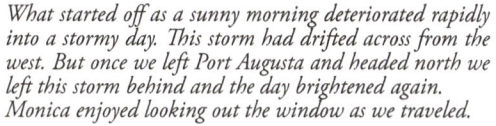

What started off as a sunny morning deteriorated rapidly into a stormy day. This storm had drifted across from the west. But once we left Port Augusta and headed north we left this storm behind and the day brightened again. Monica enjoyed looking out the window as we traveled.

The effect of recent rain was obvious as we traveled. Fresh growth, bright and green, had sprung up over what was normally dusty red earth, giving the impression of a lushness that normally doesn't exist. Even a long abandoned farmhouse that we passed didn't look so forlorn.

    It was pleasant, sitting in the train and looking out over the land passing by. The view was gorgeous because it had rained a lot over the last few weeks and where there had been nothing but desert and sand dunes when I traveled previously on the Ghan with a few half-dead desert oaks jutting above the sand (16 years earlier) it was now covered with green bushes and carpeted with wild flowers, mostly red and yellow coloured. Even the few scrawny trees looked vibrant as they stood up above the wild flowers and salt-bush and desert peas. It was truly amazing what a little bit of rain can do in an area where the rainfall is usually less than 10ml per year if any.

An alien world

Australia, to the early British settlers, was an alien world, as unlike anything they were used to in England or Europe as was the planet Mars. None of the plants were familiar, and certainly the animals belonged to another world. Not one of them was mammalian. They were very different, and one in particular were just simply weird; the platypus. It laid eggs, like reptile or a bird, it suckled its young as would a mammal, and it lived in and around rivers and lakes like an amphibian. It had webbed feet and a poisonous spine; it was covered in fine fur and had a bill like a duck. Nobody believed something like that could exist, and when stuffed specimens were shown in Europe it was thought they were fake. The kangaroo and wallabies were the most obviously different because of the way they stood tall and moved by jumping or leaping instead of walking or running.

These early settlers, or invaders as many today see them, were incapable of adapting to the land, the climate, or the environment. Most modern humans are incapable of adapting to their environment, so they change it to suit them. They tried that in Australia, by importing what was to them familiar plants and animals. The plants rarely survived anywhere other than along some coastal areas. Some animals, like rabbits, introduced for food, escaped and ran wild becoming feral pests in not time. Horses and buffalo which were used to haul goods to and from settled areas, or equipment for exploration and development, couldn't survive in the barren outback areas. They died from the heat or from lack of water. But in the far northern tropical wetlands, buffalo from Asia, brought in as pack animals became feral and now occupy huge areas of the wetlands. But it was the harshness of the inland desert area that gave explorers and early (invaders) settlers the biggest problems.

In desperation, smart entrepreneurs saw opportunities to make profits and imported camels, animals more suited to Australia's harsh desert climate. As many as 20,000 camels were brought into the country over a period of 20 or 30 years starting in 1870, mostly from the Indian sub-continent. They also brought in people who could handle these large animals, cameleers who were known as Afghans, whether they came from the Kingdom of Afghanistan or not. At that stage the Indiana sub-continent had not been divided into separate countries, it was still part of the British Empire. The cameleers were generally called Afghans, or Ghans, and they managed to open up a diverse number of trading and supply routes throughout inland Australia, and places where they congregated, such as Marree became proper towns, or centres where various camel routes intersected.

Unlike horses and buffalo, which were used to pull loaded wagons, and needed plenty of water, camels could go for days, weeks even, without water and their soft spayed feet had no trouble in sandy desert areas. But because they couldn't be made to haul wagons, the goods they carried had to be strapped on and piled on top of each individual camel. They needed lots of camels, and lots of cameleers to handle and control them.

When the railway lines were built which opened up the interior to a generally wider population with steam trains that could carry far more than the camel trains, they stopped using camels and they were left to their own devices. They didn't die off as was expected; they became feral, and ran wild in a country that suited them. There are now huge wild camel populations in the more remote areas of South Australia, Northern Territory and Western Australia; so many that they have become a problem and are being culled because they eat the sparse food the native wildlife would eat, leaving nothing for the kangaroos, and other related animals. It is not uncommon, if you are driving in those areas, to see road signs warning drivers to be aware of camels crossing the road.

Other introduced animals that have become feral and cause problems in bushland and outback areas are goats and deer, and more recently cats and dogs as well as cane toads. It seems, animals will rapidly adapt if they have no predators, and Australia is perfect in that regard. We have no large predators like the other continents have, and the only two we did have, the marsupial lion, and the Tasmanian Tiger, (both highly evolved marsupial carnivores) have become extinct. The Tasmanian Tiger only recently, the last one having died in captivity in the 1930s. Cats and dogs are carnivorous and have decimated the smaller marsupials and birds found throughout Australia.

Arriving early

The Ghan arrived in Alice Springs at 5 am and I woke up with all the noise as workers started to unload the chained vehicles. The conductor came along and banged on every cabin door and announced that we had arrived. He told us we didn't have to get off immediately, but if we wanted breakfast, we had to go to the dining car as soon as possible because it was a limited service. Most people didn't bother with breakfast, they got off and went on into town or stood around and waited for their vehicle to be unloaded. It took just as long to unload the vehicles as it did to load them in Port Augusta. By the time we got up and had our last breakfast on the Ghan we found they were already unloading our campervan and we could, basically, just drive off.

— Grab that Moment —

Absolutely beautiful! The country as we approached the gap through the mountains the Ghan would pass through to arrive at Alice Springs.

Looking back towards the gap in the mountains through which the Ghan enters Alice Springs.

We were in no rush to go anywhere at that moment, so we drove along the main street and up onto a hill which overlooked the town. Then we drove out to look at the monument dedicated to the founder of the Flying Doctor Service, The Reverend John Flynn, and visited a local outdoor museum. We drove to the nearby gorges that were about an hour's drive out of town and after that we drove back to town and parked by the river, dry as usual, where we decided what to do next.

— Grab that Moment —

   Monica taking time to read the bronze plaque which marks the grave-site of the founder of the Royal Flying Doctor Service, The Reverend John Flynn.
   The granite monolith weighing 8 tons is from the Devil's Marbles, and was placed over the grave in 1953. This was the one we saw in 1974.
   After years of controversy with the traditional owners of Devil's Marbles, the Warumungu and Kaytej people wanting the stone returned, a compromise was reached with the local Arrente people agreeing to replace the stone with a similar stone from the nearby Caterpillar Dreaming site, which was done in 1999. The stone in the pictures here was returned to the Devil's Marbles.

— John Litchen —

The inscription reads:

BENEATH THIS STONE REST THE ASHES OF
FLYNN OF THE INLAND
THE VERY REVEREND JOHN FLYNN OBE DD
FIRST SUPERINTENDENT (1912 - 1951) OF
THE AUSTRALIAN INLAND MISSION
FOUNDER OF THE FLYING DOCTOR SERVICE
MODERATOR GENERAL
OF THE PRESBYTERIAN CHURCH (1939 - 1942)
HE BROUGHT GLADNESS AND REJOICING
TO THE WILDERNESS AND THE SOLITARY PLACES

Early morning at a wayside stop just out of Alice Springs. If you look closely, there is a tabby cat poking its head out from behind the van's rear wheel. A feral cat? I had no idea it was there when I took the photo. Monica had just come back from cleaning her teeth.

— Grab that Moment —

There were a series of stunning sculptures in this museum as well. I have no recollection of who the artist was, but each sculpture depicts people emerging from the rock. They are carved into the natural rock and have such an organic live feel to them you can imagine the real people of this ancient land could actually have emerged from the stone, just as they appear in the sculptures.

— John Litchen —

We loved the campervan, it was so much more comfortable than the other van which only had a frame on which we could place a mattress. The campervan had a washbasin, water supply cooking space, seats, a proper bed, and we could stop anywhere and make ourselves a cup of coffee and sit inside at a fold-out table to drink it. The roof lifted up so we could stand up inside.

The scenery around Alice Springs was nothing short of spectacular, and we spent the whole day and the next exploring as much of it as we could.

The original plan was to drive from Port Augusta via Coober Pedy and Ayer's Rock, now known as Uluru, before arriving at The Alice. Since we couldn't do that and we were now in Alice Springs, we figured we would drive back south and then take the turn west to go to Ayer's Rock. It was a bitumen road for a short way, but the rest of the way to Ayer's Rock would be a graded gravel road or dirt road. The distance back along the Stuart highway was 199 kilometres before the turn into the Lasseter Highway to Ayer's Rock and The Olgas. From that point it was 254 Kilometres to Ayer's Rock, quite a distance, and of course, once we got there and after looking around, we would have to drive back to Alice Springs before continuing north to Darwin.

— Grab that Moment —

There were Aboriginal families camped in the dry river bed in makeshift houses constructed of corrugated iron, canvas, wooden boxes and other detritus, and I wondered what they would do if the river flooded. Occasionally it does flood as storm water some distance away rushes along the Todd river. I guess they would know when it was likely to flood and would pack up and move before the water came rushing down along the river. Apparently this was very rare, and the river is usually dry. They even hold a boat race, the Todd Regatta in which people standing inside bottomless boats hold up the shell of the boat and run along the river bed in a mad race. We wanted to see that but it was the wrong time of year, so that would be something we missed.

Monica couldn't believe that people did this in Australia.
Her impression was that the whole country was more or less urbanized like Sydney and Melbourne, or at least like some of the country towns we had visited in Victoria. She was shocked to see people living in hovels on the river bed. For her, Alice Springs was an eye-opener. I had seen people living in similar conditions in Mexico City and in the outer makeshift slums that had built up around the outskirts of that city. And no doubt Monica had seen similar places in Chile, and Brazil when she went there. But to expect to find these kinds of living situations in Australia was a big surprise to her.

Much to our shame as a nation, and as inhabitants of this nation, nothing much has changed over the 48 years since we were in Alice Springs.

We decided to leave in the evening of the second day and sleep in the Campervan somewhere along the highway so we could arrive at Ayer's Rock early in the morning. Storm clouds had been building up to the south and the air in The Alice was oppressive and heavy as the afternoon wore on. We could feel a tingle of electricity in the air because there was lightning flickering somewhere within the clouds. As it got darker the clouds glowed with a stroboscopic effect as lightning intermittently flashed.

A frightening storm

We had been driving south for about an hour. The landscape on either side of us was dead flat, with not a tree in sight anywhere. It was also pitch black except when lightning flashed, and all we could see was the small part of the road ahead lit up from our high beam headlights.

"I'm scared," Monica said and a huge bolt of lightning zapped out of the clouds and hit the ground several kilometres ahead of us. "We should turn back."

"We'll be right," I said, reluctant to turn back since we had been driving almost an hour and had probably come about 80 kilometres.

A series of lightning bolts zapped down to the ground once more ahead of us. I began to have second thoughts about going on. There was nothing out here, no trees, nothing that stood above ground level more than a metre, except for our Campervan, which was made of metal. Isn't lightning attracted to metal? I was still driving when a little off to our left a huge lightning bolt struck the grown. The thunder was immediate, rattling the van so much it almost ran off the road. It hit the ground not more than fifty metres away. The sound of it hitting the ground was phenomenal. It was like we were in a massive explosion. My ears were ringing. I couldn't hear the sound of the engine or the fact that Monica was yelling at me, presumably telling me to turn around.

"Shit!" That was too close.

I immediately stopped. Lightning continued to hit the ground, but much further away, in the direction we would have to take when we reached the turn onto the Lasseter Highway.

That was it. I wasn't going to drive into the storms because the next lightning strike might very well hit the Campervan.

I turned around and we drove back into Alice Springs, where we camped beside the river under a big tree. The air still felt electric and the sky intermittently flashed with lightning high in the clouds.

We still wanted to see Ayer's Rock, so in the morning I went to travel agent and asked about flying out there. He informed us that there were no flights because the runway had been flooded by the storm that had enveloped the rock. Water was cascading off the rock and the whole area was impassable. A good part of the Lassiter highway had turned into a bog. Cars were stuck, planes couldn't take off or land, and anyone out there would have to wait until the weather cleared before they could leave.

"How long is this going to take?"

"Days, maybe a week before anyone can come and go. Might be a couple of days before planes can fly out there again."

He looked at me as if to say do you want to book a flight?

"I think we'll give it a miss," I said.

He just shrugged.

We didn't have a lot of time, and if we wanted to be back home by the beginning of December, we had to head off for Darwin and not worry about Ayer's Rock.

"We can always come back another time," I told Monica as we drove north along the Stuart highway towards Darwin.

But of course, we never did. That's twice now I have been in Alice Springs and for one reason or another, not gone out to see Ayer's rock. Maybe one day…

Heading north

The only road north was the Stuart Highway. It was such a narrow red gravel bitumen road, hardly wide enough for two cars to pass, let alone when big trucks and road trains loaded with cattle came towards you, that it barely deserved to be called a highway. Quite a few times we were almost blown off the road by the wind from those monstrous road trains. I always made sure we slowed down when I saw one of them in the distance coming towards us so I could move off the edge of the road to allow them to pass.

We left early so we could cover a fair distance during the day. The landscape was stunning, with the early sun causing distant mountain ridges to glow an astonishingly pale golden colour. The red desert was lush with fresh green growth and a plethora of wildflowers. This was not the way I remembered it from 16 years earlier. Then it had been red sand dunes with wisps of dust swirling off them from hot dry winds.

This time the air was more humid, with tropical fronts pushing down from the north or north-west as the wet season was beginning earlier than usual. It had rained enough before we arrived on the Ghan to have turned the desert country around Alice Springs into something spectacular.

The red and golden yellow of the flowers and the variety of green foliage was a stark contrast against the deep red colour of the ground and the rocks.

Karlu Karlu – Devil's Marbles

Driving north from Alice Springs, the land gradually became dryer although the evidence of recent rain still showed with wildflowers and a rich greenness that made the scrawny trees look alive rather than half dead. The early morning sun highlighted a distant row of hills with delicate pink and pastel shades. What looked like towns marked on the map, Ti Tree, Barrow Creek, Wauchope, turned out to be nothing more than roadhouses or pubs. Tennant Creek, and much further north, Katherine, are the only two places that can be called towns. But out first stop was the Wauchope Roadhouse, around 390 kilometres north of Alice Springs, where we topped up the petrol tank and had a snack. Tennant Creek is a further 100 kilometres up the road. It was early afternoon and only a short hop to the Devil's Marbles.

Nine kilometres past the Wauchope Roadhouse and visible from the road since it actually goes through the middle of the formation, is one of the most iconic places in Australia; The Devil's Marbles. These are huge granite boulders heaped up and scattered across the country on both sides of the Stuart Highway. You can't miss them. They don't look that big until you drive off the highway and park near them. Only then do you realize their enormous size. Some are as tall as 6 metres, and they are stacked on top of each other, with many balancing precariously. A small one of these rocks weighing 8 tonnes was taken to Alice Springs in 1952 and placed upon the grave of the founder of the Flying Doctor Service, the Reverend John Flynn. It created a controversy because it was taken without permission. It was later returned to its original place and a local rock of approximately the same size was placed on the grave, which is what tourists see today.

At Karlu Karlu, the local name for the Devil's Marbles which I think means round boulders, there is now a campsite for visitors to stay, but in 1974 when Monica and I stopped to look at them, there was nothing like that there.

The boulders are millions of years old and were formed by magma in the crust upwelling and solidifying. This formation was originally covered by sandstone and as the sandstone weathered away it released the pressure on the granite layers which pushed up and cracked into huge blocks. Over subsequent millions of years with rain and wind and intense sunshine during the day with very low temperatures during the night, the granite fractured and split, and layers and slivers flaked off gradually rounding the blocks into ball like shapes. Sometimes the weight of the stone causes a boulder to split, but generally small amounts of material are constantly flaking off making the boulders even more rounded as time goes on.

The area was named originally Devil's Marbles Reserve in 1961, which is what it was called when we were passing through in 1974. It later became the Devil's Marbles Conservation Reserve in 1979 and was administered under the Territory Parks and Wildlife Conservation Act. Ownership was passed back from the Northern Territory Parks and Wildlife Service, to its original owners, the Alyawarre, Kaytetye, Warumungu, and Warlpiri peoples, at a ceremony held on site in 2008. It is now in indigenous protected area.

The name Devil's Marbles is popularly attributed to a quote from Scottish Australian explorer John Ross who was surveying the area in 1870 for the overland telegraph service. It is claimed he said: "This is the Devil's country. He's even emptied his bag of marbles around the place."

Whether that is true or not is irrelevant, but it makes a nice story for tourists, who now have a series of pathways through the Devil's Marbles with notice boards informing them about how they were formed along with Aboriginal stories relating to how the boulders became scattered over the site. There is a basic camping area for visitors as well, none of which existed when we passed though this area in 1974, let alone when I went by in 1958 on my way to Darwin.

After wandering about and climbing up onto some of the boulders to gain a better view, it was easy to see how large an area is covered by the Devil's Marbles, beyond what you can see from the highway. Devil's country is right, as john Ross claimed in 1870, from the point of view of the heat. It was extremely hot and dry, and it sucked the moisture out of you. After a couple of hours, I was exhausted and just had to take a rest before we moved on.

— Grab that Moment —

Standing beside them is the only way to comprehend their sheer size. And knowing that they have been there for millions of years adds a feeling of spirituality that allows visitors like us to sense the connection the traditional owners of the land have with

— Grab that Moment —

these massive boulders. There is an energy that emanates from them that you can feel if you stand quietly amongst them. And if you listen, the wind blowing between the cracks and crevices almost talks to you. A truly unique place.

— John Litchen —

— Grab that Moment —

— Grab that Moment —

    I fell asleep for an hour while Monica probably read one of the 20 or so books we had brought along.
    We were parked under a tree and out of the direct sun, but that didn't stop the heat. It was probably hotter here than a thousand kilometres further north in Darwin, but up there you also had the humidity generated by the start of the wet season to contend with. In my view, high humidity combined with a high temperature is much worse.

By the time we got to Tennant Creek, the sun was low and casting long shadows which only accentuated the enormous width of the main street through the centre of the town. On either side of the narrow highway, there was a median strip where cars could angle park, and then beyond that on each side was a service road where cars could parallel park, then there was the footpaths and the shops. Crossing from one side to the other was probably the widest space for the main road that I have ever seen in a country town.

We only stopped long enough to buy something to eat at the Billabong Cafe before moving on and stopping at a rest spot further along the highway where we spent the night in the campervan. Over the entire trip, we never slept in a hotel or motel or any other kind of accommodation. We stayed in the campervan, It was spacious enough for the two of us, and we could stop anywhere, anytime, which gave us a wonderful sense of freedom.

A plethora of termite mounds

The land became drier after Tennant Creek and we began to see termite mounds. They were everywhere. Monica was fascinated by them because she had never seen anything like them before. We stopped every so often so she could have a closer look at them. The further north we traveled the larger they became.

"Just wait till we get to the Top End," I told her. "The mounds are gigantic… as tall as 6 metres high, and there are millions of them."

"I find that hard to believe."

"It's true, you'll see. The weird thing is though, only in Australia and Africa and in some parts of South America, can you find termite mounds. There are none in the northern hemisphere. The termites like the Savannah country, the grasslands, and the magnetic ones, you'll find them in the wet grasslands across the Top End."

"Magnetic ones?"

"They call them that because everyone of them is crescent shaped and oriented north and south. They're not actually magnetic, but every one of them has the same shape and the narrow edges always point north and south. These are only found in northern Australia. Nowhere else."

In the soft early evening light the red earth presented muted colours whereas in the harsh midday sun, it glowed, full of energy, almost blinding with intensity of the light. In the images below the shape of the mound reminded me of those enigmatic statues on Easter Island as they sat on their haunches, staring inland, always facing away from the surrounding ocean.

The colour of the earth determined the colour of the mound seen here after a fire had burnt the grass and bushes around it. The fire was probably deliberately lit to burn off the tall dead grass to make space for regrowth when the wet season begins. The further north we went, the bigger and more massive the mounds became. The ones below are in a more tropical and wetter area.

There are more than 2000 species of termites around the world, and 350 species are found in Australia, and of those only 25 are dangerous to people's houses and other wooden structures.

The termites don't actually live in the mounds, but underneath them. The mounds have s thousands of tiny holes in them which allows the exchange of oxygen and carbon dioxide to take place. They are, in effect, the lungs of the termite colonies. They regulate airflow and moisture content. And they are very solid, especially the larger ones. If you accidentally run a 4-wheel drive into one of the big ones, you won't knock it over, you'll most likely wreck your vehicle depending on how hard you hit it.

"There could be as many as a million termites inhabiting one large mound," I said while Monica walked around the base of a particularly large mound, "and how many mounds are there across the top end of the country?"

"There are a million termites in this one?"

"And how many like this one have we passed? There are millions of them. Just the mass of the termites alone, worldwide, probably outweighs the mass of all the other animals alive. When you add up the weight of other insect species like ants, beetles, flies, caterpillars, mosquitoes, spiders and other things, their sheer mass far outweighs all human, animal, and probably plant life as well that exists. And that's not counting the biomass of bacteria that inhabit every available niche in the air, the land, in rocks and crevices underground and in the oceans. Bacterial biomass probably outweighs everything else combined.

Small magnetic termite mounds

— Grab that Moment —

Wet roads and a bogged truck

We thought we were finished with muddy roads and slush, but a couple of hundred kilometres north of Tennant Creek we found a long stretch of the highway under repair. It looked more like it had been abandoned because we saw no machinery for repairing it. It didn't look like we could drive through it either as it appeared to be very slippery and muddy. There was however, an alternative path off to the side and we took that, only to discover a couple of kilometres further along, a bogged road train truck, whose driver had also tried to go around the more impassable wet stretch.

A utility had stopped and the driver was discussing with the truck driver how to help, but to me it looked as if there was no way of pulling the truck out without extensive digging. The heavy part with the container on it was well and truly bogged, deep enough to cover the wheels' axles.

That truck wasn't going anywhere, anytime soon.

Into the tropics

As we approached Katherine the abrupt change in the plant growth and the humidity in the air was astonishing. It had rained a lot since the wet season had started further north, but it was like there was a barrier, a line of demarcation between the drier desert country and the wetter rain-forest country. An invisible barrier that we crossed without being aware of it; all of a sudden the grass was taller and lush, whereas a few minutes previously it had been dried up. The trees were more palm-like and creeks were running with water. Pandanus palms overhung the creeks and rivers, creating cool tunnels that filtered the harsh sunlight. Stepping out of the campervan it was almost like entering a sauna. It felt steamy and sticky.

Katherine was well into the Tropical end of the Territory just over 300 kilometres south of Darwin. I imagined the climate in Darwin wouldn't be much different as far as humidity was concerned. But I was wrong. That 300 kilometres made a big difference.

We stopped long enough in Katherine to take a boat trip into the Katherine Gorge. Though it is spectacular, it only gives a small indication of how fantastic the Kakadu National Park must be. Unfortunately we didn't get to see Kakadu. Now you can drive into it on an all weather road, from just south of Darwin via the Arhem highway, or if coming north from Katherine, via the Kakadu highway. The two highways intersect at Jabiru, deep into the Kakadu National Park, but in 1974 it was a very difficult place to access because there were no roads. I flew across part of it to Oenpelli 16 years earlier (in 1958) when working for the Northern Territory Agricultural Department, to do a survey of wild buffalo The two highways that traverse Kakadu jointly terminate at Oenpelli.

Beautiful and serene, Pandanus shrouded creeks near Katherine.

In the Katherine Gorge, spectacular...

There are, we were told, many rock paintings in the Katherine Gorge, but we only saw this one, well above the flood line, and beneath an overhang. It was difficult to discern since we were not allowed to get close to it. The boat driver pointed it out as we passed by and all I could do was snap a telephoto shot of it.

Overwhelmed by the humidity

We drove into Darwin late in the afternoon. It had been raining and the roads were wet, but the sky was clear. There were huge cumulus clouds building up out to sea and no doubt they would drift in over the town and dump more rain a bit later. I remembered how this happened many times during the wet season, day and night, and after each rainstorm, everything seemed cooler, until the sun came out and the water started to evaporate. Then the humidity would hit you...

...and the first thing that struck us was the humidity.

The instant we stepped out of the campervan, in fact, the instant we stopped moving, with no air flowing through the open windows, we started sweating. Our clothes stuck to us. We stood in the street like a couple of drowned rats and looked around, finding it difficult to breathe. It was like the air contained an invisible mist, that when breathed in started to choke you. This only lasted a few moments, and we adjusted to it. At least I adjusted to it. Monica was still wheezing slightly.

"*No me gusta nada este lugar,*" she said. "*La humedad me está matando.*" ("I don't like this place. The humidity is killing me.")

"You get used to it after a while," I said.

She gave me a strange look and shook her head. "*No te creo.*" ("I don't believe you.")

We wandered about for an hour or so until it began to get dark. We drove down to a beach slightly out of the main part of Darwin and set up the campervan for the night. We cooked something on the little camp stove and when it got much darker we settled down to sleep. Only we couldn't sleep. It was so hot and sticky that we felt like we were choking. Sweat drained out of us making the sheets on the bed as wet as if it had rained on them.

Then it rained. It pounded down with so much noise our ears were ringing. We had to shut the windows or the rain would get in, and once we'd done that, it was impossible to sleep. We could hardly breathe, the air was so thick. And it was windy too. It blew the rain in sheets across the beach and the car park where we'd positioned ourselves under a large tree. The branches rattled and banged above us and I began to worry that they might snap and fall down on top of us.

"We can't stay here," Monica said.

"You're right, but we can't go anywhere while it's raining like this."

Turning the wipers on to look out the front windscreen, I couldn't see anything. It was like we were parked under a waterfall. We just had to endure it. Eventually it stopped and the humidity dropped a bit and we managed to get a little sleep.

As soon as we woke up in the morning we decided without saying a word about it to each other, that we would leave.

I looked out over the beach and the water was muddy and grey. Dirty white breakers pummeled the shoreline. And beyond that, out to sea there were huge billows of white cumulus clouds building up again for another storm.

I pulled the roof down and made it tight, we packed away our damp bed and sheets, started the engine and drove out of Darwin.

— Grab that Moment —

The streets of Darwin not long after we arrived. It had recently rained just before the top photo was taken. What cannot be seen in the photos is how humid it was.

Both of us found Darwin somewhat depressing. It wasn't just the enervating humidity, it was the place itself. It seemed a lot less exciting to me this second time around. It was more rundown, more dilapidated, and there were too many drunks. I was a lot younger the first time I came here and that probably was why the city seemed exciting, but this time around at 34 years of age, the place just looked like a dump.

Only one way to go

There was only one way to go from Darwin and that was south.

It was relief to be moving again, because the air coming in through the windows as we drove along gave the illusion of freshness. It covered up the humidity, which if we were motionless, would be almost unbearable. I couldn't help wondering how I managed to spend a complete wet season in Darwin 16 years earlier. A wet season and a dry season. But then I was only 18, and at that age nothing bothers you.

We drove through Katherine and continued south. Our intention was to reach the Barkly Highway which goes from near Tennant Creek across to Mount Isa and Cloncurry in Queensland where it changes its name to the Flinders Highway and continues on to Townsville on the east coast.

But as we approached Daly Waters, we decided to take a different route rather than follow the same road we used coming north. We turned left, towards the east and took the Carpentaria highway that goes to Boraloola.

60 kilometres before Borraloola you make a right turn onto another highway, The Tablelands highway, which runs from Borraloola south to the Barkly highway before it runs into Queensland. This would give us a chance to see some different country from what we had seen when we drove north along the Stuart highway to Darwin.

What I underestimated was the distance along the Carpentaria highway until it joins the Tablelands highway, and how far that goes until it reaches the highway into Queensland and the distance from that point until the first town in Queensland, Camooweal, where we could get fuel. It was almost 900 kilometres. There were no places to stop for fuel, and the names on the map were those of private properties, not towns or roadhouses.

There is now a roadhouse at the point where the two highways join, about 60 kilometres out from Borraloola, which is now a great spot for tourists wanting to fish for barrumundi and mud crabs. It was reputedly a lawless town used by smugglers fifty years ago.

As we approached the turn off I realized that even with the two fuel tanks tied on the roof above us, we wouldn't have enough petrol to get all the way into Queensland. The tank in the campervan was three-quarters empty after driving more than 400 kilometres from Daly Waters where we had topped it up as well as filling the ones on the roof. It was another 60 kilometres into Borraloola where we could buy petrol, and even with driving back the same 60 kilometres, we should just have enough to drive all the way south along the Tablelands highway, turn left (east) onto the Barkly highway to go into Queensland where the first town we would come to would be Camooweal. We had no choice. We had to drive on into Borraloola and buy petrol, then drive back to the highway junction before heading south.

The McArthur River where it runs through Borraloola in the middle of Narwindi Aboriginal land. In the picture to the left there are five people doing stuff along the river bank, fishing, washing, but it is difficult to see them at first glance. Above: parked by the roadside in Borraloola after filling up with petrol.

— *Grab that Moment* —

There was a sign on the river bank which said: **Beware of Crocodiles**, and Monica berated me afterwards because I didn't tell her before we sat on top of the river bank to eat lunch. I actually didn't see the sign until after we got up to leave, after I had taken two photos of the river.

I pointed across to the other side of the river.

"Look, there are people over there. Fishing or doing stuff. I don't know, but they don't seem too concerned about crocodiles."

"You should have told me. What if one came up the bank and attacked us?"

"Come on. We were twenty feet above the water level. There's no way it could run up and grab us if there was one in the water. We would have seen it the moment it came out of the water in plenty of time to get up and out of the way. Do you think those people over there would be at the water's edge or in the water if there were crocodiles around?"

"I don't know," she mumbled. "You should be more careful."

She got back into the campervan and waited for me to get in the other side. It didn't take long to get back to where we had to turn south. From there on it would be a long haul to the next town which was Camooweal in Queensland, about 700 kilometres of nothing but flat grasslands.

The Tablelands Highway, looking south. Dead straight for hundreds of kilometres, and dead flat also. It was also a lot dryer than I expected, considering the rain and wet weather back in Darwin about 800 kilometres north west of here.

This was a good place for Monica to get in some driving practice.

We had to pull over almost at the point where the Tablelands highway reaches the Barkly highway, to fill up the tank. Those two full tanks on the roof were pretty heavy, but they had enough fuel to take us another 400 kilometres, which would see us in Queensland and the town of Camooweal. After that we would find many towns on the way where we could fill up with petrol, and not have to worry about the tanks on the roof rack.

— Grab that Moment —

Camooweal looked like a ghost town with abandoned stores falling to pieces in the main street. After filling with petrol at a service station we parked beside Freckleton's old general store while we walked around to stretch our legs. Like the butcher shop, that store had seen better days, and no longer functioned. The building next door, which didn't look much better, had replaced it and that's where we bought petrol. Camooweal is actually part of the city of Mt Isa even though Mt Isa is 188 kilometres further east. There are only 208 residents of this small town living there at the moment. I doubt if there would have been any more than that when we stopped to fill up with petrol in 1974.

— Grab that Moment —

We had been gone now for about four weeks and I was beginning to wonder how our house was progressing. It was supposed to be finished when we got back, but knowing how long it was taking, and how many delays had occurred, I was doubtful that much more would be done. We needed to be there to prod them, to keep reminding them, to make sure they finished the house as they had promised. As a result, the drive across to Townsville on the tropical East Coast was virtually non-stop. There were places along this outback highway that we could have visited, the Qantas Museum, the site where hundreds of dinosaur fossils had been discovered, lots of fascinating places, but we simply didn't have enough time. Of course, I promised myself I would come back, we would come back another time to have a better look at outback Queensland, but like going to Ayers Rock (Uluru), this has yet to happen. (*And 48 years later, unfortunately, may never happen.*)

It was a welcome relief to arrive in Townsville, to leave the flat tablelands way behind, to feel the warm tropical air instead of the burnt dryness of the interior, to see fishing boats and yachts in a beautiful harbour, to smell the saltiness of the sea air.

Parked beneath a giant native fig tree on the foreshore in Townsville.

But we couldn't spend too long in Townsville; it was still a long way to go to get back to Melbourne. After a couple of days we drove down the coast as far as far as Rockhampton, then we took a more direct inland route from there to Goondiwindi on the NSW Qld border, and then straight south to Melbourne through Moree, Gilgandra, Dubbo , Forbes, West Wyalong, Naranbera and on into Victoria via Echuca and Shepparton. We didn't really stop anywhere except for meal breaks, brief rests, to sleep, and to fill the van with petrol; we just kept going until we got home.

No change

Unfortunately, when we got back, nothing much had progressed with the house from the way it was before we left. As soon as we walked into the head office they were all over us with apologies and excuses about the delay in completion, and sincerely promised that we would be in our house by Christmas, only three and half weeks away.

It had to be completed by then as the building trade closed down for five weeks over the Christmas New Year period. But not only that, in the contract, it stated that if the work had not been completed by the final time stated, the company would have to pay us a penalty for every day it was delayed ...and you could bet they were not willing to do that.

The site became a hive of activity with plumbers, and gas-fitters, plasterers and painters, and right on the last two days before the holiday shutdown, we were being led through the house for an inspection to see if everything was up to scratch. We were too excited to finally be in the house to notice any faults like misaligned doors or stuff like that. Everything looked fine as far as we could see. It was only later that we noticed how rough some of the work was, and that was obviously because of the last minute rush to have it all done before the annual shutdown.

How it was looking as we left for our trip to Darwin.
It looked exactly the same when we got back.
Nothing had been done during the time we were away.

— Grab that Moment —

Brickies hard at work finishing the walls.

Almost done; at lockup stage.

Two weeks after we came back from the trip to Darwin, lock-up stage was reached. If you look closely, you can see the bricks from the level of the air vents down looks different from the brickwork above. The bricks used for the lower part were a different size to those used above. Also the colour of the mortar was different,darker, than that used below. But I figured that once we had a garden established, the difference would not be noticeable.
The gaps between the bricks used on the upper part of the house are obviously wider because the bricks used were slightly smaller in length. This could be clearly seen at the front especially between the windows. Along the side walls it wasn't so noticeable.
Monica is checking out the carport.
The house at this point had reached lock-up and was waiting for the interior to be completed.

Before we moved into the house, Dad celebrated his 50th year in Australia on the 12th December 1974. He arrived in 1924 on a ship that looked so decrepit it was a wonder it hadn't sunk on the way over. There was a big party with all the family and many of his compatriots and friends celebrating well into the night. It was a fantastic night. He might have been old, around 76, assuming he was born in 1898 as he claimed, but he could still hold his own leading the dance around the lounge room. What is it about Greeks and dancing? Zorba had nothing on Dad, but Zorba epitomized that Greek spirit that I often saw in all of those old guys who had migrated to Australia (and elsewhere) in the 1920s. There is something about dancing, that really gets to them. When they hear music from their homeland, they can't help themselves. It sends shivers up my spine.

We had Christmas dinner that year at Mum and Dad's place, the family home, in Benbow street, and it was there that Mum told us Darwin had been destroyed by a cyclone, Cyclone Tracy. We couldn't believe it. We had just been there the month before. But it was true. The total devastation was almost too much to comprehend. It looked like an atomic bomb had hit it.

We watched the news coverage on TV and constantly had to remind ourselves that had we taken our trip a month later, we would have been there when the cyclone struck.

Part Seven

Disappointment and excitement

Moments of disappointment

It was hard to believe that when we got home and went out to the house, which was the very first thing we did, that nothing had been done while we were away for those 5 weeks. It was at lock up stage, but looking in through the windows we mostly saw just framework, no plastering. The floor had been laid so that was something. It was only a few weeks to Christmas. We were supposed to be in by then. I couldn't see that happening so I went to the builder's headquarters in Footscray, and kicked up a fuss. I also reminded them that if it wasn't finished and ready for occupancy by the date on the contract, (24th December 1974) they were liable to pay me $1000 per day for every day it went over time.

They assured me it would be finished on time, and that they would have a team out there the next day to commence plastering.

They did, and they also had electricians out there to put all the fittings in place, plumbers to connect the water and install the bath tub, the shower recesses in the bathroom and the en-suite, a bidet as well as a second toilet and connect everything to the sewer. As soon as the plasterers were finished a team of painters came in and painted the interior. The wooden floor was polished and varnished, doors were fitted in all the rooms and the kitchen was set up. There were no tiles laid as I was going to organize that separately.

It was absolute chaos for the three weeks prior to Christmas, but they got everything done.

It was the middle of the morning the day before Christmas Eve, when they called and invited us to come out for a final inspection. We could hardly wait to get there.

There was a lot of rubble lying around the site which I expected they would clean up, but they didn't. Everyone had knocked off that day and went off for their annual holidays. No building work would be done until the end of January(1975) which included a site clean-up.

Ignoring the rubble, we made our way inside and were escorted through the house by the company representative. He was jovial and friendly and took us through and showed how all the doors were fitted squarely and that everything had been completed as per the contract. Everything we had asked for was done.

We were given a certificate of occupancy from the council stating the house was ready for occupation. He gave us the keys to the front and back door and took off.

We stood there for awhile, gazing with pride at our very own home.

"Let's go and get some of our stuff," I said.

We drove back to Benbow street and got some of our things together, loaded the van and took them to our new house; bean bags, a few boxes of books, a large circular rug and a smaller matching rectangular one to throw on the floor. The rugs were bright and colorful and they immediately made the place appear more welcoming. There was nothing else there yet. No curtains on the windows, nothing like that.

"We'll have to pin up a sheet or two to cover the windows until we can get some curtains," I said as we stood in the bedroom at the front of the house. The afternoon sun was shining right into the room.

Monica was standing at the window looking out onto the front yard which was nothing more than churned up dirt scattered with broken bricks and tiles and pieces of wood. Anyone driving past or walking by in the street could see in, at least at night when we would have to put on the lights. During the afternoon, the sun shining on the windows would reflect back onto the street making it impossible to see in.

"We definitely need something here," Monica agreed.

We were in our own house, and it felt fantastic.

As the afternoon wore on, I went to switch on the lights and found the electricity was not connected. We had no power. Not only that, When I went into the kitchen to make a cup of tea I discovered we had no gas connected either. I thought the plumbers would have done that, but obviously they hadn't.

I immediately rang the building company and had trouble finding anyone there who wasn't at their Christmas party. When I finally got someone who could do things, he told us they would have someone out there immediately to connect the electricity, but it was too late for the gas. That would have to wait until the trade came back from holidays the last week of January.

'Immediately' didn't happen. The electricity didn't get connected until after Boxing Day, so we had no power for three days.

This didn't bother us too much because we stayed at Benbow street where we had been since we were married. It wasn't our intention, but without power, we didn't have a choice.

We had Christmas dinner at Benbow street, at which time we found out that Darwin had been totally destroyed by Cyclone Tracy and that thousands of residents were being evacuated to other places including Sydney and Melbourne. Seventy percent of the city and suburbs had been destroyed and would have to be cleared and rebuilt. It was actually worse than the destruction done by the Japanese bombing raids during World War Two. It was hard to imagine, but soon enough we saw video and pictures on TV and it was real mess.

We moved in as soon as the power was connected, and all we had was our queen bed, a fold-able camp table and chairs, the two rugs we'd already chucked on the floor, my drums, boxes of books records and so on.

We had no lounge chairs, kitchen table or any other stuff like that. We hadn't needed any of that when we were living at Benbow street because Mum and Dad had all that.

For a few days we sat on the floor on rugs, cooked with the portable camping stove, or an electric fry-pan. We took cold showers because the gas had yet to be connected and there was no hot water, but it was summer with temperatures in the mid to high 30s, so we didn't mind even if we had to wait a month for that to be connected

Paul helping me move some stuff into the house. He's carrying the camp table we used on our two recent trips. Below: carrying in our mattress for the bed. The bed base is still in the van.

Relaxing on the floor with the weekend newspaper.

Making the house livable

I cleaned up the rubble, broken bricks, cut pieces of roof tiles, offcuts of timber, lumps of unused cement, pieces of plaster and other stuff left by the builders and got rid of it. The next thing we did was to get a concreter in to concrete the carport and the driveway. These guys didn't take time off like the rest of the building trade, and they came the first week in the new year and did the job. I planted a few trees and bushes and laid out a lawn. We had a brickie come in and build a brick fence all the way around the property at the rear, because the wooden fences separating us from our neighbors were so dilapidated, they were ready to fall over and would have to be replaced anyway. He also laid the sandstone on the back entrance which made the place look much better. We got the Holland Blinds people to come out and install sun blinds on the three front windows where the afternoon sun blasted the building heating up our bedroom. Once the trees strategically planted in the front grew, we wouldn't need the blinds, but until that happened, they gave us some privacy as well as blocked the hot sun. In no time the place started to look like a house that was being lived in. A Spanish acquaintance was a tiler and we got him to come in and lay tiles in the kitchen and the bathroom.

Although we were yet to obtain any furniture, we had lots of space and we were in our own home.

We couldn't have been happier. Monica was ecstatic and enthusiastically did her exercises on the floor in the bedroom.

In February we bought a lounge suite and a coffee table, a dining table and chairs and a table for the kitchen. By then the place started to look lived in. I hung a couple of paintings I bought from the art gallery in Williamstown on the wall to complement the New Guinea statues and drums lined up around the wall. In the spare room I built shelves for my records, tapes, amplifier, turntable and tape-deck, moved my drums in there, and this room became my study or office. I got a desk where I could sit and write with the small electric typewriter. There were no desktop home computers available in those days. It would be another ten years before home computers started to become affordable.

At the beginning of February, I decided to lay cork tiles through the dining and lounge rooms, as well as the small entrance way. They gave a nice softness to the floor and also acted as an insulator to prevent cold coming up from under the floor in the winter, since it was a raised floor and not a concrete slab. Cork tiles also gave it a more elegant appearance, not to mention it was beautiful to walk on barefoot. In the passage and the bedrooms, I laid a carpet with the help of my brother Phillip who had done this in his own home. He had the tools for stretching the carpet and was big help. Finally, I had a builder friend come in and build bookshelves along one wall of the lounge room. Once that was done and the books were stacked on the shelves, everything looked great. Apart from removing an inefficient gas heater from a side wall and replacing it with a better one on the opposite wall where more heat could be radiated into the room in the winter, the house remained unchanged inside until we eventually sold it. The garden of course continued to develop as trees grew, and plants went through their annual cycles.

The first couple of days after moving in... sitting on the floor... no furniture other than my drums and some carvings from New Guinea.

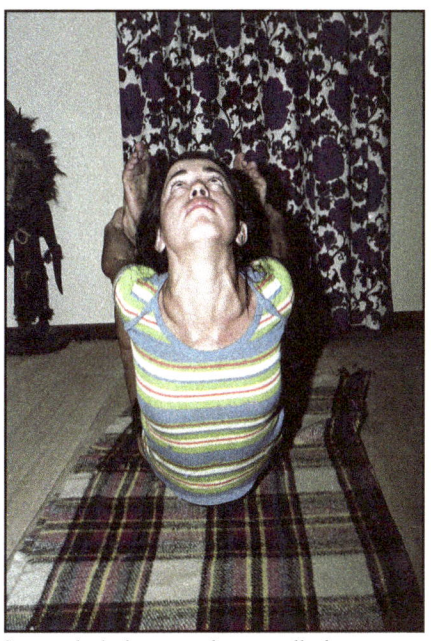

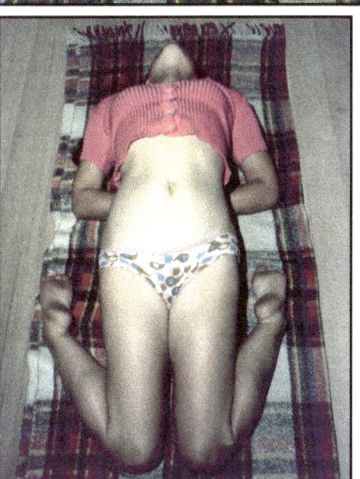

On the floor in the bedroom, enthusiastically doing her exercises. We bought some ready made curtains to replace the sheets we'd temporarily used to cover the windows.

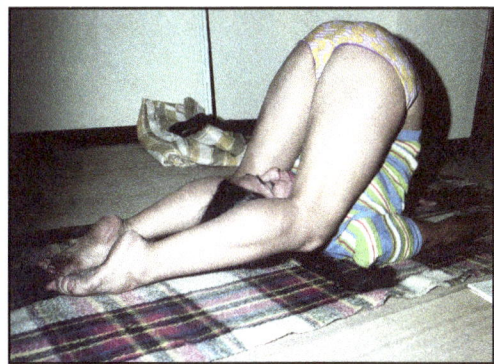
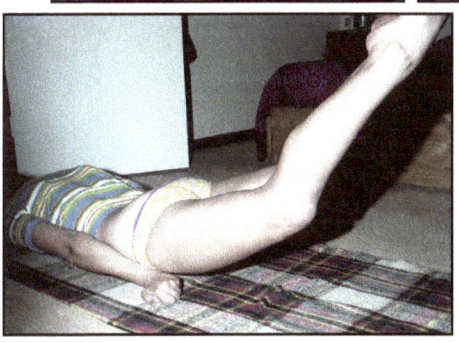
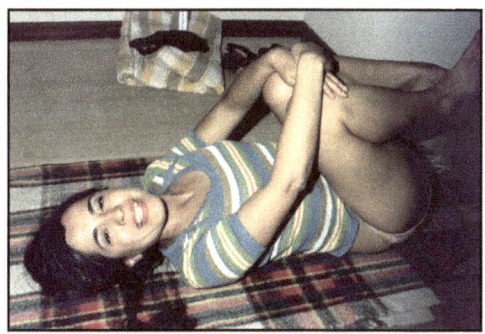

With the cork floor done, and some furniture, the place really started to look lived in.

    With the driveway concreted, access to and from the house was easy, and with a few trees and other plants forming a front garden, the place looked like a proper residence at last. The sun blinds made an enormous difference to the front which was our bedroom, and en-suite. The lawn still needed to develop, but it was taking shape.
    The back yard as well was transformed into a place that looked like you could have a party there with a barbecue built in along the side wall that the brickie built. He also paved the back porch with sandstone.
    All of this was done in the first three months we lived there.
    After that I built a pergola across the back of the house and around the side to link with the carport. It added character to the yard.

— Grab that Moment —

Changing jobs

At this stage, Monica gave up her work at Berkley Apparel in North Melbourne. It was too difficult to get there from Hoppers Crossing. She was also not happy with the son of the original owner who had taken over the business and didn't treat the workers as well as his father had.

I bought her a small Mazda car which enabled her to come and go from Hoppers Crossing, which if you didn't have private transport, was an isolated place. A train was the only public transport I was aware of at that time. There may have been buses, but I never saw one. She had to learn how to drive and had to have a car of her own.

I spoke to Merv Binns at Space Age Books, whom she knew through me, and asked if he had any vacancies. He hired her to work part time in the office taking mail order book sales. To get there she would drive to Hoppers Crossing station, park, and take the train to Flinders Street station, and either walk up to the shop in Swanston Street, or take the loop underground and get off at the station underneath the corner of La Trobe and Swanston Streets. Then it was only a hundred metres or so to walk to Space Age Books. She was familiar with the shop and with all who worked there because she had seen us making the Antifan Film to promote the Australia in 75 Worldcon. She also came with me to Sydney when I went there to promote and present the film for its premier at a national convention, before the film was sent over to the US.

Around September 1975 we discovered that Monica was pregnant.

An exciting end to the year

We were going to become parents.

That was exciting, but it was a concern with her being isolated at Hoppers Crossing once she gave up work. She was worried that she would be 36 years old when the baby was born, and 36 was quite old to be having a baby.

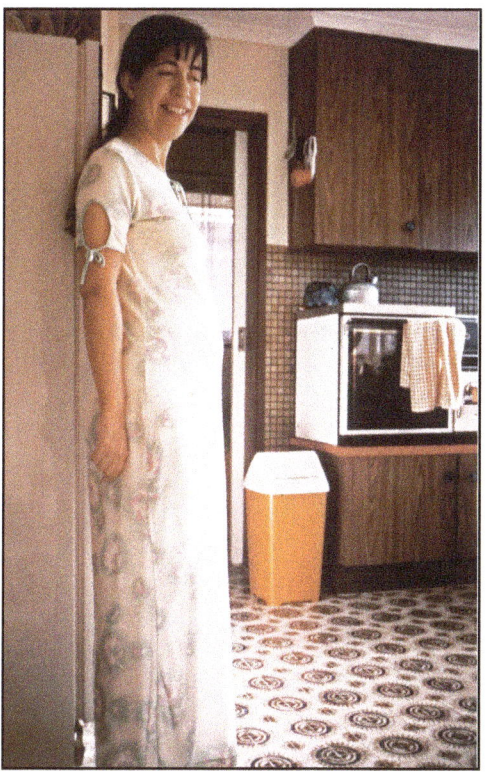

But everything seemed to be going fine. We decided to bring her mother over so she could have some emotional and physical support during her pregnancy. Monica was over the moon once the idea of her mother visiting started to sink in. She couldn't wait to see her again.

They wrote letters to each other every week. It had been five years since she had seen any of her family, and only knew how they were getting on via the correspondence with her mother. She couldn't wait to catch up on all the gossip first hand once her mother arrived. She missed her mother as well as her brothers and their families.

Having her mother with us would be a big help for her.

I went to Qantas headquarters in Melbourne and organized the flights to bring her to Melbourne from Santiago via Easter Island and New Zealand. There was a bit of paperwork to do but eventually it was arranged. Her visa to visit was for 6 months.

Señora Marina arrived at the end of November.

Monica was ecstatic. It had been at least five years since she had seen her mother, and they talked non-stop. I had no idea of what they were talking about, and switched off while driving home.

We had prepared the spare bedroom for our visitor. We bought a single bed and a small dresser with a mirror which she could use. Monica helped her unpack and settle in.

A couple of weeks earlier we had bought a small colour TV which we placed in the lounge room. It was an AWA set. AWA was an Australian company and they made very good electronic gear, and the colour on their TVs was phenomenal. They vanished once the market became flooded with Japanese and Korean TVs. Mum and Dad had dumped their gigantic black and white Admiral TV and replaced it with a large Sharp TV, which had pretty good colour.

I later bought a Phillip's video recorder which was connected to the TV to record programs we were unable to watch when they were broadcast. Phillips invented the video recorder and it was an enormous machine that used a large cartridge which could record just one hour. This was before the Japanese came out with two competing systems, Betamax and VHS, after which Phillips vanished. They even closed their service factory in South Melbourne. Betamax from Sony was a superb system, while the competing VHS couldn't match it for sharpness and clarity, but unfortunately became the more popular because of advertising and the fact it was cheaper. It ended up dominating the market worldwide. Betamax vanished and VHS lingered for years until DVDs, and much later Blue Ray discs, became the standard.

It's all very different now but back in 1975 it was an exciting new device.

When the cassette got jammed, I took it to the factory in South Melbourne and the technicians there replaced the whole loading mechanism with a new one while I waited. You wouldn't get that kind of service today.

I guess they had a reputation to maintain. Phillips had invented the cassette recorder which Sony made famous as their *Walkman* radio cassette player. I think they hoped they would do the same with their video recorder, but the whole thing was too big and cumbersome. It took the Japanese to re-invent it and make it smaller, more compact, and more easily workable. Eventually Phillips switched over to using the Japanese versions of their invention so they could maintain a presence in the market.

We went to Portarlington for Christmas along with the whole family and all the kids. The photos here are from inside the lounge room. Monica and her Mum were very happy together.

— Grab that Moment —

Fred, Phillip, and Paul, examining the shattered windscreen.

Apart from the weather being dull, the only damper on the day was Fred arriving with a shattered windscreen. A car in front of him just down the road a bit, had flicked up a small stone, and it smashed into the windscreen which didn't shatter but became a matted mass of tiny breaks almost impossible to see through.

The same thing happened to me years later while driving over the Westgate bridge. I was in the third lane from the edge and there were two trucks in the two left lanes. On my right side in the fourth lane was another car parallel to me. It was peak hour, and the traffic was moving fast. Ahead of me I could see a piece of wood had fallen off a truck at some stage and was lying on the road right across the white painted line. I couldn't move right because I was hemmed in by other cars traveling faster than me, and on my left were a number of trucks and other commercial vehicles. I saw the truck ahead in the immediate left lane try to avoid the piece of wood but it had nowhere to go other than to sit in the lane it was in. The rear wheel clipped the edge of the piece of wood and flung it up into the air. I couldn't move left or right and could see it flipping over and coming directly at me. I was hoping it would fly over the top of the van but it didn't. I flew straight into the middle of the windscreen which shattered making me blind. I leaned over as far to the right as I could to avoid the wood if it came through the glass, but it just bounced off and over the top of the van. I heard a screech of brakes behind me as the car behind tried to avoid being hit by the same piece of wood. All I could do was lean out of the driver's side window so I could see ahead. I couldn't stop. I had to keep going over the bridge and down the other side, after which the traffic spread out and I could work my way over to an emergency stopping lane.

It doesn't take much; a tiny stone, a small plank of wood, but traveling at high speed, if it hits a windscreen, it will shatter it. Thankfully, windscreens are made with safety glass that doesn't break into slivers that will cut you to shreds. It becomes a mosaic of tiny squares and rectangles of glass held together making it impossible to see through.

In the emergency lane I punched out the rest of the windscreen, then turned around and drove back over the bridge and down to the service station in Newport where I regularly had the van serviced. Theo, the owner, ordered a windscreen to be sent out and he fitted it as soon as it arrived. I was back on the road a couple of hours later.

We quickly forgot about Fred's smashed windscreen as dinner got underway. As usual, each of us brought something to the table so Mum wouldn't have to do much cooking. I brought a roast leg of lamb, Zara a duck cooked with an orange sauce while Fred brought his famous abalone salad. Fred no longer drove buses but had been abalone diving professionally for a long time. Phillip brought salads, and Christine a lovely chicken. Mum, as always, made the plum pudding. But for the kids, the whole focus was on opening their presents. They literally took over the house, while we looked on. Monica's Mum sat quietly on the lounge watching everything. She was content to sit and hold young Dione who was probably about 9 months old at that time. Since she couldn't speak English she remained rather quiet, but she did enjoy herself.

Exchanging gifts.

— Grab that Moment —

With Christmas gone, we entered the new year (1976) by taking Señora Marina on a trip to Ballarat and Sovereign Hill, the historical recreation of what Ballarat was like during the gold mining rush a century and a half earlier. It was a hot day and a slight wind blew dust everywhere, stirred up by horse drawn carriages loaded with tourists driving along the packed earth streets. There was a blacksmith working to show how things got done back in the old days. There were huts showing how the miners lived, and all kinds of workshops, with everything operating with steam or with human muscle power. There was a bakery where we had lunch, and while Monica and her mum enjoyed an ice cream under a veranda, I went down to have a look inside a reconstructed gold mine. Talk about claustrophobic! How those early miners worked in such cramped places deep underground is beyond anything I could comprehend. The early Chinese settlers had the right idea; they opened businesses like laundries and restaurants, market-gardens and hardware supplies, to service the needs of the miners who often paid them with gold they had dug up, many of them becoming quite wealthy compared to many of the miners.

After visiting Sovereign Hill, it was a relief to sit beside Lake Wendouree where magnificent trees provided welcome shade from a very hot sun.

— Grab that Moment —

Happy together in front of the entrance to a Chinese Temple at Sovereign Hill.

Enjoying ice creams in the shade.

Horses were used in many ways in the 1890s; for stage coaches, public transport, working the milling stones to crush the rock dug up from the mines, for milling hay, and they are everywhere at Sovereign Hill giving us a glimpse into the past.

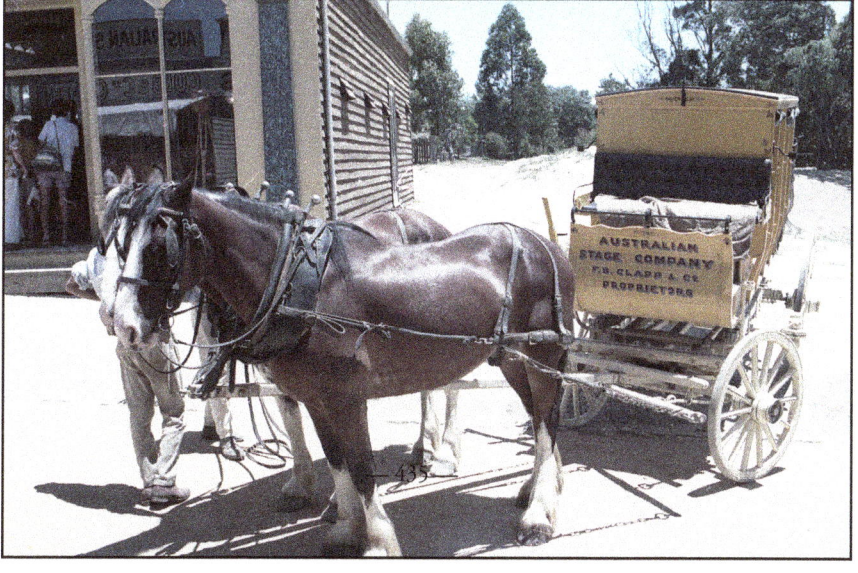

In the shade, under the most magnificent trees seen anywhere.

These incredible trees were probably planted when the swampland that existed here was drained and constructed to form a lake. Some of them certainly look as if they are over 100 years old.

Back from Ballarat Monica and her Mum in one of Melbourne's iconic shopping malls, and at St Kilda open air art market.

Part Eight
Cyclones, wild weather
and shipwrecks

Cyclone David

On the 13th to the 19th of January (1976) a massive cyclone formed off the northern coast of Queensland. Its effects were far reaching, from New Guinea as far south as Lord Howe Island. It produced enormous waves and swells which combined with extra high tides caused massive damage to heron Island even though it passed well to the north. As it crossed the coast it unroofed thirty houses in Yeppoon and the waves did considerable damage to Yepoon's Rosslyn Bay Harbour where the breakwater was destroyed along with the yachts and trawlers sheltering behind it. It brought prodigious amounts of rain as it moved inland and dissipated into a heavy tropical storm, traveling inland as far as the point where the Northern Territory, South Australian and Queensland borders intersect. It produced 12 metre waves at Sydney heads. It forced shipping all along the coast from central NSW into Queensland to seek safety. A 3000 tonne cargo vessel from Monrovia bound for New Guinea from Brisbane was tossed mercilessly by the huge waves after leaving Moreton Bay and the captain turned his ship back to Brisbane. Everything on board was smashed.

"It's the worst sea I've ever seen," he said when back in port. "The waves must have been 50 foot high! We were tossed around so much I thought we were going to sink. I've been at sea for over 12 years and seen lots of bad storms, but this one was terrifying."

Tides were up to a metre above normal levels and waves peaked 8.9 metres along the coast.

Once Cyclone David had degenerated into an inland storm producing the usual floods all the way down into central NSW, the weather settled down along the coast into cloudy and rainy weather interspersed with the odd moment of sunshine. It was the wet season up north, not the best time for a dive trip.

Fred suggested the Middleton Reef trip to me.

He and Rommy had previously been on a trip on the Coralita to Saumarez Reef the year before and knew Wally Muller from that trip. Saumarez Reef is about 300 kilometres out north east of Gladstone, and is a large coral reef and island with scattered coral sand cays near the Swain Reefs which indicate the beginning of the Great Barrier Reef.

Like me, they had read about the Coralita in Australia's most popular Skindiving Magazine and that had prompted them to take a trip, a holiday away from Abalone diving in cold water. On that trip to the Great Barrier

Reef the professional diver on board was Neville Coleman, whose articles describing marine species often appeared in *Skindiving in Australia and New Zealand.*

When Fred received a letter from the secretary of *Barrier Reef Cruises*, Wally Muller's charter business, explaining that they were doing a trip to Middleton Reef, he and Rommy decided immediately to go. Fred called me and asked if I was interested.

Of course I said yes.

Fred contacted Wally Muller, the skipper of the dive boat TSMV Coralita, who told them he was having the boat's annual Commonwealth Certification inspection in Brisbane, which was why the Coralita, normally operating out of Yepoon, was not wrecked when cyclone David passed over the coast a few kilometres north of the town. He was also making some repairs and was berthed in the Brisbane River at Wright's Shipyard. He was planning to take some fishermen from Coffs Harbour out to Middleton Reef. It would be a shakedown cruise after the annual inspection. Besides the weather further north was not conducive taking divers out to the Great Barrier Reef.

"There is good diving out at Middleton Reef," he told Fred, which was more than enough to convince Fred to take the trip.

Fred and I were regular readers of Barry Andrewartha's *Skindiving in Australia and New Zealand,* previously known as *Skindiving in Australia.* In many issues there were stories about divers charting a luxury dive boat called the Coralita. Neville Coleman, a marine biologist and enthusiastic diver often travelled aboard this lovely boat as he documented marine species all around Australia. He had many articles published in *Skindiving in Australia and New Zealand* prior to starting his own magazine *Underwater*. This later became *Neville Coleman's Underwater*, and then *Underwater Geographic.* Another well known (at the time) diving personality was John Harding, who was an underwater filmmaker who had also started his own magazine, *Fathom*, which was in a roundabout way, instrumental in us deciding to go to New Guinea. John filmed his girlfriend Jocelyn in many underwater sequences and the two of them would often tour around Australia showing the films they made and telling stories of their diving exploits. They too often traveled on board the Coralita.

I think it was a policy of the owner, Wally Muller, that he always had an experienced diver or diving person who was known within the diving community to host activities relating to diving for guests whenever the Coralita was being used as a dive boat. His own crew were all expert divers as well, so they were always there to assist guest divers during the charters. Reading the exploits of these people also gave an insight into the locations the dive boat traveled to in Queensland and elsewhere along the Australian coast.

Wally Muller was the captain (and owner) of the TSMV Coralita, which was based at Yeppoon in Queensland, north of Brisbane, on the coast just past Rockhampton, with Keppel island offshore at the start of the Great Barrier Reef. Most of the trips the Coralita took were north into the Great Barrier Reef rather than south. Reports of the journeys and chartered expeditions were thus often spectacular with some of the best diving spots in the clearest of water featured regularly. It was enough to make any skin-diver's, scuba-diver's and spear-fishermen's mouth water.

The Coralita weighed 100 tons and had been designed especially for cruising in coral reef waters and shallow tropical seas such as the Coral Sea. She was 79 feet long with a beam of 20 feet, and draught of 7 feet. Powered by two diesel engines, the cruising distance was 2000 miles. There were 8 passenger cabins, with two of them self-contained double suites. Four cabins were twin berth with hot and cold running water, but showers and bathrooms for gents and ladies were separate. The other two cabins were a bit smaller and located on the main deck with portholes open to sea air. A total of 16 passengers could be accommodated very comfortably. Carried on board were 22 scuba tanks, 2 air compressors, lead weights and belts, flippers, masks and snorkels. Each diver had to bring their own regulator. The Coralita also was fitted with two Doppler sonar scanners for charter as a hydro-graphic survey vessel, radio telephone for voice and telegraph messages to anywhere in the world, gyro and magnetic compasses, electronic echo sounders, radio direction finder, radar and automatic pilot. On top of that it had a licensed bar and served food of gourmet standards to all passengers and crew.

"You picked a great time for a dive trip in Queensland," I said to Fred. "It's the cyclone season. Haven't you been watching the news?"

"We're not going to Queensland, other than to board the Coralita. She's at Wright's Shipyard in the Brisbane River. We're going out to Middleton Reef, and that's 400 kilometres straight out from Coffs Harbour, so it's New South Wales."

"Not much difference Fred. Cyclone David may have crossed the coast into central Queensland, but gale conditions extend all the way from New Guinea down as far south as Lord Howe Island. The sand has vanished from the Gold Coast beaches and there is scarping right back to the edge of some of those high-rise blocks."

"By the time we get there, it will have settled down."

"I saw on the news the council was dropping concrete blocks in the front of one building to stop the waves washing away any more sand."

"You worry too much."

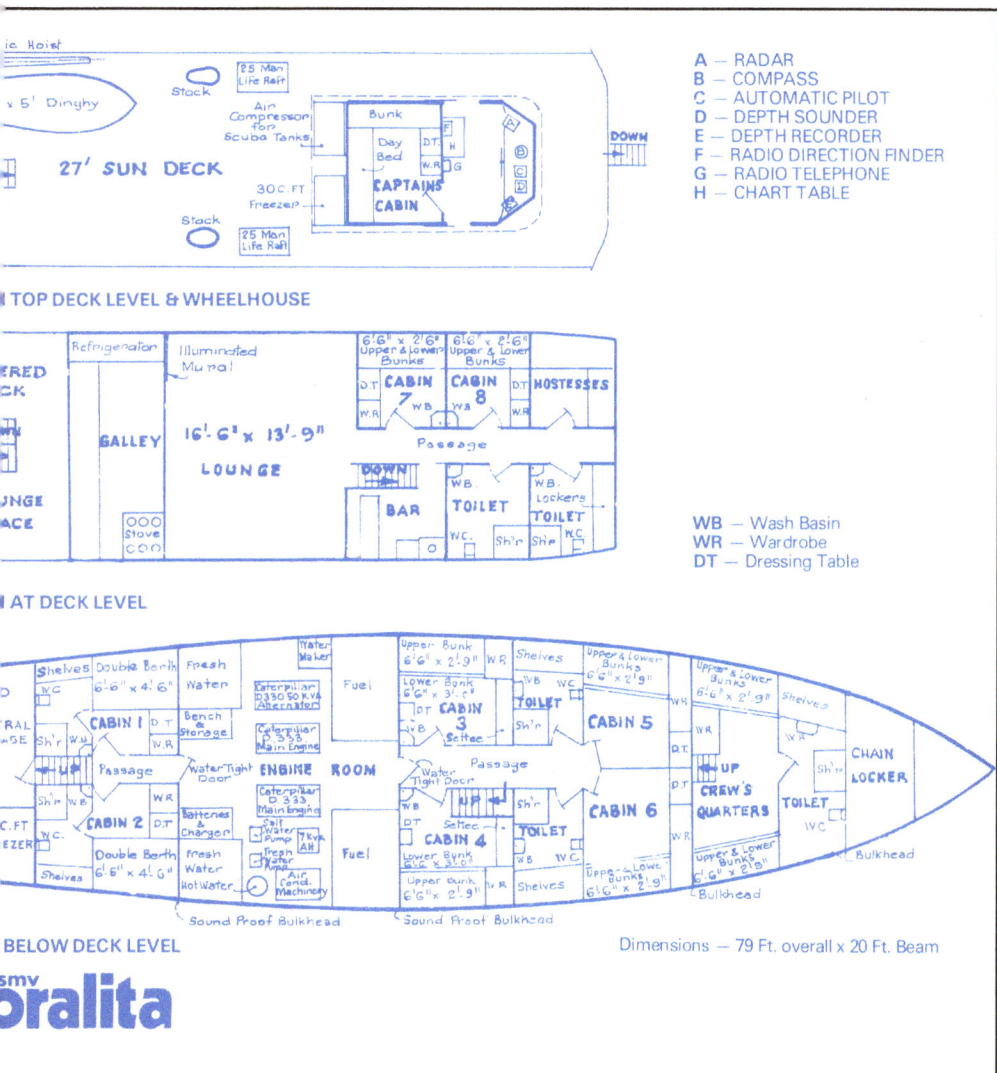

"There's already another cyclone forming up there, in the Solomon Sea."

"That's a long way away from where we're going. It's unlikely it'll have any effect on us."

While I still looked skeptical, Fred added, "Look, if Wally Muller thought there would be any problems, he would have canceled the proposed trip. He knows the area. He's been out there before many times."

19th February 1976

We packed our flippers, masks and snorkels, regulators, camera gear, and clothes into my campervan, and off we went; Fred, Rommy, and myself again. We had to drive up via the east coast since most of the highways in central NSW were cut in various places by flood waters and swollen river systems as a result of the massive amount of rain dropped into southern and central Queensland by the remnants of Cyclone David.

I don't think Monica was too happy about me taking off on a trip while she was three months pregnant, but her mother was there and she had a lot of catching up to do. She wouldn't miss me all that much. We weren't going to be gone long anyway.

Once we got into northern NSW Fred and Rommy couldn't resist stopping at every chance to buy mud crabs; any crabs for that matter, but mud crabs especially; they were a luxury in Melbourne and weren't seen that often, but up here in the more tropical coastal country they were available almost everywhere.

Two very fine specimens.

21st February 1976

Entering Brisbane from the Pacific Highway we went straight to Wright's Shipyard along the lower reaches of the Brisbane River. And there was the Coralita moored beside a short pier. From a distance, she looked quite small. But looks can be deceiving. The sky was grey and it drizzled with rain, but the Coralita looked more impressive as we walked along the pier towards her.

The Coralita at Wright's Shipyard. Fred and Rommy are standing on the aft deck while Wally Muller, the Skipper, is exiting a side door.

"Anyone aboard?" Fred called as we stepped onto the deck.
Wally Muller, the skipper was there. "Welcome aboard," he greeted us with a big smile.

"Glad to be here," Fred said. "Not very nice weather though."

"I tried to call you," Wally said, "to tell you we would be delayed for a few days because of the weather, and because there are still some jobs to be completed on board, but you'd already left."

A quick look around confirmed that. Her decks were a scramble of scattered tools and equipment. The crew had been cleaning up after the obligatory annual inspection and certification, but had stopped because of the incessant rain.

"We'll be ready to depart on Monday. Pick a cabin and bring your stuff on board."

Since we were the first passengers, we had our pick of the cabins. Inside, your perspective soon changes. The whole interior is beautifully designed and appears much larger than we imagined it would be from our first impression as we walked towards her.

Over a couple of stubbies after we'd stowed our gear, Wally said, "the rain was a blessing in disguise. The port of Brisbane has been closed since Cyclone David hit the coast, which has given us plenty of time for extra maintenance. I know we were supposed to leave today, but I'll make it up at the other end."

Since we would only get in the way, we decided to go over to my uncle Jack's place in Stafford on the other side of Brisbane. This delay meant we would get to spend a weekend in Brisbane. After visiting Uncle Jack (Lofty), we went to visit a friend of Rommy, Merv who had been his best man at his wedding. He lived much closer to where the Coralita was moored.

9 am 22nd February 1976

It had rained continuously since we had arrived in Brisbane. Everything was damp, humid, sticky.

Gale force winds were being whipped up by a continuing tropical low depression off the coast near Gladstone with southeast wind gusts between 60 and 70 kilometres per hour. This depression was currently moving north west at about 28 knots, but it kept changing direction. It changed direction five times that first night we were there, and the weather forecast more or less said *it is highly unlikely that this low would develop into a cyclone because it is being fed by cooler waters*. This was a remnant of what had been Cyclone David after it crossed to coast the week before. High winds and three metre waves had closed all the beaches.

23rd February 1976

It was still raining. It just kept alternating with steady drizzle and relatively calm to gusty winds with pounding rain that cascaded off the roof because the gutters are too full to handle it. Not once has it looked like clearing.

"It's been like this for the last two months," Lofty said as we drank our first coffee for the day around his kitchen table.

"Why would you want to live up here," Fred asked.

"You get used to it."

"Not me," Rommy said. "I used to live here, but I couldn't stand it and moved to Melbourne."

"And the weather's better in Melbourne?"

"It's different."

Enough said. The weather is always shit when you don't like it, and when you do, then it's fantastic.

The radio updated the weather warnings every half hour. *The coast road is now closed and the inland is flooded as far south as central NSW.*

"You were lucky to get here," Lofty added.

As Sunday progressed the rain lightened, and later that day we went to visit Rommy' friend and best man at his wedding. We left the campervan at his place and he drove us over to Wright's Shipyard where we boarded the Coralita. The decks were clear and she looked ready to go. We stayed on board since Wally said we would be departing first thing in the morning.

The Coralita at Wright's Shipyard in the muddy Brisbane River.

24th February 1976
Fred and Rommy shared one cabin while I had the adjoining one to myself. I slept well and when I came up on deck at 8 am a miracle had occurred. Overnight, while we had slept, the storm had moved out to sea and dissipated. The sun was shining. I could hardly believe it. We'd had constant rain for days on end it was hard to imagine the sun was still up there somewhere shining. Now we could see it.

"How good is that?" Fred said as he stood beside me.

It was already hot and muggy. The sky was still a bit patchy but a sluggish breeze was pushing the clouds out to sea. The river was muddy and swollen with flood water coming down from inland, but with the sun shining everything looked so much better.

We had breakfast, prepared by Wally's wife Denise, who was responsible for all the cooking and catering. Joining us was their son Roy, alias Boris, who was one of the crew along with Terry, who did everything from taking care of the divers and filleting the fish caught to serving wine at dinner. Joining us as breakfast was finished was Richard Weir, who represented Australia at the recent world skindiving championships in Peru. He was accompanied by his girlfriend Lucia Macuga from Nambour. The others who were to accompany us on this trip we would pick up in Coffs Harbour.

It was 10 am when we left.

Cruising down the river was beautiful at first. On both sides there were many hills shrouded with abundant greenery with the occasion top of a building, usually a block of flats, sticking up above it. Sometimes on the higher ground a bit back from the river, the sun glinted off the windows of luxury houses. There was hardly any traffic on the river. We saw a few barges and a couple of fishing boats, and one small yacht heading slowly downstream. As we passed it, someone on board waved to us.

An hour or so downriver, the land flattened out and became industrial and a lot less interesting. There seemed to be lots of factories serviced with their own wharves. There was the Ampol Refinery on our right with a huge flame burning methane above its distilling tower, and what appeared to be a golf course on our left. Shortly after that we left the river and headed out into Morton Bay.

"I'm going to take the south passage," Wally told us as we headed into Moreton Bay.

We looked blank. We had no idea what he was talking about.

"Instead of going north and around the top of Moreton Island, where all the commercial shipping has to go, we'll go south and through the gap between Morton Island North Stradbroke Island."

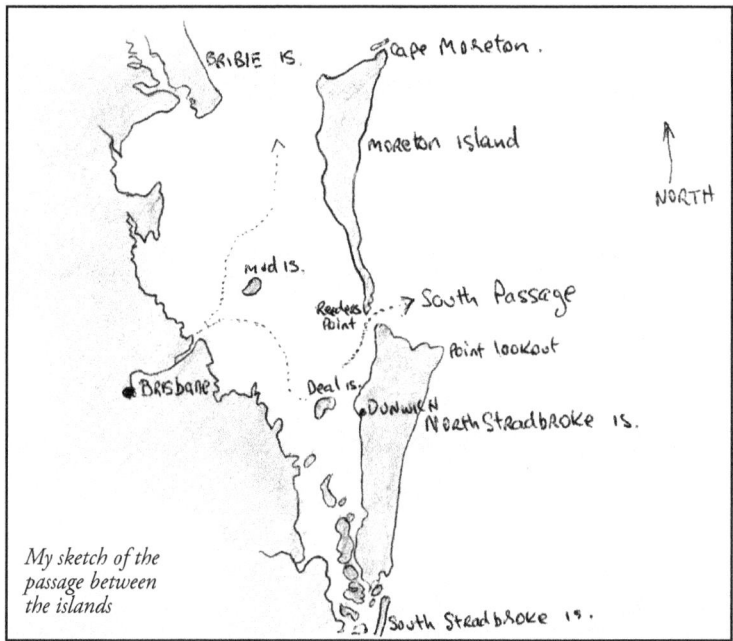

My sketch of the passage between the islands

He spread a chart on the dining table and pointed to where the south passage was.

"We'll stop by Deal Island and have lunch while we wait for the tide to come in. It's a pretty shallow bar between the two fringing islands and we have a seven-foot draught. There are still lots of big waves out there and we'll need all the clearance we can get. Going that way will save us about six hours of travel time."

We passed Mud Island and several smaller islets. Morton Bay is home to dugongs but we didn't see any because the water was discolored with run-off from the rivers and creeks feeding into Morton Bay, but especially from the Brisbane River which carried enormous flows of muddy water after all the rains they'd had. We Passed an oyster farm and finally dropped anchor close to Deal Island. Not far ahead of us was the large mass of North Stradbroke Island and nestled in amongst the trees we could just discern the small town of Dunwich.

We had lunch, beautifully prepared by Denise, while we waited for the tide to come in.

Terry, Richard and Boris were on deck battening down everything that was loose and checking everything else in preparation for an expected rough trip over the bar. In fact, because it was still windy and there were still lots of large waves left over from the recent storms, we were promised a rough trip all the way down the coast to Coffs Harbour.

After lunch, waiting for the tide to rise enough to allow passage between the islands.

At 2pm, when the tide was as high as it was likely to get, Wally told Terry to haul up the anchor, and once again we were under way.

We followed the channel which was about half a kilometre offshore from North Stradbroke Island. It ran parallel to the coastline until the island degenerated into a series of sand dunes which finally disappeared into the sea, forming the long bar of the South Passage over which huge waves were breaking and smashing up in a confusion of white water and windblown spray.

"That looks pretty rough," Rommy said as we looked at the messy water between the two large islands.

The sand dunes continued underwater between the two islands where they emerged again almost a kilometre away as the sand dunes of the southern end of Moreton Island. Most commercial fishing boats or other boats like the Coralita could only cross this sand bar at high tide. The only alternative was to head north and go right around Morton Island. The passage at the northern end of Moreton Island was deep enough for ocean liners and cargo boats of all sizes, but it would take at least six hours to go all the way around and to come back on the ocean side to the spot we would get to if we went through the South Passage over the sand bar.

"It's a bit rougher than I expected," Wally commented as he concentrated on steering towards the centre of the space between the islands. Then he turned around and smiled at us. "But it won't be problem."

As we got closer, we could see the waves were much bigger than they had looked when we were some distance away. They were enormous. The long fetch of the ocean beyond had allowed the wind to push the waves up to a huge size. No wonder the beaches along the Gold Coast to the south of us, and those further north had suffered considerable damage.

"Here we go," Wally said. We were in the wheelhouse with him where we got a good view. The others on board were below decks in the lounge or sitting by the bar.

Wally timed it so that as we entered and got close to the shallowest part a huge swell lifted us up. Gunning the motors. The Coralita surged up the wave front. She slid over the top, and as we drifted down into the trough behind, he pulled back on the motors. The bow punched into a wave and water sprayed up over us, over the whole length of the boat. The Coralita shuddered as she hit the bottom of the trough.

Aiming at slight angle to the next wave barreling towards us Wally gunned the motors again. The Coralita surged forward and up diagonally to the wave front. On one side of us it started to break, but Wally steered towards the side where the wave was still rolling forward. The Coralita leaned over and slipped a bit on the face of the wave, and then suddenly we were over it, or the wave had rolled on by underneath us and we were sliding down the other side.

And that was it. We were through. Ahead of us was the open ocean full of huge swells and rolling waves, but they weren't breaking as they did closer to shore. We rode up and down, punching through the odd one which sprayed water and foam all over us.

"That wasn't too bad," Fred said.

"Easy as," Wally said.

Rommy and I said nothing. We were enjoying the boat's movement as it headed straight into the oncoming waves. A smooth ride up and down over and over. It's hard to tell, but I thought the waves were at least 4 metres high.

"There's a current running south," Wally explained, "so we should make good time once we're in it."

"But we're not heading south," Rommy said. "We're going straight out."

"The current at this time of year is about four kilometres offshore. As soon as we hit it, we'll turn south."

Half an hour later, with the coastline barely a smudge behind us, we turned south to run parallel to the coast. Coffs Harbour was 186 nautical miles south. It was late afternoon and we wouldn't get there until early the next morning.

The waves were now hitting us side on. We were no longer punching into them. The rolled us over to the starboard side and as the waves moved underneath and past us heading towards the shore, we then rolled back the other way to the port side, only to be hit a minute later with another wave rolling us over. The Coralita still moved up and down, although not as much as when we were punching directly into the oncoming waves. It was this sideways rolling combined with the forwards up and down that played havoc with my balance. I started to feel queasy.

"Do you want a sea-sick pill?" Fred asked me.

"I think I'll be right. I just need to get some fresh air."

"I took one," he said as he staggered across the lounge to a seat beside the bar. "Just in case…"

The constant rolling and twisting gets to you after a while. It was taking me longer than usual to get used to it, to adjust to the movement. I went out on deck and the waves rolling towards us seemed bigger than ever. The wind was certainly stronger. Maybe I should lie down, I thought. And that's what I did. I went down to my bunk and tried to sleep, but I kept getting rolled from side to side. The good thing was that after a while I felt comfortable with no sensation of nausea at all.

It was getting fairly dark so it was quite late when Wally came below and called everyone to dinner. I guess the others had come down for a rest as well. I jumped up quick enough, but suddenly I broke out in a sweat. I was dizzy, and had to hang onto the bunk or I would have fallen over. Staggering out into the passage I bumped into Terry who asked, "Where's everyone?"

I couldn't answer. At that moment my stomach gave a lurch and whatever lunch was left down there started to come up. I just made it to the toilet where I spewed everything up. I was shivering and sweating. There was no way I could eat anything.

I staggered back to my cabin just as Fred and Rommy appeared from theirs. They looked fine.

"Coming up for dinner?" Rommy asked.

I couldn't answer.

"Should have taken a pill," Fred said.

Up yours!

I laid down on my bunk, and almost immediately felt better. The dizziness and the nausea vanished. But every time I tried to get up, my head would start spinning and my stomach would start dry heaving. I gave up trying and laid there until eventually I fell asleep.

The Coralita at Coffs Harbour.

25th February 1976

I woke up to discover that although we were still moving, there was no up and down or side to side movement. I felt exhausted, but not sick or dizzy. I went up on deck and discovered that we had arrived at Coffs Harbour and were making our way into a completely sheltered port.

Very soon we were tied up beside a low concrete wharf. The crew were busy topping up the water tanks and taking on fuel for the long haul out to Middleton Reef and back.

Fred, greeting Bill Baxter as he arrived and showing him the layout on board the Coralita.

As we had breakfast, I could see people wandering about the concrete wharf looking at the Coralita. Perhaps they were envious of us being on board such a luxury boat. More likely, boats like the Coralita didn't often come into small ports like Coffs Harbour.

After a while, we were joined by two gentlemen from Gunnedah, further inland on the other side of the coastal range, Bill Baxter and Linsdsay Eather, and they came on board with fishing rods and a carton containing a dozen bottles of scotch whiskey.

"Just in case they run dry," they told us. "We brought our own."

Shortly after they arrived and settled in, John Harding and Jocelyn Edwards arrived with their camera and diving gear. By the time everyone was sorted, and their gear stowed, it was lunchtime. Again, Denise excelled, serving a beautiful lunch which we all enjoyed together.

We left at 1pm. A lovely smooth run out of the harbour and past Mutton Bird Island.

Leaving Coffs Harbour.

Middleton Reef is about 300 nautical miles due east of Coffs Harbour, about thirty-two hours of travel.

The sky was overcast, and the seas were heavy. The Coralita rolled constantly, so much that at times it was hard to stand up let alone trying to do anything else.

"Give me one of your pills, Fred." I wasn't going to get sea-sick again.

Whether that helped, or whether I was now used to the movement of Coralita punching into the waves, riding up and down with the occasional sideways twist, I don't know, but I didn't get sick or even feel dizzy again. Bill was fine also, but Lindsay kept saying he preferred fresh air and stayed up on deck for the first few hours. Of course, he kept a glass of whiskey handy at all times. Jocelyn was sick and John didn't look the best. Both of them agreed it was one of the roughest trips they've had on the Coralita.

At least it was until we were about half way to Middleton Reef. The sea further out settled down enough to allow Bill and Lindsay to do some trawling and they caught some fine fish which Boris, hanging over the side gaffed and pulled in. These fish were quickly filleted by Terry and found themselves the main course for dinner later in the evening.

It's impossible to imagine how immense the Pacific Ocean is until you try to cross it. I spent four weeks crossing it to reach the Panama Canal on my way to Europe on board the Ellenis back in 1964, and that was crossing from Australia to The Americas. Imagine how long it would take to traverse the Pacific from north to south, at least four times the distance. This time we were traveling only a short distance, a bare 500 or so kilometres from Coffs Harbour to Middleton Reef. Even so, looking at the seemingly endless ocean surrounding our tiny boat made me feel insignificant.

After a few hours, you begin to lose your sense of time. Minutes stretch into hours while nothing around you seems to change. It always looks the same. The water was so dark that sometimes it looked black. Most of the time it was a deep navy blue colour. The sky was again overcast and grey, which sometimes made the ocean look ominous.

Mutton birds followed us, gliding with stiff wings just above the crest of a wave. Sometimes a wingtip would touch the water creating a tiny splash of almost fluorescent white over the dark surface of the wave, then the bird would spin off in a different direction. With a couple of flaps of its wings it would gain enough altitude to soar and glide until another large wave presented an opportunity to repeat the performance. I never saw these birds catch any fish. They never stopped to sit on the water as water-birds on land do. They just glided, endlessly, silently, above the waves.

The day stretched into night and the next day was the same, riding up and over the waves, moving forward with a variety of sea birds following in our wake.

27th February 1967
At the end of the second day of traveling we arrived at Middleton Reef at 8 pm. It was dark. Wally took us around the lee of the reef where it was reasonably calm and we anchored there for the night. The Coralita was steady, with hardly any movement at all. Everyone felt fantastic, and excited for what we would be doing the next day. Denise again served a magnificent meal of the fish the boys had caught during the day.

In the wheelhouse above, the radar clearly showed the positions of all the wrecks above the waterline as well as the sections of reef where big waves broke over.

"Even though we can see all of that, it's too dangerous to enter the reef at night," Wally told us.

Impatient or otherwise, we would have to wait until morning before entering into the lagoon protected by the surrounding reef.

From a distance the Runic looks as if she is sailing along, bat as soon as we got closer it was obvious she was stuck hard and fast on outer edge of the reef. She had driven right up onto it fifteen years earlier. This was our view as we entered the main channel through the reef, the edge of which can be seen behind the Runic where there is a line of waves.

The back half of the Runic. The part broken off was sitting right behind the main part of the ship, but after Cyclone Colin had passed over us, it had been shifted by the waves almost 100 metres away from the main body of the ship.

28th February 1976

We were all awake early, as soon as the sun came up. Wally took us through the gap closest to the wreck of the Runic, which is the largest vessel stuck hard and fast on the reef. It's the most visible of all the wrecks scattered around the extent of the reef.

Technically, Middleton Reef and the nearby Elizabeth Reef, are situated in the Coral Sea. I didn't know the Coral Sea extended so far south. To me it was the South Pacific Ocean.

What is remarkable about these two reefs is that they are the southern-most platform reefs in the world.

Middleton reef is 550 kilometres from the New South Wales coast and 220 kilometres north of Lord Howe Island. Geographically, they are part of the underwater platform known as Lord Howe Rise. Elizabeth Reef is about 40 kilometres closer to Lord How Island as well as being the same distance from the New South Wales coastline as Middleton Reef. Both reefs are now a Marine National Park Reserve managed by the Government of Australia under the National Heritage Trust. This wasn't the case when we went there in 1976; it was proclaimed as a nature reserve in 1987 to protect the two reefs' fragile marine ecosystems. Before that, both reefs were favorite fishing spots for people from the mainland as well as from Lord Howe Island. They went after a rare species of black cod. These fish are now protected as well and you cannot take them. But back in 1976 no one realized how rare this particular fish was, and there weren't, as far as I know, restrictions on catching them then.

Unfortunately for sailors and their ships, Middleton and Elizabeth Reefs sit right in the middle of a major shipping lane and at high tide are practically invisible, which is why there are so many shipwrecks on these reefs, especially the larger Middleton Reef.

Middleton Reef is 8.9 kilometres long by 6.5 kilometres wide and from above it is kidney shaped, with two main entrances to a lagoon inside the outer reef. Elizabeth Reef, separated by the 45-kilometre-wide deep oceanic pass, is 8.5 by 5.5 kilometres and is roughly pear shaped. Both reefs contain a sand cay that is not completely covered when the tide rises. With Elizabeth Reef the sand island is about 400 metres in length by roughly the same width when the tide is low with much of the surrounding flat reef is exposed, but the flat reef and much of the sand island is covered at high tide. Middleton Reef is protected by hard coral outer reefs and an extensive flat area of reef. The main entrance to the central lagoon is on the north side. Its sand cay, known as The Sound, measures 100 metres by 70 metres. The lagoon is mostly sandy with scattered parches of reef.

200 years of shipwrecks adds considerable marine archaeological significance to the Marine Reserve that protects both reefs and the surrounding areas. (The reserve covers 1,880 square kilometres.)

Middleton Reef is a tiny speck lost in a vast ocean, but at first light, as we entered the lagoon and dropped anchor safely inside the reef, it seemed to stretch to infinity all around us. In the distance ahead we could see a tiny white line where the waves were breaking against the outer edge of the reef. The water in the lagoon between that distant reef edge was a multitude of shades between dark blue to a dazzling pale green. To our right was the wreck of the Runic, etched against a brooding overcast sky. To our left, the paltry remains of an earlier wreck showed above the water just inside of where the bigger ocean waves were breaking over the outer edge of the reef.

Wally brought the Coralita in slowly and carefully, and we anchored above the position where a Japanese trawler lay intact in about 10 metres of water. While Wally went aft to start the air compressor to fill the scuba tanks we went and got our wetsuits, regulators, cameras and whatever else we needed to dive. You could actually swim down to the wreck below us without the use of scuba gear, but you were limited to how long you could hold your breath.

Middleton Reef may be a tiny speck in a vast ocean, but standing by the bow of the Coralita in the middle of the lagoon, the edge of the reef is barely discernible on the horizon ahead. The hint of white you can barely see are ocean swells breaking against the reef. The clear blue water beneath us indicates a white sandy bottom whereas the darker coloured water ahead is a large area of flat coral reef.

Lucia Macuga and Richard Weir, part of the crew who traveled down from Brisbane with us, happy to have some good weather the morning after we arrived. Little did we know it would soon change for the worse...

While John and Jocelyn were getting their cameras, ready Richard went over the side and swam over the wreck below us. Fred and Rommy were right behind him. A few minutes later Fred swam back to the dive platform at the back of the boat and called up.

"It's like in a movie," he said. "The whole thing is just sitting there intact. It's hardly even covered with coral."

Then Rommy popped up and said "there are fish everywhere. I've never seen so many. Can you pass me my camera?"

I handed it to him and he disappeared instantly.

A few minutes later I was in the water with my Bolex in its underwater housing filming the cod swimming over the wreck. Rommy had brought some pieces of left-over fish scraps from those Terry had filleted the day before and proceeded to feed one of the giant black cod while I filmed it. Lindsay and Bill were on the deck midships with their fishing lines in the water and any trevally they caught were instantly filleted by Terry. He passed the scraps to us to use underwater to attract more fish so we could get photos and film of them feeding.

After sucking the fish out of Fred's hand, the cod backed off a safe distance before swallowing it.

The only downside was that a strong current was running into the lagoon and it stirred up the sand. It wasn't as clear as we'd hoped mainly because of the recent after effects of Cyclone David, which although not coming anywhere near Middleton Reef, had produced severe storms with huge waves that extended all the way from New Guinea to Lord Howe Island. We had to make sure the current didn't pull us too far away to swim back up to the Coralita.

We weren't there too long before the sky became cloudy and grey which meant it wasn't as bright underwater as I would have liked. John Harding had twin lights on his camera housing. They only lasted fifteen minutes before needing to be recharged, but if you only switched them on as you started to film a scene, quite a bit could be achieved before they became too dull to be effective. The light made a huge difference. They brought out the colors that are lost by absorption of the water. I didn't have lights and relied on natural light. I suspected my film would be somewhat lackluster in comparison to that which John shot. But on seeing the film later, we were surprised at how good the quality was considering the conditions under which we filmed.

I filmed Fred as he placed a bag of fish scraps on the deck of the sunken trawler. And as he moved back to position himself with his camera to take photos, something huge came up behind him and shoved him out of the way.

"It gave me a bloody great shock," Fred recounted later. "The damn thing swallowed my flash. I had to pull it back out of its mouth. It went for the bag of scraps but it couldn't swallow it."

It was one of the giant black cod that hung around the shipwreck.

I filmed Fred as he kept pushing it away far enough so he could get some scraps out of the bag.

"As soon as I offered the fish scrap to the cod it snatched it right out of my hand."

And that I filmed. He hung on to another larger scrap and the cod twisted and wrestled until Fred was forced to let go. Finally, the cod swam away with the fish tail still protruding from its mouth. It came back moments later for more and Fred obliged, but this time he didn't hang on. He let the cod take it. It could have swallowed Fred's arm; the fish was that big. Hanging on like that was dangerous, but Fred can be like a big kid when he gets excited, which is why he hung onto the fish tail and wrestled with the cod. What an experience that was!

Getting close to film a beautiful black cod.
It was heading back to Fred to grab some more fish scraps.

Getting ready for a dive without scuba gear. I am holding the Bolex movie camera in its housing. Rommy is behind me, and Lindsay is beside the table used by Terry to Fillet the fish the boys caught.

Hanging onto the wreck of the Japanese trawler, John Harding shoots a scene with Jocelyn feeding trevally.

We spent the morning diving around the trawler and then moved to a new spot after lunch.

Lindsay and Bill threw heaps of bait over the side which attracted a large school of Silver Trevally. They circled furiously, snatching at the pieces of bait floating down. Quite a few were caught by the boys and Terry immediately filleted them and put them on a tray to go in the freezer. The Coralita had the capacity to freeze and store as much a 2000 pounds, around 850 kilos, of frozen fish. On the bottom below, Jocelyn was filming John Harding as he hand-fed fish scraps to the circling trevally.

A couple of small whaler sharks swam around, attracted by the smell of the fish bait and the struggles of the fish caught, but no one took any notice of them. They were not much over a metre long and kept away from the divers in the water who were quite large compared to the sharks and probably for the sharks, intimidating.

Lindsay Eather with a fine specimen which became our dinner that evening. Fred couldn't resist having a picture taken with this fish.

Some fine fish were caught by the boys and these ended up in the freezer until they were served later for dinner.

In the afternoon, Wally took the Coralita out and we ran around the edge of the reef several hundred metres out so the boys could do some trawling. Rommy tried his hand and caught a respectable kingfish. The others also caught kingfish as well as bonito. Boris did his thing, hanging over the side and gaffing the caught fish as they were brought in close. How he managed this without falling in was remarkable. At times he scrambled over the Coralita like a monkey up a tree.

Back inside the reef later in the afternoon Wally anchored us at a spot where previously he had the foresight to establish a mooring. He had taken a five-ton anchor from one of the wrecks around the reef and placed it in a strategic position in what he considered the safest part of the lagoon. At the time he established this mooring Cyclone Yulan was in the area and had approached to within 150 nautical miles of the reef. He lashed the Coralita onto the anchor and had no trouble sitting out the wild weather. This incident had been documented by John Harding and printed in his magazine, **Fathom, vol 1. #8**. Little did we realize that we too would be doing the same thing in a few days' time as Cyclone Colin now forming in the Coral sea far to the north, would move rapidly down the coast towards us.

After dinner, Rommy caught his first shark. Jocelyn called me to come and have a look and I took a flash photo of him about to pull the shark onto the dive platform at the rear of the boat. It was four feet long, not much bigger than the couple that had swum around with the trevally earlier. He released it. Quite a few sharks were caught in the evening, but they were accidental catches. The boys were after something better and each shark caught was a nuisance, and was released back into the water.

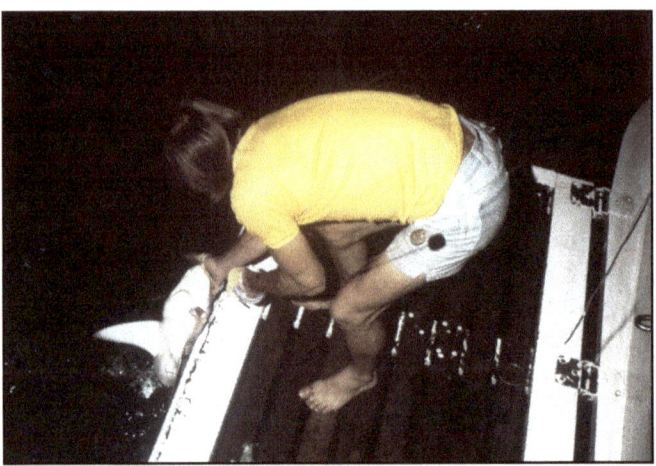

29th February 1976

This was a leap year so we had an extra day in February. It didn't make any difference to the weather. It was still overcast with an ENE wind blowing. Lindsay and Bill caught a lot of what they called Lord Howe Island Blue fish as well as the ubiquitous trevally. They also landed a Red Bass which Terry said was poisonous. After a couple of photos were taken, they threw it back in.

The Runic was our next objective.

By the time we anchored next to the Runic it was raining. A heavy swell prevented us from getting too close. Fred and Rommy, John and Jocelyn all went in to swim over closer to the Runic. Bill was busy pulling in Blue fish one after the other. I grabbed the Bolex and using the zoom lens shot some close views of the waves smashing into the side of the Runic. I panned along the length of the ship.

The Runic is a 14,000-ton cargo-passenger ship which ran up onto the reef about fifteen years earlier. Up until the last couple of years, it had been in excellent condition. Some idiots climbed on board a couple of years ago to salvage from it what they could and they set fire to it in order to kill rats which had been marooned and breeding on board since it ran up onto the reef. Someone else, or perhaps the same idiots, blew a hole in the side to make it easier to gain access while they stripped whatever metals they could find that might have some value. After that, the waves had been able to enter the ship and it quickly began to rust away and deteriorate.

Rusted and broken, the Runic was a sad sight. Yet seen from a distance, it looked magnificent, almost as if it was sailing along unharmed.

Since we were there in 1976, the Runic has rapidly deteriorated and has fallen over onto one side and is nowhere near as visible or as magnificent as it once looked. Other shipwrecks have been added to those already there.

The rain was getting heavier, and Wally came down to tell us that as soon as the divers were back on board we would move back into the safety of the lagoon. The wind was getting stronger and the waves bigger. We could see the waves smashing into the side of the Runic, entering and exiting through the hole blown in her side. Rommy came back with several pieces of brass, and he and Fred climbed back on board. John and Jocelyn were already back. It was much calmer inside the lagoon and the rest of the afternoon was spent trying to film some whaler sharks, but they were nervous and agitated which made it difficult to get near them. It very quickly got too dark underwater to do any filming so we returned to the Coralita, where we enjoyed a glass of whiskey from Bill and Lindsay's stock which was rapidly diminishing.

Cheers everyone! ...with hefty glasses of whiskey from Bill and Lindsay's stock.

1st March 1976

The wind was still blowing from the NE, gusting to 30 MPH. The surface of the lagoon was very choppy, yet when I jumped in, I was surprised to find visibility was still good. There was a strong current running so I stayed close to the Coralita while diving with only a mask and snorkel. Wally had tied a long rope to the dive platform so that if the current carries anyone away from the boat there is something to grab and hang on to for a rest, or to pull yourself back to the boat. Down on the sandy bottom, John Harding was again hand feeding a school of trevally which circled around so densely packed I could hardly see him in the middle of them.

A huge black Cod was slowly swimming along the bottom so I followed it and managed to get a couple of shots with my Nikonos camera before I had to go back up to breathe. Fred took the pictures of me taking pictures of the Cod.

It didn't take long before the visibility in the water became cloudy with stirred up sand. The tide was moving out and there was bit of a current to contend with, but overall, it was fun diving down without any scuba gear.

— Grab that Moment —

We moved several times before lunch but couldn't seem to find a good spot. Right after lunch Rommy caught a large black cod on his fishing line. He took longer to haul it in than usual because John Harding was filming the action. Right after a couple of photos were taken, Rommy put it back into the water but it seemed to flop about helplessly on the surface, unable to swim down. Apparently, its swim bladder had expanded making the fish too buoyant. John tied a cord around its tail and dragged in deeper down until the air in its swollen bladder became compressed by the water pressure enabling it to swim away on its own.

"It was really slow and disorientated," John told us after he came back on board. "I think it was suffering from shock."

"Wouldn't you, if you'd been dragged out of the water with a big hook in your mouth? And then dumped back in?"

"You know what?" John went on. "There doesn't seem to be as many black cod out here as I remember. There were a lot more here a couple of years ago."

"Trouble is," Wally said, "is that they taste so good. There are a couple of fishermen who come out here from Lord Howe Island regularly to fish for them. They don't take a lot, because they want the stock to last, but even

Rommy and the black Cod he caught.

Not one to miss an opportunity, Fred had to have a picture with the same Fish.

— Grab that Moment —

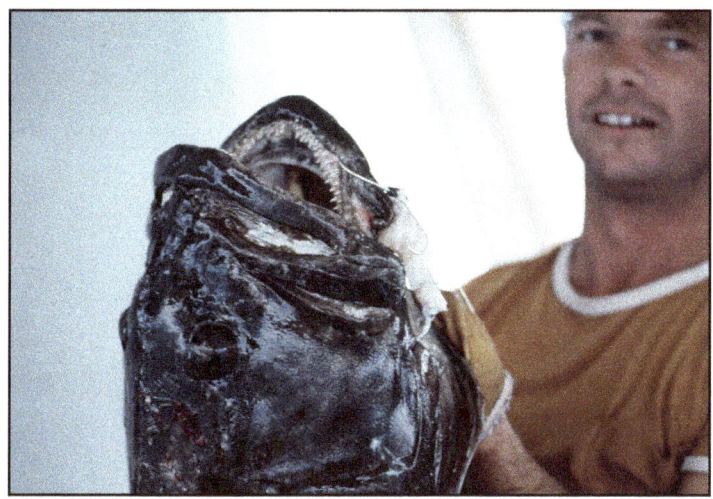

what they do take is too much. I don't think there'll be too many of left at all in a few more years. They'll be extinct as they are along the NSW coast."

That would be a pity. They are a beautiful fish to see underwater. You can actually swim up close enough to touch them. They'll take a fish right out of your hand and then hang around waiting for more. They even follow you around to see what you are doing.

Not only the cod; the other fish are equally as tame. Rommy grabbed a passing king-fish by the tail, but of course he couldn't hang onto it. It shot away the second his hand closed around it. Blubberlips and Red Bass will swim right up to you. Clouds of Trevally will hang around waiting for you to feed them. Who says fish don't remember? People like John Harding have often fed them on trips out to the reef so the fish hang around divers waiting for morsels of food to be dispensed. It's simply beautiful to be amongst them.

It's fortunate that Middleton and Elizabeth reefs are so far out, 550 kilometres due east of Coffs Harbour, that not too many people can get out there.

Again we moved; this time to a channel where there was an old wreck and some canons. Who knows how long that wreck had been there, but it was a long time ago. Wally had promised a canon to a friend with a private museum in Mooloolabah, or someplace like that. There were three canons lying in a sandy gully in about forty feet of water. Most of the wreck had rotted away, but it was the same wreck that he had taken the 5-ton anchor from to establish a secure mooring inside the lagoon. Although he tells people that the anchor came from the Runic, one look at it will tell you it's a different kind of anchor, something much older, something from a ship that went down more than a hundred years earlier.

A heavy swell was making it difficult to anchor, and the Coralita kept dragging it in the sand. Richard went over the side with a rope attached to a small buoy. He swam along the side of the reef until he located the canons. He dived down and tied the rope to one of them. He waited with the buoy until Wally swung the Coralita around. We drove into the current and moved slowly and cautiously towards the buoy. Terry must have been driving the Coralita because Wally was on the deck behind the captain's cabin where a small derrick capable of lifting one ton was located. He lowered a tangle of ropes down towards Richard so he could tie them around the canon. Richard grabbed the ropes and swam down to the canon where he tied the ropes around it. Terry stopped the motors and we drifted with the current. Wally started the derrick and slowly dragged the canon up from the sea floor.

The Coralita was rolling heavily in the swell and the weight of the canon didn't help. John Harding was in the water filming from underneath. I quickly put my Bolex in its housing and jumped off the dive platform into the water to film the canon being raised from below. As soon as I got underwater, I felt the current dragging me along. I swam back up to the surface and discovered that the Coralita was at least ten metres away and I was being dragged away from it at a rapid pace. I swam as hard as I could without making any headway. But I noticed as I kept swimming, the Coralita was coming closer towards me because it too was being dragged along by the current. I brushed against the rope Wally had left out behind the boat and gradually pulled myself along it. In a few moments I was against the dive platform and climbed back on board. By this time the canon had been raised to just under the surface. I took a couple of shots from underneath the stern of the Coralita, then I climbed on board to film it as it was hauled out of the water, swung over the railing and lowered onto the deck.

It took three guys to get the canon on board. Richard, Boris and Terry guided it over the rail and lowered it onto the deck, then tied it securely so it wouldn't roll around and cause any damage. The Coralita then moved back inside the lagoon where it was safer and we anchored for the night.

— Grab that Moment —

Richard dropping into the water at the stern of the Coralita, taking down some ropes to tie onto the cannon so it could be hauled up out of the water. There was a strong current running in this channel which made it dangerous as well as stirring up sand and algae which made visibility rather poor. The images above are from the 16mm film I shot with my Bolex camera.

Once the cannon reached the surface I came back out and took the other photos with my other camera, a Nikon F1.

— Grab that Moment —

Finally, the canon is on board.

Unfortunately over time, almost 50 years now, the movie film has deteriorated with color shifts to the red end of the spectrum. The other negatives also have faded or have had color shifts, but not to the same extant as has the 16mm movie film.

2nd March 1976
We actually caught a glimpse of the sun that morning, but the wind was much stronger and still blowing from ENE.

We were all around the dining table finishing breakfast when Wally said "Listen up everyone. I have an announcement."

Suddenly everyone was quiet. The only noise was from the wind outside and the rumble of waves smashing into the hard reef edge some distance away.

"You all know another cyclone has formed in the Solomon Sea, but that's a long way north of us. What you don't know is that it is now moving south. It's traveled towards the Queensland coast and is about 300 miles off, about as far off the coast as we are at the moment. It's also moving south or south east at a rate of fifteen knots. The report I received says that 200 miles from the eye, the winds are blowing at 120 miles per hour. The barometric reading is," and he consulted a sheet of paper he held, "955 millibars, that's 2 millibars less than the reading for Cyclone Tracy that devastated Darwin a few years back." He put his notepaper down, and looked at us with a serious expression. "We are in for some bad weather. Some really bad weather. Cyclone Colin is about 550 miles north of us and moving towards us."

The silence continued for a moment and when nobody said anything Wally asked a rhetorical question. "So, what do we do? Warnings have been issued for all coastal regions as far south as Coffs Harbour. We can't return, it would be too dangerous. The seas will be enormous and the wind, ferocious. We would be half way across when it hits and there's no way the Coralita would survive that even though she's a good boat."

He was delighting in scaring us. You could see it on his face.

"So, what can we do? We do nothing. We stay here. As long as we stay inside the reef, in the lagoon where I've placed that big old anchor, and we tie up to it, we'll be fine. The prediction at the moment is that the cyclone will pass between us and the coast, the worst we'll get is a lot of strong wind. Once we've tied onto that anchor, nothing will shift us."

Outside, the sun was shining, but a lot of heavy cloud was building up to the north of us. It was unmistakably the storm front. High above, long streaks of cloud were being torn apart and stretched by the wind. Much bigger waves were beginning to roll in and smash onto the fringing reef around us.

"That looks like the clouds we saw when we went through the Zone of Convergence on our way to New Guinea," I said to Fred.

The clouds to the north were black underneath with huge bulbous heads reaching high up into the sky. They stretched as far as we could see across the northern horizon. It was like a wall rolling slowly towards us.

After he'd finished his soup, and before the main course was served, Wally, at the head of the table, told us that it was likely Cyclone Colin would hit us soon.

"I don't like the look of that," Fred said.

It didn't bother Rommy. He was aft with Bill and Lindsay throwing lines over the side to catch fish.

We moved to a couple of spots in the lagoon but there was little to see. Currents were stronger than they had been the day before as much more water was pushed into the lagoon and then sucked out again. It was still clear underwater, but most of the fish seemed to have vanished. Lucia tried diving with scuba gear for the first time. Richard helped her. She flooded her mask and came back up with Richard by her side. She had trouble breathing through the regulator, but she had guts; she kept trying until she got the hang of it, and with Richard's help she managed a respectable dive close to the Coralita.

After lunch the wind picked up and the water in the lagoon became very choppy. We measured wind gusts up to 50 miles per hour on the Coralita's anemometer. The barometer was still dropping.

The wall of cloud approaching was much blacker than before.

It was starting to get rough and choppy even inside the lagoon.

Wally explaining to Richard how to tie onto the 5 ton anchor 10 metres below us.

John Harding preparing to follow Richard down to film him in action.

3rd March 1976

Nothing much had changed overnight. The water in the lagoon was clouding suspended sand and plankton making diving unpleasant. The boys did a bit of fishing but caught very little. The waves pounding the reef were much bigger than the day before and the wind seemed stronger than ever.

We dropped anchor at Wally's mooring which is marked by a small red buoy.

Richard put on his scuba gear and went over the side near the bow where the anchor chain went into the water. He took with him a couple of lengths of very strong and flexible cable. The wind was howling and blowing sea spray so hard it became difficult to walk around on the deck.

Hanging on to the anchor chain, Richard pulled himself along it hand over hand until he reached the sandy bottom where the giant anchor lay embedded about 10 metres below. Using the lengths of extra cable he took with him, he lashed our anchor and chain to the giant anchor.

When he came back on board, Wally allowed the Coralita to drift backwards away as extra anchor cable was released. He didn't stop until we were three times the distance away as we had been with the single anchor cable and chain.

"Three lengths should do it," Wally said. "We need the extra slack and spring. Nothing will shift us now, not even a 200 mile an hour wind."

We were all hoping he was right.

— Grab that Moment —

Frames from the 16mm film I shot.

Richard, ready to go, thinking about what he has to do.

...carefully stepping over while hanging on because the Coralita was heaving up and down...

...ready to put on his mask before grabbing onto the anchor chain...

Wally watches anxiously as Richard grabs the anchor chain and begins to lower himself down to the water...

Still hanging onto the anchor chain it's easy to see how much pressure the waves were already expending as the wind and outgoing current made them bigger and choppier.

We knew the cyclone was closer, but had no idea how close. The last reports we'd received over the radio were several hours out of date. Wally tried contacting Sydney, Lord Howe Island, and Brisbane, but couldn't get through. By late afternoon, the wind ripping sea spray into us had passed 60 mph which was the highest the on-board anemometer could register.

Finally, Wally got through to Brisbane and he was told Cyclone Colin had veered back out to sea and was heading in our direction and would certainly hit Lord Howe Island. That meant it would go right over the top of us. He didn't tell us that, at least not right away.

What he did was get Terry to help him take down the awnings and pack them away. When we saw that, we knew we were in for it. Everything loose lying about on the deck was brought inside. Anything too big to shift was lashed down tight. After there was nothing to do but wait.

The wind got much worse quite rapidly. It was literally screaming and you hardly hear yourself think, let alone talk. Not only was the wind lashing us with spray ripped off the waves smashing on the outer reef, it also pummeled us with rain which came at us sideways rather than straight down. If you stuck your head out of the door it would be blasted with stinging needle-like spray that was a combination of sea and rain. Sometimes this would clear slightly and we could see as far as the reef edge where gigantic waves smashed into it. They were big enough to completely bury the wreck of the Runic which stood normally high up above the reef. All we could see momentarily was a shadow of it lost beneath breaking waves.

It was scary, but there comes a time when you can only be scared so much, after which you kind of become numb; you endure it without thinking, and if it goes on long enough, you push it into the back of your mind, and start to relax. There was nothing else to do but wait.

Up in the wheelhouse, Wally had the radar on which showed clearly where the Runic was as well as the waves breaking on more prominent areas of the fringing reef. He had the engines on idle, and if the Coralita was to be blown back by the wind, rather than the waves, which it was during the worst moments of the oncoming cyclone, he would inch forward to maintain our position, relative to where we were before the wind increased. It would be absolutely terrifying to be in a ship blown onto this reef during a storm. But we felt quite safe where we were because Wally seemed relaxed and not the least worried about what was happening around us, and by the fact that Denise went on to prepare the evening meal totally unperturbed as she normally would.

Over a glass of wine after dinner Wally read with some amusement, a passage from one of his favorite books. It was a navigation book published by the USA Government printing office. He read to us the descriptions of how a cyclone was formed and the various stages it goes through as it develops. After a suitable dramatic pause which allowed us to once again be aware of the ferocious wind ripping over us outside, he quoted, "Only the best ships survive. Lesser boats do not!"

When none of us commented, he smiled and said, "I don't know about you blokes, but this fella intends to survive."

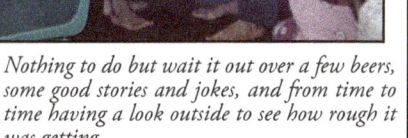

Nothing to do but wait it out over a few beers, some good stories and jokes, and from time to time having a look outside to see how rough it was getting.

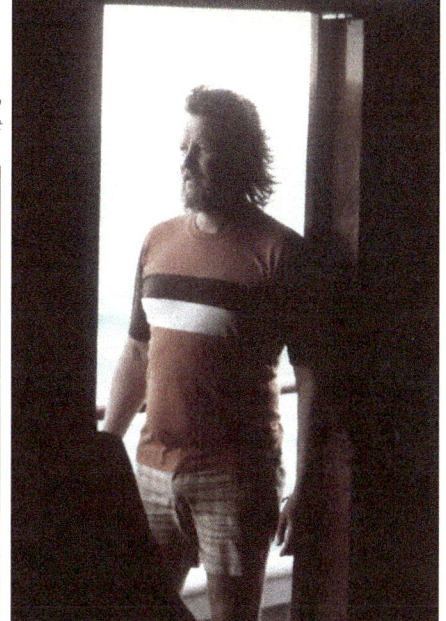

The worst of the cyclone hit us during the night while most of us were asleep or at least trying to sleep. The fact that we even tried to do this speaks well of the confidence we had in our captain, Wally Muller. He is a fine seaman and he knew exactly what he was doing.

It is almost impossible to photograph big waves at sea and make them look as big as they appear when you see them. They always look flatter and smaller. In the image above, the giant waves produced by Cyclone Colin are smashing onto the fringing reef, breaking completely over the wreck of the Runic which can just be seen as a shadow when the wave passes and flattens out inside the lagoon. That gives an idea of just how large the waves were because the Runic is a big shipwreck. The spray blown by the wind, and the rain, blasted the Coralita. It felt like needles cutting into you when you ventured out onto the deck. It also made any photo look as if you were peering through a haze or fog. It was hard to get a sharp image.

4th March 1967
Up in the wheelhouse Wally looked very tired. He'd been on watch all night while we slept, and he kept the Coralita exactly in position.

The winds abated and the sky above cleared. Huge waves still battered the fringing reef but the water in the lagoon had flattened out and John Harding went in with his scuba gear and his camera to see what it was like. Fred and Rommy dived in as well.

A few moments later Fred came back and said, "You won't believe how clear it is."

I decided to have a look and was amazed to find at least 40 feet of visibility. Most of the sand in the lagoon was fairly heavy and had settled quickly. Out here there was no silt from rivers or anything coming off the land into the ocean. There was nothing but very deep ocean water all around Middleton reef, nothing in suspension that would cloud the water. There was only the gravelly sand inside the lagoon and most of that had already settled.

"I wouldn't stay in there too long," Wally called over the side. "We're in the eye of the storm, and we're going to h get hit again very soon."

"We shifted the anchor," John Harding announced when he came back on board a few moments later. Already the wind was freshening as the eye moved over us.

"How much?" Wally asked.

"I don't know, ten or fifteen metres?"

"That must have been some wind," Wally stated.

He made sure we had enough room to swing around because the wind was rapidly picking up again. And once again, we made sure we were battened down because very soon it was the same as it had been the day before. Winds blasting rain and salt spray at us, massive waves smashing into the other side of the reef, as the cyclone Colin continued on its way towards Lord Howe Island.

We were much more relaxed this time, sitting by the bar, swapping stories, actually having a good time, while the wind outside screamed in the rigging.

We stayed one more night to allow the waves out in the ocean to settle down before leaving.

Waiting for the waves to calm down in the lagoon. Jocelyn is sitting on the dive platform. She later geared up and joined John Harding to shoot more fish feeding.

Fred also went in for another short dive and came back with a weird kind of crayfish, or Morton Bay Bug, only it was a different species.

Standing by the wheelhouse, I was happy to see the end of the cyclone and the start of some clear weather.

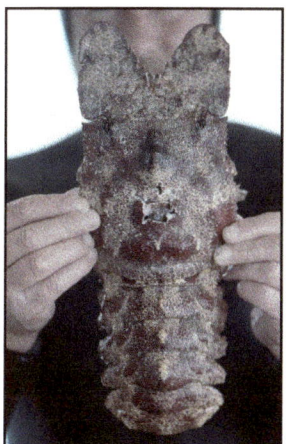

It is called a Red Flapjack, or Squat Crayfish. Arctides Antipodarum It is found in shallow south eastern waters, and is occasionally seen by skin-divers although it is not very common.

Denise cooked it and I'm sure it tasted just like any other crayfish. There wasn't enough for everyone to try but Fred said it was great.

One last look at the Runic before leaving Middleton Reef. The piece of wreckage to the left was the broken off aft of the ship and it had been sitting right behind the main part of the wreck. It must have weighed hundreds of tones, but the cyclone shifted it almost 100 metres away from the rest of the ship.

Wally in the wheelhouse guiding us out of Middleton Reef and into the deeper ocean. Even though we had waited for the waves to flatten before leaving, they were still enormous, at least 30 or 40 feet high (10 to 15 metres) and as the Coralita rode up and down them, they came at us on an angle so we rolled from side to side. With Boris standing on the table and balancing as the boat rolled about him it is easy to see just how much movement there was. While he stayed vertical, the boat rolled at least 45 degrees to either side of the centreline. He had a great time, while the rest of us stayed in one place and hung on, You simply could not move around while the boat rolled so much so continuously.

It was a huge relief to finally arrive at Elizabeth Reef three hours later.

5th March 1976

Elizabeth Reef is about three hours cruising from Middleton Reef. Very similar to Middleton, it is a slightly smaller pear-shaped reef rather than a kidney shaped reef, and it too has many shipwrecks, but they were not as visible to us as the ones at Middleton reef.

Travelling the forty nautical miles across deep water to Elizabeth Reef, the swells were enormous but smooth. No breaking tops, just huge rises up and down, and this was after the winds had blown from the opposite direction which tended to flatten the waves a bit. They were much higher than the Coralita which rolled from side to side, up and down, but the movement was relatively smooth. No one felt sea sick, but you couldn't stand up or walk about much with such extreme movement. All you could do was stay in one spot and hang on. Boris (Roy), Wally's son, enjoyed himself trying to remain upright on the dining table which had been folded and was flat on the floor.

He remained vertical while the boat rolled around him.

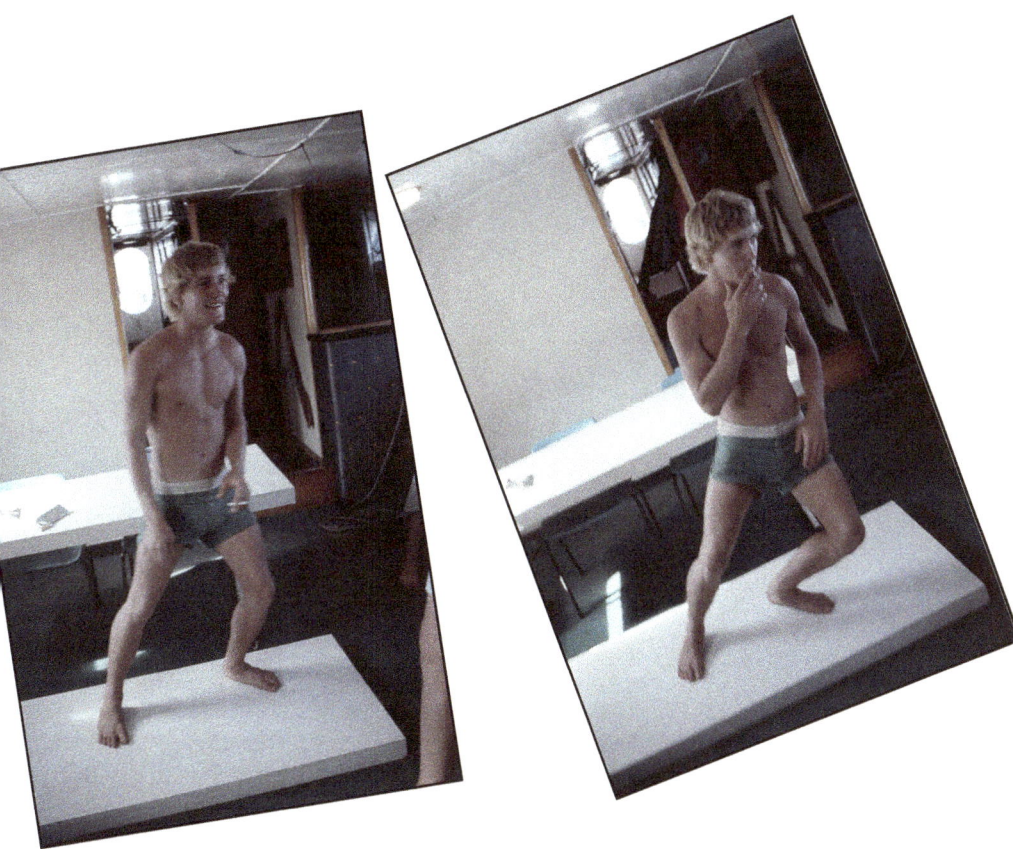

The tide was out when we arrived at Elizabeth Reef, and because the lagoon is much shallower than the lagoon at Middleton Reef, we couldn't go inside very far. We anchored in a channel where a strong current was running. It was mid-afternoon.

Looking over the side, the water was very clear, we could see every grain of sand beneath us. There were schools of surgeon fish swimming around and lots of small sharks.

"You've got time for one dive," Wally said. "I don't want to stay here overnight, so get to it and make the best of it."

I grabbed the Bolex in its housing and went over the side I didn't use any scuba gear, just a mask and snorkel. It wasn't all that deep and quite easy to swim down. Richard was already in the water looking for something to spear. He didn't shoot anything but did disturb a butterfly cod which swam slowly along the sandy bottom. I followed it for a few moments filming it. Wally and Denise went snorkeling in a shallow area looking for shells to add to their collection on board.

There were lots of small sharks swimming around and they seemed quite agitated. They became a nuisance swimming towards us and snapping and humping their backs before suddenly veering off. Bill and Lindsay were fishing from one side of the Coralita and I suspect the struggling their catches made while being hauled in was what attracted and excited the sharks. I got out of the water. Standing on the aft deck above the dive platform John Harding said 'They're going into a feeding frenzy."

It was only then I noticed the sun was low down so it was later than I had expected.

With everybody out of the water, we started throwing in the carcasses of the filleted fish the boys had caught and this attracted many snapping sharks to the rear of the boat. They swam just under the surface, dorsal fins cleaving the water as they snapped up the fish thrown into the water. Boris, Rommy, John and Fred were all on the diving platform and if a shark swam really close one or the other tried to grab it by the tail. Needless to say, none of them successfully managed to hold onto one.

Wally appeared after a few minutes of this. "Fun and games are over boys," he said. It's time to get moving."

The dive platform was hauled up and locked in place and the Coralita edged its way out of the channel and back into deeper water as the sun sank beneath the waves on the horizon.

— Grab that Moment —

A small shark taking the fish scraps we threw in just off the dive platform. The shadowy forms of other sharks can be seen just beneath the surface.

6th March 1976

We traveled all night and arrived at Lord Howe island early in the morning. The sea around the island was rough in the aftermath of cyclone Colin, which had gone right over the top of the island. The sun was rising but we still couldn't see to go through the entrance in the reef into the lagoon so we anchored offshore for about an hour.

When it was bright enough to clearly see the entrance through the fringing reef, Wally took the Coralita in and we anchored inside beside the channel through the reef. We couldn't go further in because the lagoon was very shallow. To go ashore we had to use the Coralita's dinghy to ferry us over to the short jetty.

From the dinghy ferrying us ashore, the Coralita is seen anchored just inside the fringing reef.

The cyclone hadn't done much damage as far as I could see, but one of the locals told me later that most of the fruit on the trees had been blown off. One or two trees had been uprooted and a couple of roofs partly damaged. Bill's sister, who lived on Lord Howe Island told us all the avocados on her trees had been blown off, and none of them were ripe enough to salvage.

Fred and Rommy and myself, hired bicycles for 50 cents each and road all over the island, at least as far as the few roads there would allow. We had a Bar-B-Q in the afternoon and saw a movie that night.

From the 16mm film, Fred and myself on the bikes we hired to ride around the island.

The Bar-B-Q in the park by the waterfront. It was late afternoon.

— Grab that Moment —

Approaching Lord Howe Island after traveling overnight from Elizabeth Reef. The island was partially hidden by clouds, the remnants of which came from Cyclone Colin. It was clearing and looked like it would be nice day.

7th March 1976

We helped shift some moorings in the harbour, before leaving early in the afternoon.

Wally was having trouble with a generator so he decided we wouldn't go over to Ball's Pyramid, a spectacular rocky formation jutting up high out of the sea an hour or so away. He was also having a problem with the desalinating plant, so there was no running water, or fresh water other than what was left in a small tank. It was time to head back to the mainland where these things could be fixed. It was nice to see the sun after all the bad weather we'd had and spent most of the afternoon up on deck enjoying the sunshine as we headed back to Coff's Harbour.

With a strong current assisting we made good time and arrived at Coffs Harbour 11 pm the same night instead of the next morning.

Bill and Lindsay, as well as Jocelyn and John Harding left us in Coffs Harbour.

Chatting with Rommy and enjoying the view as we leave Lord Howe Island.

Jocelyn with John Harding taking a picture of me taking a picture of them, as we leave Lord Howe Island.

— Grab that Moment —

For the technically minded, below are the charts and satellite images from BOM, the Bureau of Meteorology, for Cyclone Colin as it passed over Middleton Reef.

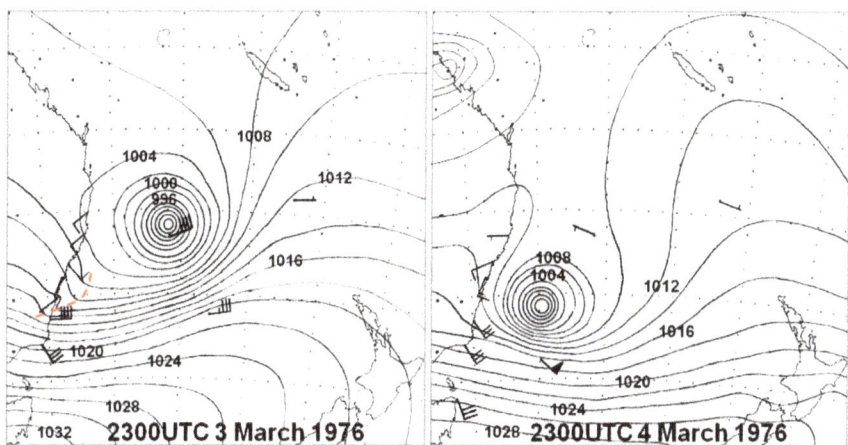

Figure 2 Mean sea level pressure analyses and wind observations for 2300UTC 3 March 1976 (9am 4 March local time) and 2300UTC 4 March 1976 (9am 5 March local time).

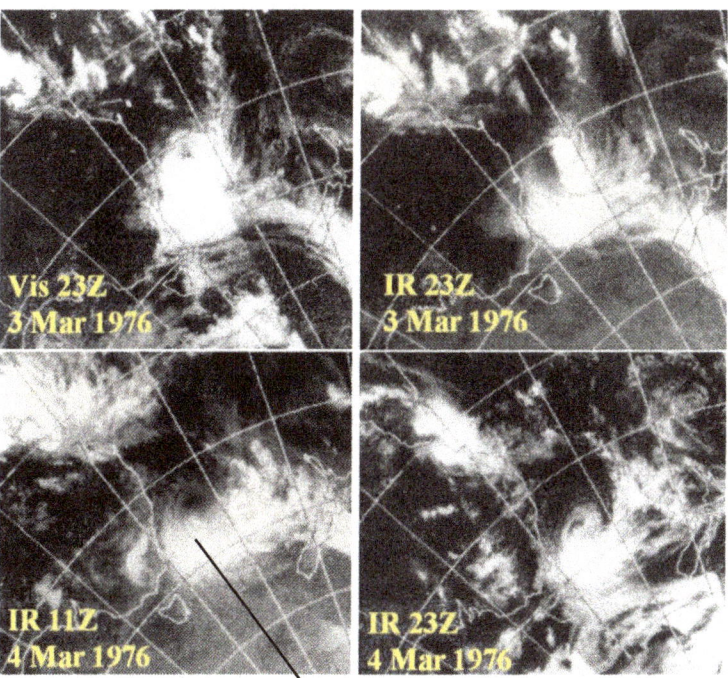

Figure 4 Satellite imagery of reintensification of Colin as a deep Tasman Sea low from 2300UTC 3 March 1976 to 2300UTC 4 March 1976.

We were right in the middle of that!

8th March 1976
Fred, Rommy and I stayed while Wally fixed the generator and the desalination plant. We had to go with him back to Brisbane to pick up my campervan which we had left at Rommy's friend's place.

A bit of minor excitement occurred when Wally discovered that Boris had filled the fuel tank with water by mistake.

Boris laughed it off. "I did something much worse than that last year," he said. "I filled the bloody water tank with diesel oil. You should've heard what the old man said then."

The trip back to Brisbane was hard, punching into the current, with the wind and waves hitting us side on, yet the South Passage bar was a breeze. We anchored in the Brisbane River, not far from where we were when we first went on board, and had our last dinner. Wally cooked since Denise had already flown back to Yepoon from Coffs Harbour.

We stayed on board that night and in the morning said goodbye to Wally and the crew. Rommy called his mate and he came and got us. After picking up the van we left for Melbourne via Toowoomba where we dropped in briefly to say hello to Colin Boreham (from Finschhafen in New Guinea) who had moved there to study at the University.

Part Nine

Becoming Parents

Coming Home

"You could have been killed!"

That was the first thing Monica said to me the moment I stepped through the front door. She didn't look unhappy or angry, but it was not what I expected her to say when I got home.

"It was all over the news on TV, about cyclone Colin going coming down the Queensland coast then veering out over to Lord How Island," she continued when I got inside. "We were worried sick. With a baby on the way, what could I have done if the boat you were on sunk?"

"It didn't happen, we were okay, quite safe…"

"But it could have."

"It didn't."

"But what if it did?"

Arguments like that just go around in circles and nothing changes.

"We weren't expecting another cyclone to form so soon after David," was all that I could offer.

David had formed mid-January and tracked towards the Queensland coast from the Solomon Sea. By the 19th of January it had crossed the Queensland coastline and tracked inland as a diminishing tropical storm. It caused the floods that swept down into central New South Wales which made it impossible for us to travel that way to get to Brisbane. But nobody expected another cyclone to form so soon after that one which is why we thought it was safe to go up there, and why Wally Muller also thought it was safe to take his proposed trip on the Coralita out to Middleton Reef and Lord Howe Island.

We knew it was the wet season, cyclone season, but usually when a tropical cyclone forms in the east, the next one after usually forms across on the other side of the country in the north west, and that's what was happening as we drove up the coast to Brisbane. There was a cyclone forming off the Kimberly Coast.

No one expected another cyclone to form so soon after again in the hot waters of the Solomon Sea south of New Guinea. But it did, after we left Coffs Harbour, and it tracked across to the Queensland coast, as they all do, and then veered back out to sea. It zigzagged all the way down the coast until it veered out from the Gold Coast towards Lord Howe Island. Since Middleton and Elizabeth Reefs are between Australia's east coast and Lord Howe Island, in a line drawn from Brisbane to New Zealand, it would pass right over the top of us while we were out there. It ended up dissipating somewhere further south in the Tasman Sea.

Señora Marina kept well away until we'd finished discussing that possibility. Once I'd dropped my bag in the bedroom and the cameras in the room I used as a studio, she appeared and announced that she had prepared something to eat. After that things went back to normal. I sent the films to be processed the next day and went back to work at the dry Cleaners. Phillip then took some time off for himself.

When the film and the slides came back, I wrote an article for Barry Andrewartha and his **Skindiving in Australia and New Zealand** magazine and sent it to him. He published it a couple of months later.

I didn't realize until much later that he stated in a caption accompanying one of the photos that we had survived Cyclone David. It should have been Cyclone Colin. David had dissipated before we headed out to the reef. Cyclone Colin was the only one I mentioned in the text of that article.

A difficult birth

Over the next few months, the days seemed to fly by and before I knew it was time for Monica to go to the hospital for the birth of our son Brian. Señora Marina of course stayed with her in the hospital, while I was at the shop in Douglas Parade. The Williamstown hospital was not very far away and several times during that day I took went around to see how she was doing. She was worried. She was nervous. We had arrived at the hospital early in the morning and it was now well into the afternoon. It seemed it was taking an extraordinarily long time for the baby to come. She didn't want me in the room when Brian was born, which was disappointing but I didn't insist so I waited elsewhere.

She was having difficulty giving birth, probably because she was an older mother at 36, and because it was also her first time. Some mothers have no trouble giving birth, but Monica seemed to find it extremely hard. Perhaps the baby wasn't positioned properly. Whatever the reasons, the doctor and the midwife eventually had to use forceps to assist with the birth, and this upset Monica. What made it worse for her was they insisted on placing the baby in a humidicrib in a different section to where they keep the other newly born babies. They wouldn't let her hold him as is the normal custom. She complained to such an extent that the doctor, Dr. Peers, took me aside to explain that everything was fine. It was procedure.

"Whenever a there is a forceps delivery, the baby always goes into a humidicrib for 24 hours, in case there are complications."

"Are there complications?"

"Not at all," she said. "Come with me and I'll let you see him, then you can reassure Monica that everything is fine."

I followed the doctor to the room where the humidicribs were installed and saw Brian. He was asleep, completely naked and showing that everything appeared to be normal. There wasn't even any bruising on the sides of his head where they had gripped with the forceps.

"See," she reassured me. "He's perfectly normal."

Up until then, for some reason, I had not taken any photos of Monica and her mum since January and our trip to Ballarat. This time I had my camera with me. I wanted a picture of Monica in the hospital with Brian and her mum. I had already taken a photo of the two of them, so I took a couple of shots of Brian. He wasn't in a humidicrib, but was in a standard cot, which was a sign that everything was normal. It was the 2nd of June, and he was born at 3.27 pm after a very long labour. It was about 4 pm when I took the photos. I went back to Monica's room and told her everything seemed to be okay.

"Estás seguro que todo está bien?"

"Si. Está bien. No te preocupes."

"Why wouldn't they let me hold him?"

I couldn't really answer that other than to repeat what the doctor had told me, that it was standard procedure when a forceps birth occurred. Eventually she calmed down. Dr Peers came back and told her that the nurses would bring Brian to her shortly, which allowed her to settle down.

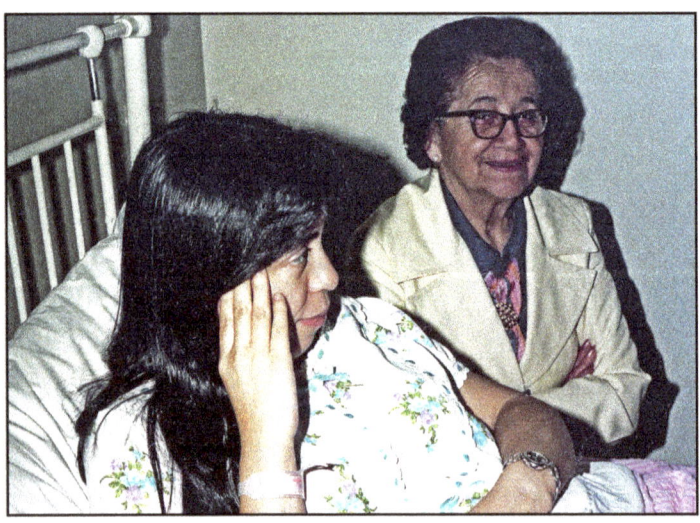

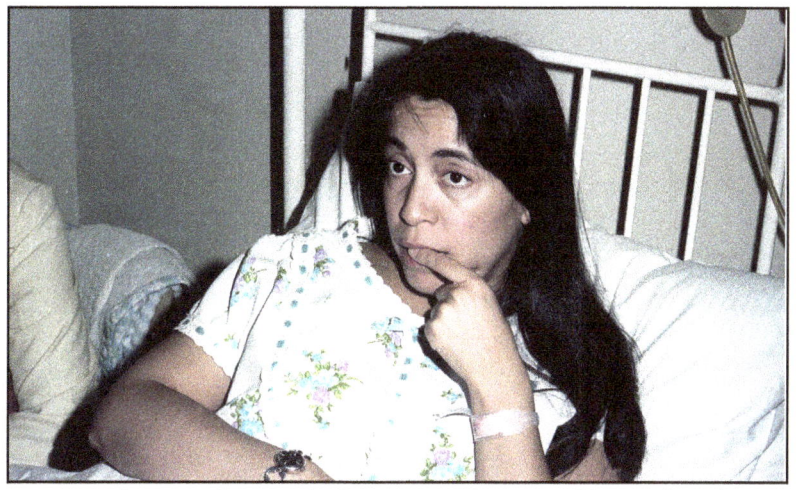

Monica, a short time after giving birth to Brian. Looking worried because the midwife and the doctor had not brought the baby in for her to hold, to see that he was fine. A few moments later the doctor took me to see Brian so I could reassure Monica that he was fine.

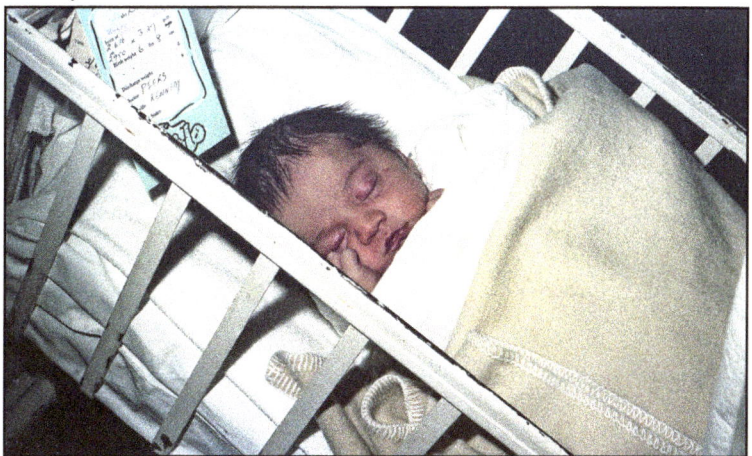

Our very first photo of Brian. I took this before Monica had seen or held him.

The text on the tag above says Room 28.
Forceps.
Born 2-6-76 at 3.27 pm.
Birth weight: 6 lbs 8 oz.
Dr. Peers, Midwife, Kennedy.

Her face lit up when the nurse came into the room with Brian and she saw him for the first time.

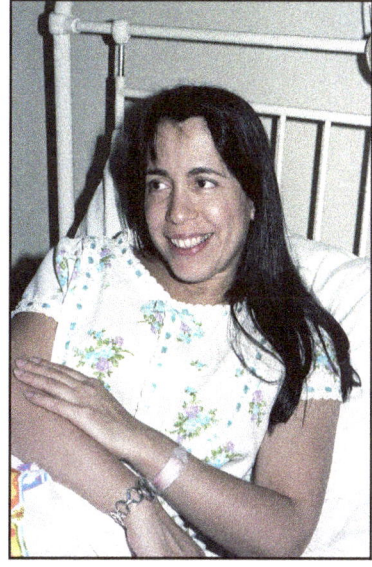

She stayed in hospital for a couple of days to make sure Brian was okay and that she was okay with breast feeding him and doing other stuff needed to look after him.

At one stage, women with their new-born babies used to stay in hospital for at least 5 days, but it seems now they've cut the time in hospital back to 2 or 3 days at the most, unless there are difficulties.

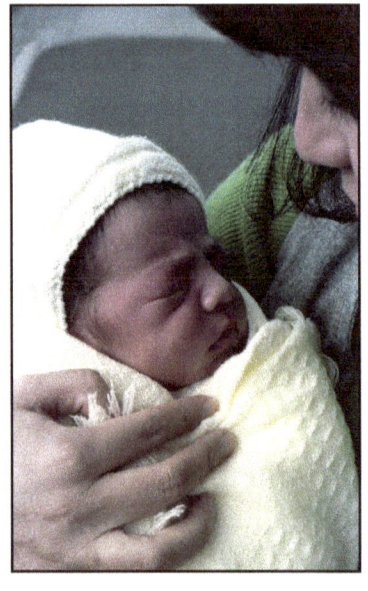

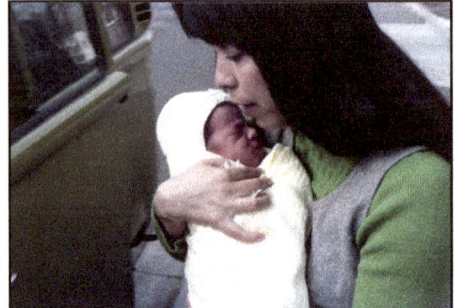

Leaving Williamstown Hospital.

Arriving Home.

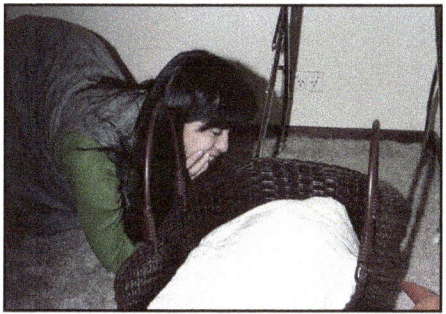
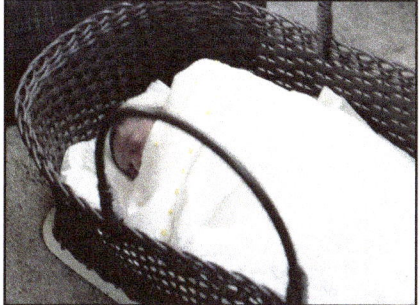

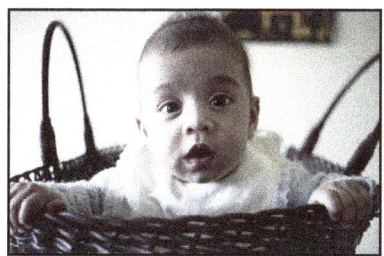

Brian remained asleep all the way home. I have no idea where we got that gigantic basket to carry him in.

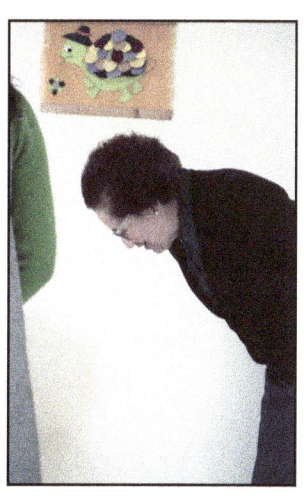

Now we were on our own, but at least Monica had her mum to help her.

He loved being in that basket. In those first couple of weeks she would have him in the basket and take him with her wherever she went in the house so he could see whatever she was doing.

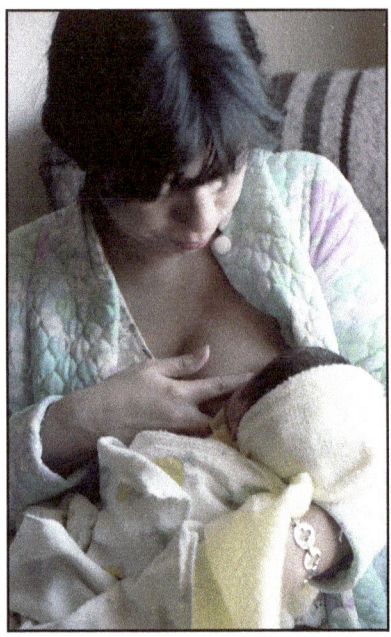
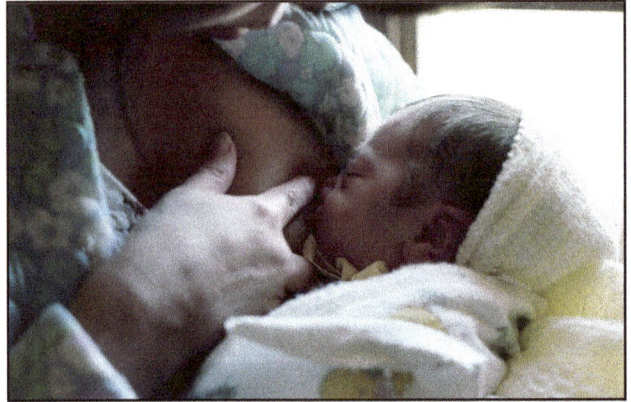
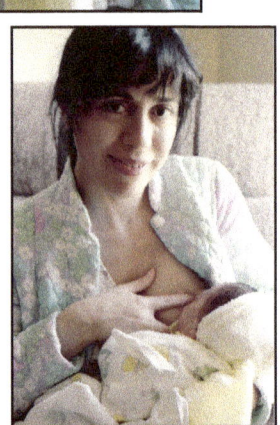
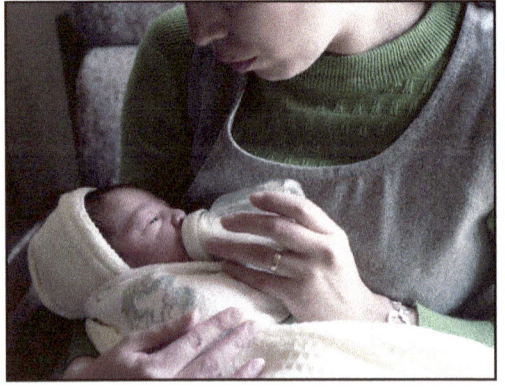
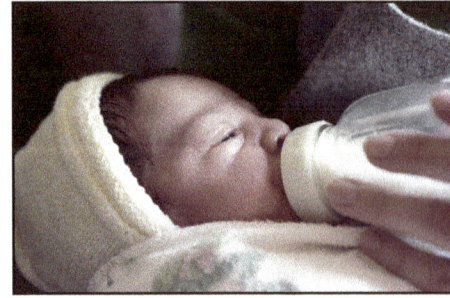

Coming home, settling in...

It was all new and exciting.

I had no idea of what to do so I left Monica and her mum to figure out how to feed Brian, dress him, wash him, all that stuff you need to do with a new-born baby.

Apparently Monica didn't have enough milk to breast feed all the time so she had to bottle feed as well.

When it came to changing nappies (diapers), the great advantage we had over what our mothers had was disposable nappies. No more washing and bleaching dirty nappies, folding them, pinning them on anymore. You simply pulled them out of a packet, and put them on, and when they were changed, they went into the garbage. It made that part of looking after a baby much easier. Of course, there was still washing and bathing, and that was not always easy for Monica.

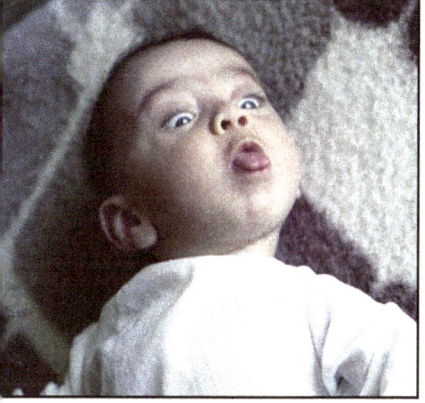

While Monica had been in the hospital I had hung from the ceiling a couple of mobiles, bright cheerful things, that would attract Brian's attention with their movement. We tried to make his room as bright and cheerful as we could because this, we believed, would stimulate his curiosity. They were only made of cardboard and paper, but they looked good.

— Grab that Moment —

With Paul in 1956.

The day after coming home from the hospital.

I was nervous at first to be holding Brian.

It had been twenty years since I'd held a new-born baby, and that time it was Paul. In 1956 Mum came back from hospital with a new baby, Paul, and now twenty years later, twenty year old Paul was enjoying my nervousness as he watched me hold Brian in the back yard of our Woodville Park Drive home a few days after we got back from the hospital. Although I felt awkward, I did my best to hold him and remain relaxed, enjoying this moment in the winter sun.

Brian had his own room. We didn't want to get into the habit of having him sleep in the same room as us, which would have been convenient when he woke up in the middle of the night, because it would harder for him to adapt later to being in his own room. He was in his own room right from the beginning.

We kept the doors open so if he woke up and cried we would hear him and one of us would get up and see what was wrong. Unfortunately, Brian was not one of those babies who slept all night. Some people tell you *their's* does, but everyone I knew had not had a baby that slept all night, so I took that with a grain of salt.

We got used to waking up several times a night and getting up to see to Brian. It became part of our routine. It did mean that we were often very tired by mid afternoon. Luckily Monica had her mum at home and she could take a nap knowing her mother was there to see to Brian when he woke up while she was sleeping. I couldn't do that because I had to go to work. And this meant that at night it was usually Monica who got up for Brian rather than me, even though I woke up too. I would quickly go back to sleep while she attended to Brian.

Bathing him was a challenge for Monica. She did it in the kitchen where we had a table and plenty of space, using a basin big enough for him to fit into at first because he was so small. He splashed a lot and made one heck of a mess. Often she wore her bikini when bathing him because she would get just as wet as Brian did. After the bath she would lay him on a blanket on the table beside the basin and dry and dress him. Later when he got a bit bigger she moved into the bathroom to bathe him in the bathtub. It didn't take long before he had enough strength in his legs and arms to stand up and hold on. Bathing him became much easier then.

The first time she gave him a bath I thought she looked terrified. She was uncertain, and seemed awkward holding him. She was extremely cautious in everything she did, which made it take longer than expected. Brian didn't stop crying. He obviously hated being immersed partially in water. It had never happened to him before. He hardly moved while in the water being supported by Monica who held him up by the back of his head while she washed off the soap she had earlier rubbed onto him. He calmed down once she took him out of the water and laid him down on a huge fluffy towel so she could dry him. She overdid the talcum powder that first time after his bath before dressing him. But it was all a learning curve, and as she did this every day she got better and more efficient at it and Brian became more accustomed to it. So much so that he kicked and splashed which is why Monica ended up wearing a bikini top to avoid getting her clothes drenched when she had to give him his bath.

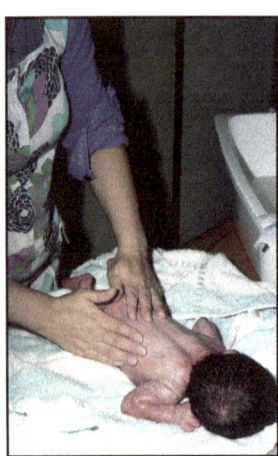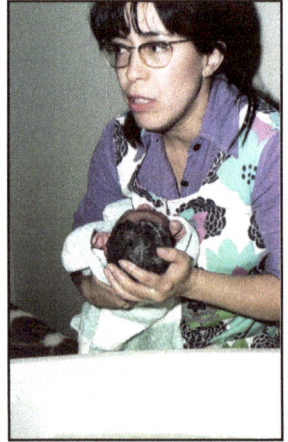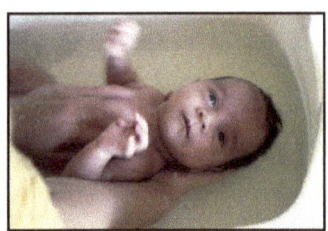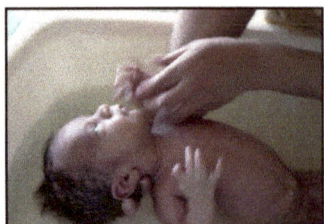

First bath: soaping his back, supporting his head, starting to wash him.

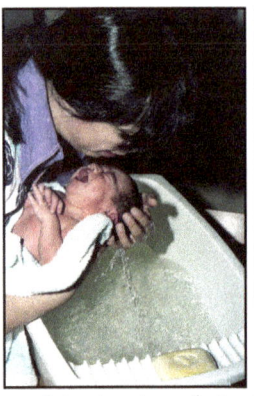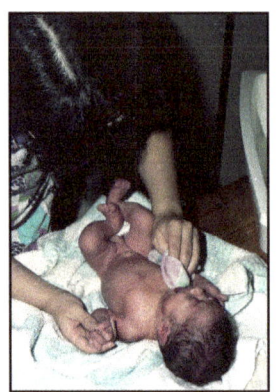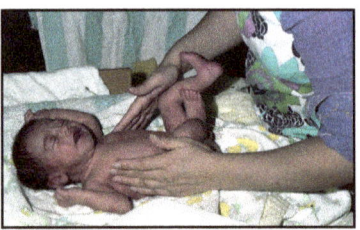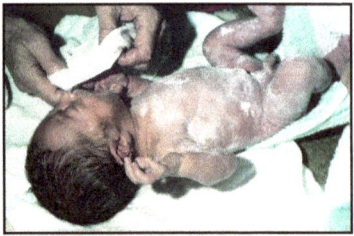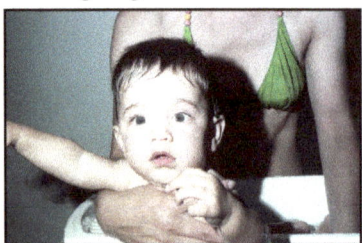

Brian is crying as he is taken out of the water and wrapped in a soft towel. Placed on the table beside the baby bath, he started to calm down once he was dry. Still not sure of what she was doing, Monica overdid the talcum powder a bit before she dressed him.

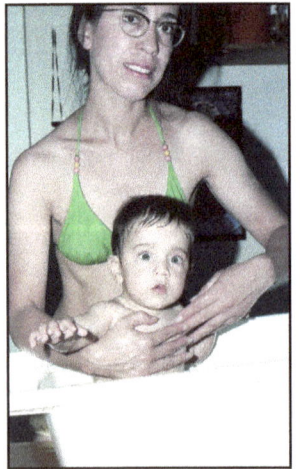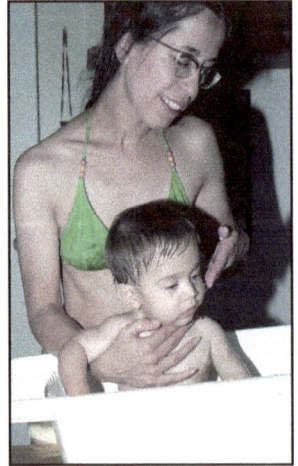

A few weeks later, both participants were quite confident and because Brian splashed a lot of water around Monica wore one of her bikini tops to avoid getting her clothes wet.

— Grab that Moment —

A couple of months later when he was stronger in his arms and legs, she moved him to the big bath in the bathroom where if water got splashed around, not much of it got onto the floor, as it had in the kitchen. He was able to stand up in the bath tub and hold on with his hands.

It was a lot easier to bathe him as well as to dress him afterwards. By then he was enjoying his time in the bath.

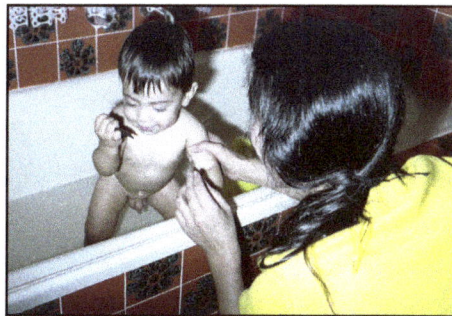

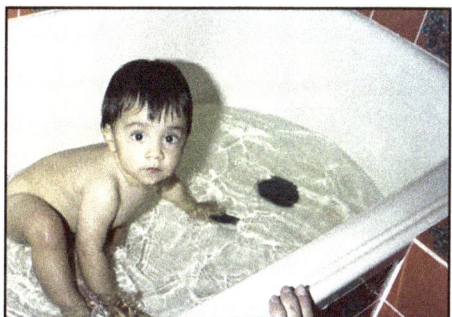

3 months later he was able to stand and hang on without any trouble.

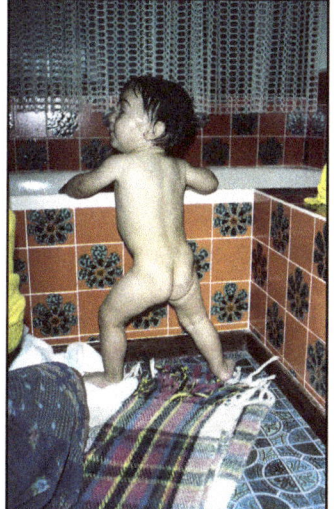
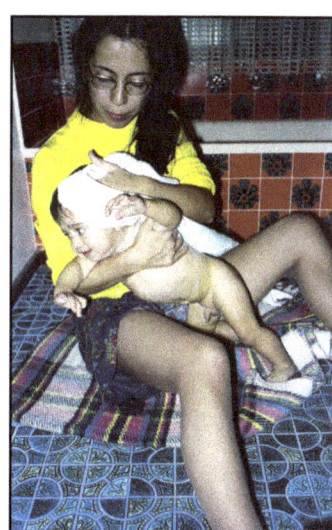

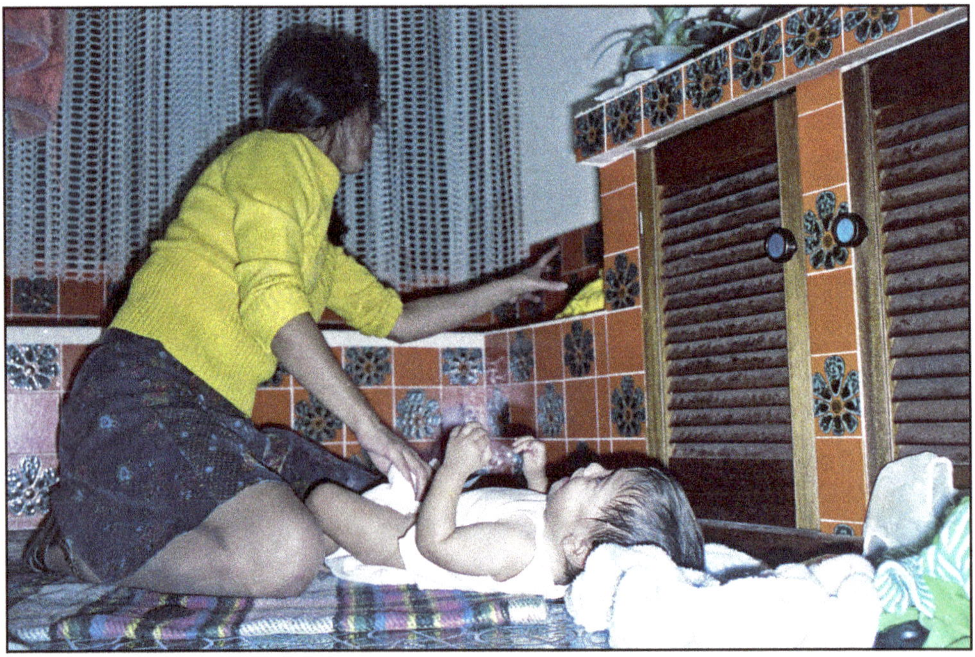

It was a job and a half giving him a bath and getting him dressed.

She had no trouble keeping Brian entertained, while at the same time entertaining herself. In fact he kept us both entertained and enthralled. At other times it was hard work, having to change nappies and feed him and clean up afterwards, but that was something every parent does, but with Brian being our first, and as it turned out later, our only child, it was all new and a bit daunting.

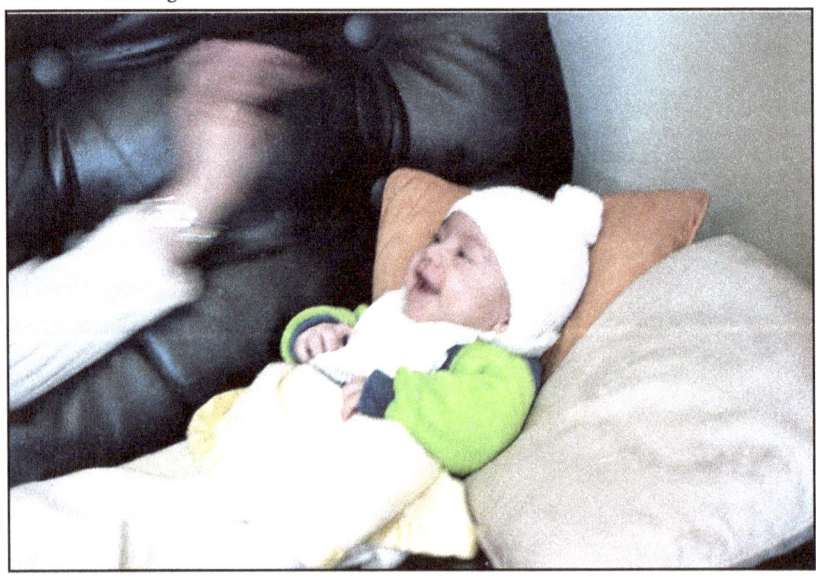

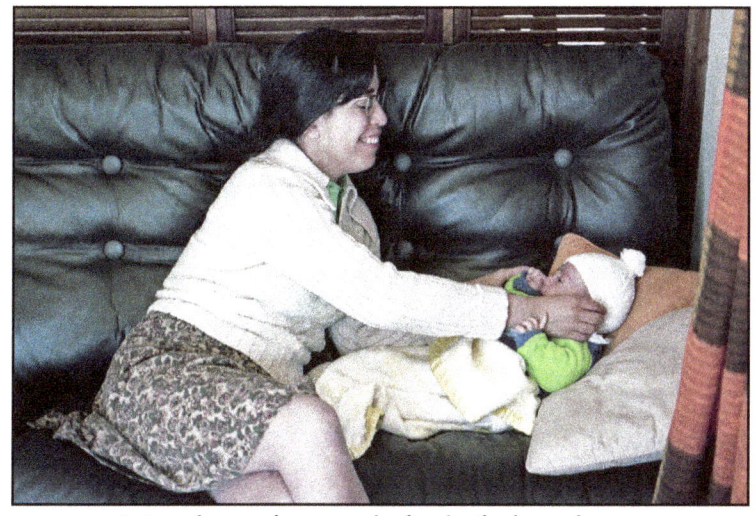

*At Portarlington about a couple of weeks after he was born.
At home in our backyard two months later.*

I was amazed at how rapidly he started to grow. In a matter of days he started to show a distinct personality and seemed to enjoy being held by Monica, and of course Monica's mum. It didn't take Monica long to feel comfortable holding him. Even I got into the act.

La Señora Marina

Monica also took Brian in his pram for a walk every day, accompanied of course by her mother. I believe it's good to take babies outside for walks so they get to see the things around them in the environment. It helps stimulate their mind, curiosity and imagination.

My mum always had me taken for a walk everyday in Williamstown when I was a baby. When she couldn't do it herself she got a lovely cheerful lady, Nellie Brown, to do it for her. Nellie would take me down to the Strand where we could see the yachts sailing or anchored, fishing boats, tug boats and big ships coming and going.

At Hopper Crossing there was nothing like that. Monica would take Brian down the road to the shopping centre where there were many things that could grab the attention of a new baby. She would do a little bit of shopping at the supermarket and return home. Our garden had evolved quite well by this time and she would spend a lot of time outside in the back yard with Brian as well.

To go to a park or public gardens, you had to leave the suburb which was why I made sure Monica had a car. On weekends, we would go together somewhere in Melbourne, where there were many beautiful parks and gardens to stroll in.

Taking a stroll through the beautiful Fitzroy Gardens which are adjacent to the Treasury Gardens next to Victoria's Parliament House. The white stuff on the grass is not snow, but the petals of late blooming flowers that are falling before Winter gets into its colder months.

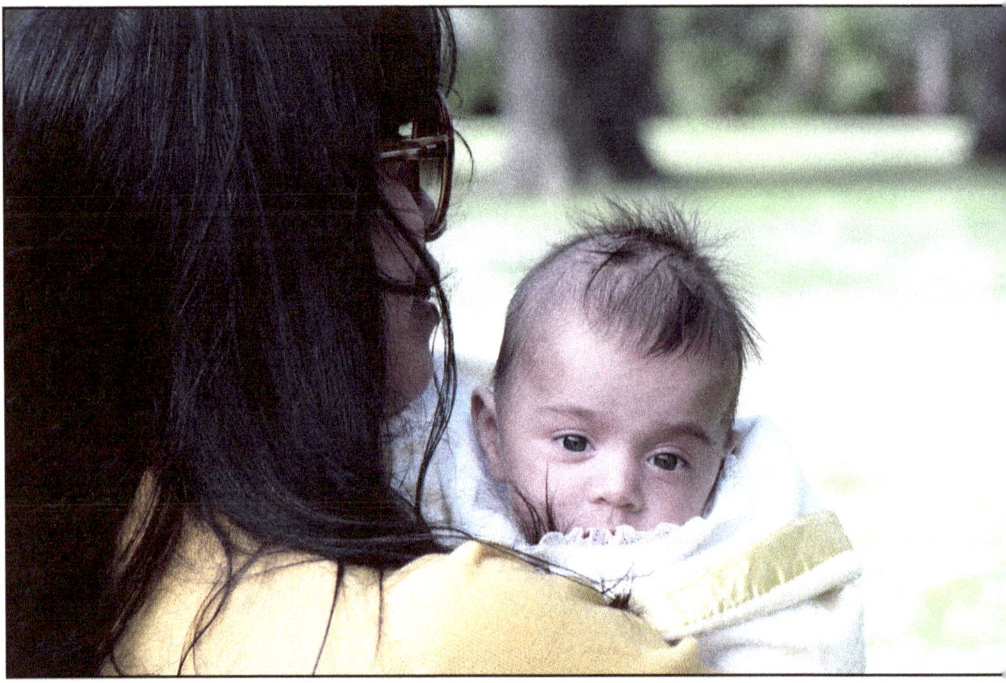

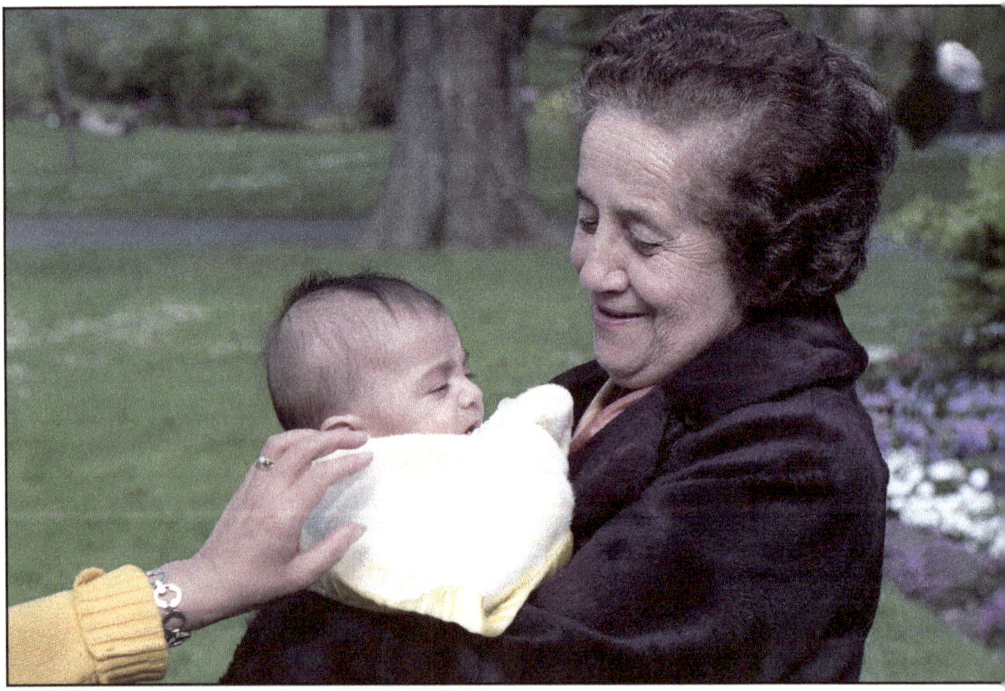

— Grab that Moment —

Monica and her Mum enjoying themselves...

A beautiful sunny winter's day to be in the park.

A happy day – a sad day

It started off as a happy day.

The winter weather was beautiful. Sunny with a clear sky and a temperature that was almost warm, considering it was the middle of winter. Melbourne can be like that. It can turn on some absolutely gorgeous days followed by completely shitty days. It could change from one extreme to another within minutes, no matter what time of year. This particular day was one out of the box!

It was the day Brian was to be christened in the same church where Monica and I had been married, and where Phillip and Nijole had christened their two girls.

Brian was just over a month old and the reason, I suspect, that we were to have his christening so soon was because Monica's mother was due to return to Chile. She came at the end of November 1972, and had Christmas with us, and was with us throughout Monica's pregnancy. She came on a six month's visa, which ran out the month before Brian was born. We got Dr John Silver to issue a medical statement saying she was unwell and unable to travel at that moment. The letter suggested she would need several months to fully recover. On that basis we managed to get her visa extended for another three months which meant she would be with us until the end of August 1973, a good time to leave because the weather in Melbourne was almost always shithouse in August with freezing days, drizzling rain, and icy winds. But what the extension meant was that she would be here with us when Brian was born and for the first two months of his life.

What I find odd now, is that I never took any photos of the actual christening. I could have, I should have, but I didn't. As the parents, we sat aside while the God-parents took part in the ceremony. All I remember about it now was Brian crying; he obviously didn't like being splashed with water, especially in a place he was unfamiliar with. Initially he didn't like having a bath either, but since that happened every day at home, he soon got used to it and as he grew bigger and stronger, he enjoyed it.

After the ceremony in the church, everybody came back to our place in Hoppers Crossing and we had a wonderful afternoon. It was one of those events where the whole extended family came together, along with our close friends Wally and Betty, with their son Russel. Fred, Zara and David were there, Phillip and his two girls, Melina and Anne, Christine, Morgan and Michael, George and Verga, with two of their three children, Alexandra and Nick, my cousin Mick, (the oldest son of Dad's brother George, who, like Verga, was born in North Epirus and migrated to Australia in the early 1930s) his second wife Anna with their son George, Mum's brother Eddie,

Mum and Dad along with Paul who had turned 20 a couple of days after Brian was born, and Us, Monica and her mum, Brian and me. There were stacks of food eaten, drinks consumed, much laughter, and good conversations while the kids ran around the yard and played. By now, the house and the garden were well established and looking good. Everyone wanted to hold Brian and so lots of photos were taken that afternoon.

You could not have wished for a better day.

Who could have foreseen that it would end with a tragedy?

Arriving at our house in Woodville Park Drive. Melina leading the race to see who gets inside first. Anne is following while David looks on.

More arrivals: George Crinis standing by the chair. Anna and Mick arriving followed by Paul. Fred is sitting down.

The extended family group.
Left to right: Paul, Fred with Dione, Mick, Anna, George, Mum, and behind her Dad. Morgan and Monica are standing behind Senora Marina who is holding Anne. Next to Monica is Christine holding Michael, then there is Alexandra, Zara with Melina and David in front. Between Zara and Phillip is uncle Eddie, and standing behind me next to Phillip is Wally.
Not in the photo because they were inside were Verga, Betty and Russell (Wally's wife and son) Georgie and Nick, and Tony who was a little older than Dione but does not appear in any photos taken that day.

Verga and George.

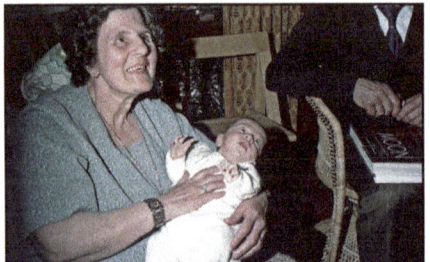
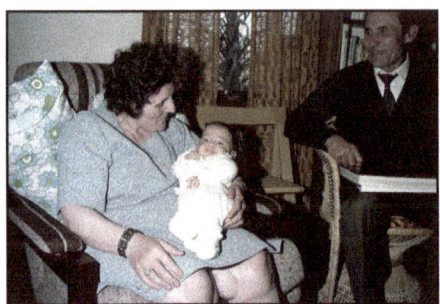

Above: Verga is delighted to be holding baby Brian.

Zara enjoying a drink and a chat with Mum.

Paul, as well as Dad, couldn't resist holding Brian for a photo.

And of course, Mum also got into the act.

— Grab that Moment —

Phillip enhancing the photo....

Phillip and Anne.

Below: Georgie, Anna and Mick.
George, Alexandra and Nick.

Melina and Anne couldn't resist showing everyone how well they could stand on their heads.

Dione, Fred, Zara, and David.

Wally, Russell and Betty Shaw.

Michael, Christine and Morgan.

Monica, Paul, Mum, Señora Marina.

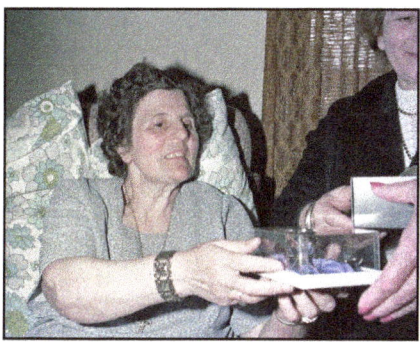 

As the afternoon wore on and the temperature dropped a bit, it was winter after all, the sky lost its blueness and became a pale grey misty colour which made the photos soft rather than contrasty. People started to drift off, to go home. Mum and Dad stayed a bit longer. Mum helped with the cleaning up, washing dishes, that sort of stuff. I shared a Turkish coffee with Dad and Paul. Eventually they also left. By that time, it was dark. We settled down; Brian was put to bed in his room, and we settled into the lounge chairs to watch a bit of TV.

A tragic end to the day

Around 9 pm, the phone rang.
"Who could that be?" Monica asked.
We weren't expecting anyone to call that late in the evening.
Late, unexpected phone calls, are always not good in my experience.
It was Mum on the phone.
"Mick's dead," she said bluntly. "He had a heat attack in the car on the way home."
"On the way home from here?"
He had left with Anna and George several hours earlier.
"No. After leaving your place he went to a friend's place in Carlton. They'd gone home and left Georgie there and then went over to their friend's place for his name day."
Name days are days of Patron Saints. It is a Greek custom not to celebrate birthdays on the day a person was born, but on the day of the Patron Saint who bears the same name given to the child after they are christened. Many older Greeks, like Dad, never actually knew what day they were born, and often only had a christening record or certificate. Children in remote villages and towns were not christened until about a year old since infant mortality was high and church fees or the obligation to pay something to the church was often prohibitive. If a child lived for the first year, then the parents

would invest in the christening, at which time a name was given to the child. A person celebrating their name day opens their house to friends and visitors who come to celebrate with them. Mick and Anna probably went to a couple of friends places for their name days, and would have eaten and drunk something at each place.

"He was on the way home from a friend's place and had just driven into Lygon street when he said to Anna he wasn't feeling too good. He pulled over to the side of the road, and died right there in front of her. He had a heart attack."

I didn't know what to say. I must have mumbled something because Mum continued telling me what had happened.

"She didn't know what to do. A bus driver saw she was upset so he stopped to see what he could do. She told him her husband had just had a heart attack and was dead. The driver called an ambulance and they took him to the morgue. He also took her home. It was only a short distance away from home where it happened."

"Is there anything we can do?"

"Paul is going to drive me over, but they need someone to identify the body, to verify it is Mick. Anna is too distraught to do that."

"I'll do that. I'll come and get you and we'll both go over there."

Monica was upset when I told her what had happened.

"They need someone from the family to go and identify the body," I explained to Monica. "Anna's too upset to do it, and Georgie is too young, so I said I'd do it. I don't know how long this will take…"

I collected Mum and we went over to Carlton. There were a lot of Greek women already there comforting Anna. I told her I would go and identify Mick.

"I want come too," Georgie said. "I want to see him."

"Okay with me." But when I called the morgue, I was told I couldn't come until the next day.

Some sort of protocol?

I told them I was already here and could come over right away.

"You have to wait until tomorrow."

It was 10-30 by this time.

"What if I come over after midnight?"

"What?"

"Tomorrow starts after midnight."

"I don't know…"

"You did say I couldn't come to identify the body until tomorrow. If I come after midnight, it will be tomorrow. I've come all the way into the city from the country. I don't want to go back now and come again tomorrow when I'm already here. If I wait a couple of hours, technically it will be tomorrow and I can then identify the body."

"What relation are you?" the man asked.

"I'm his cousin, and I'll be accompanied by his son. His wife is too distraught to come and see him."

"Oh, okay."

"Does that mean yes? We can come after midnight?"

"Yes, I guess so."

He still seemed hesitant, so to prevent him from changing his mind, I said, "We'll be there at ten minutes after midnight. Thank you," and hung up.

The Melbourne Morgue was down by the Yarra River along the Flinders Street Extension. When we got there the streets all around were empty. It was poorly lit and looked like a scene from a horror movie. It was also very cold and I started to shiver. Georgie and I found the entrance and went inside to encounter one person, the person I had spoken earlier to on the phone. He was the only one there.

"I've got him ready for you," he said.

We followed him into a small room that had a huge window on one side. There were several hard wooden chairs lined up against the wall opposite. A blind was drawn down on the other side of the window so we couldn't see in.

"Wait here," he said before stepping out of the room and closing the door.

I'd never been to a morgue before so this was a bit strange.

"Where is he?" Georgie whispered.

Before I could think of a reply, the blind on the other side of the window rolled up to expose another room, brightly lit and very stainless steel clean. There was gurney in front of the window. On it was a body covered by a large sheet. The attendant peeled back the sheet covering the head and shoulders of the body so we could see. He then left the room.

It was Mick alright. I expected his face to be contorted but it wasn't. It was relaxed, almost as if he was asleep. He looked perfectly normal except for the paleness of his skin. The brightness of the overhead light made it look washed out.

We stood silently for a few minutes and Georgie mumbled something that sounded like 'goodbye Dad' but I couldn't be sure. The man reappeared and came close to the window. "Is that Mick Litchen?" He asked through a grille above the window.

"Yes, that's him," I said.

He pulled the blind down and we waited for to come back into the room where we were.

He came in with some papers we had to sign confirming the identification.

"We'll release the body later today, or tomorrow. An autopsy will have to be performed to confirm cause of death and a report made for the coroner. After that you can have a funeral parlour come and take the body."

And that was it. It was one o'clock in the morning. I took Georgie back to Carlton, told Anna what had happened and what to expect, collected Mum and took her home, and finally got home to Hoppers Crossing at 2 am.

What a day! It started off as a happy day, but ended up a very sad day with the sudden death of my cousin. The photos I took of him and Anna and Georgie earlier that afternoon were the last pictures ever taken of him, and it was nice to see they showed him happy and enjoying life.

You never know what can happen next, so it's best to enjoy every waking moment as much as you can, because there may never be any more.

Another sad day

When you are not thinking about it, time passes very rapidly, and in no time at all it was time for Monica's mother to return to Chile.

Monica didn't want her to go, but she knew she had to. Her visa extension was running out and it was unlikely that we would be able to get another extension.

She would miss her mother; they were very close. From the time Monica had arrived in Sydney five or so years earlier, they had written letters to each other every week without fail. In a chest of drawers in our bedroom, the bottom drawer was packed tightly with all of the letters from her mother.

Of course she had to return. Monica's three brothers, two of whom were married with eight children between them, were there. Her oldest brother Hugo, (the science fiction writer and journalist) was a grandfather because two of his older children had children of their own, and they also missed being able to see their great grandmother, Señora Marina. And no doubt Señora Marina missed the family over there as well as her friends in Santiago. She had been almost a year in Australia.

"*No quiero que se vaya,*" Mónica told me with tears in her eyes. "I don't want her to leave."

"I know."

"It'll be years before we can see her again."

That was the reality. Traveling with a new baby was not something either of wanted or thought we could do.

Of course, we expected to go to Chile one day. I wanted to meet the rest of Monica's family, and I had never been to Chile or anywhere else in South America. I had been to Mexico where I stayed in Acapulco for eleven months, but that was in 1968.

The day came, the flights had been confirmed, and we headed to Tullamarine, Melbourne's international airport.

It seemed a much longer drive than usual, but I suspect that was a subconscious feeling. We didn't want her to leave. The traffic was normal for that time of day. I didn't drive slower than expected, because we did have to be there by a certain time. It was just that we knew we wouldn't see her again for a long time, and that's what made the drive to the airport seem longer than usual.

Monica, holding Brian, walked with her all the way into the airport terminal and through to the check in and on to the departure gate. Beyond that we were not allowed. They hugged and kissed with eyes full of tears.

We watched as she walked along the tunnel to board the plane until she was lost amongst the other passengers who were also boarding.

We hung around to watch the plane take off, then we went home.

The house seemed empty without her, but what neither of us considered was the possibility that we would never see her again.

Part Ten

Mucking about with boats
Filming Underwater

— John Litchen —

On one of Fred's early boats, out on the Bay on a summer's day. These days were a lot of fun.
The feeling of freedom, of being outside of the everyday world where all those people were driving to work or travelling on public transport, or having to be at certain places at specific times; we were free of that, with the wind and salt spray blowing in our faces, we could drift along with the movement of the water and the waves, dive in wherever we wanted or whenever we felt like it, or simply just lean back and sun-bake a bit. Those were the days I'll never forget.

Abalone diving... just having fun

Fred and his dive partner Rommy, about to get into the water to collect abalone off the reefs near Point Cook.

On this particular day around 1970, Fred came across a shovel nosed shark, sometimes called a skate, which he grabbed by the tail and hauled it up for us to have a look at. It went back in after the pictures were taken.

There weren't too many abs there, and both of them came up with empty bags, so they moved to another spot.

Abalone diving, and the starfish threat

Fred had long given up bus driving and had been a professional abalone diver for many years, sometimes working Rommy initially as partners, and later as separate divers. Rommy later moved down to Apollo Bay to live and work while Fred stayed in Melbourne and primarily worked Port Phillip Bay.

One of the things he couldn't help noticing as the decade of the seventies progressed was an ever-increasing number of giant starfish proliferating in the Bay. These massive starfish, *Coscinasterias Calamaria*, had eleven arms and were slowly decimating the shellfish populations within the bay. Cockles, mussels, abalone, as well as almost anything else unable to swim or run away were attacked and devoured. It was at the same time that the Great Barrier Reef was being attacked by another starfish, the Crown of Thorns.

Where both of these starfish populations came from is a mystery, but all around the world there seemed to be similar proliferations of predatory starfish. Was this something new? Or was it nothing more than a cycle that repeats over time.

The starfish increase dramatically and destroy much of what exists in the reefs along the shoreline and around islands, then when they have no more food they vanish, die off, and the reefs come good again. Only to repeat the same cycle many years, or even decades later. Is it only because we are now exploring underwater that we have become aware of them, never having seen this kind of plague before, or is it really something brought on by increased shipping, pollution and dumping of garbage in the oceans? No one has answers because no real studies have been made.

There is a feeling of panic, that these creatures will devour so much of the reef inhabitants that reefs around the world that reef ecosystems will be permanently disrupted and the reefs will not recover.

You can't kill them by chopping them up as each piece will often grow back into a new individual starfish. If you cut one in half, you would end up with two. If you chopped one into four or five pieces and threw it back into the water you would end up with four or five regenerating starfish. They seemed not to have a natural enemy so there was no stopping them. Sometimes divers would collect as many as they could, that were destroying an abalone or mussel bed, bring them back to shore where they would dump them on land and let them dry up. That was the only way to kill them. You would often see piles of dried starfish beside popular boat ramps around the Bay. But it made no difference. *Coscinasterias Calamaria*, continued to proliferate in Port Phillip Bay.

Fred had talked to several local newspapers, and they had reporters write articles about the starfish ruining the Bay, but it made little difference. I often accompanied Fred on his dives so I could film or photograph him in action as an abalone diver. Since it was news, and had been reported in several regional newspapers Channel 9 decided to do a story on the starfish in the Bay and contacted Ted Aitchison the official representative of the Port Phillip and Westernport Bay Professional Fishermen's Association and he told them to contact Fred Glasbrenner, an abalone diver who's been trying to get something done about the starfish for the last 12 months. And that's how it was set up.

The GTV 9 news team with Stewart Scocroft, the reporter would meet us at the Altona boat ramp as soon as weather permitted going out on the Bay. He had already spoken to Fred about underwater sequences and naturally Fred told him about me, and that we would have no trouble shooting the underwater scenes required. This was in April 1977 just after Easter, and the weather in Melbourne was not good. It had been wet and windy and the Bay was churned up, meaning visibility underwater was not good. The news team would have to wait, like us, until the water settled enough to allow underwater photography.

Coscinasterias Calamaria *up close as it attacks an abalone. We can see some of the thousands of tiny legs with suckers underneath its arms. The water was full of suspended sand and other matter since the weather had been stormy for days, churning up the whole of Port Phillip Bay.*

Saturday morning, March 12, 1977.

With wind gusting up to 20 knots from the south-west, it was a bad day for any kind of underwater photography. The news team from channel 9 were anxious to do their story, but bad visibility underwater prevented them. Since I had recently obtained a new housing for my camera, I wanted to test it underwater before we went out with the TV news team. Fred and I left the Altona boat ramp and punched into choppy water all the way across to Point Cook where there was some protection from the wind and the waves.

Once the anchor was dropped, I hopped over the side with the empty camera housing to dive down and test it for possible leaks. It worked fine, as expected, but it's always best to be sure. You wouldn't want to stick an expensive camera in it only to find water leaking in when you got deep enough. That had happened to me some years earlier in Tahiti when a Perspex housing which had worked fine for a while suddenly developed a crack while I was underwater at Moorea, flooding the housing and the Bolex 16 mm movie camera with sea water. I threw the housing away and carried the salt gummed Bolex all the way to Mexico City where I found a representative organization that could strip it down and clean it. I never wanted that to happen again.

The water, all the way from Altona across to Point Cook, was filthy, full of suspended sand, smashed fragments of sea lettuce, and fine silt washed in from creeks, but there was no hiding the huge numbers of *Coscinasterias Calamaria*.

They were all over the reefs as well as on the sand between reefs, no doubt crawling from one location to another. Visibility was less than a metre, absolutely useless for filming, but I could get a couple of close-up shots.

Fred had started the compressor and suited up in his wetsuit when I got back to the boat. Using the hookah both of us dived in a wide circle around the boat. Fred collected some abalone, but there wasn't much there that hadn't been attacked by the swarming starfish. I took some photos and we returned to the boat.

"We'll come back tomorrow," Fred decided when he got back into the boat.

"If it clears a bit overnight, I'll be able to shoot some test rolls of movie film."

Not even sea-urchins are safe from the dreaded Coscinasterias Calamaria.

Sunday, March 13th 1977.
The wind had dropped overnight and the Bays absolutely flat. The water had cleared somewhat and the sun was shining. A perfect day. Rommy turned up with his boat and deckhand, while Fred and I were accompanied by my younger brother Paul who was acting as Fred's deckhand for the day.

In his hurry to get his boat in the water, because the boat ramp was occupied and there was a long queue of cars with boats on trailers waiting to get their boats into the water, Fred decided to back down over the sand to the side of the boat ramp. He had often done this, but on this particular morning, with the tide way out, the exposed sand was deceptively soft, being mixed with fine silt, and mud washed in by the recent storms.

The inevitable occurred. The trailer with the boat got bogged, barely into the water. And as Fred tried to pull it back out the Holden van he was using also got bogged.

"Bloody typical," Rommy said.

There were other Ab divers there waiting to launch their boats. They hadn't worked for weeks because of the bad weather and were anxious to get out there and collect their quotas. Fred borrowed a car from one of them and tried to tow his van out of the mud. When that didn't work, he borrowed a 4-wheel drive, and with a long cable, managed to pull his Holden Van back up onto firm land.

After that there was a huge effort to push the boat off the trailer into the water since the trailer was also bogged. The boat had to be dragged across the mud into the water and them pushed out far enough for the prop on the outboard not to dig into the bottom once it was lowered and made ready to use. The trailer had to be dragged up out of the mud.

Rommy was smarter. He used the boat ramp which had a much firmer base to it and launched his boat. He then moved it along to the spot where Fred was still trying to push and pull his boat into the water.

"If anyone's going to get bogged, it'll be Fred," one of the other Ab divers commented.

"Why didn't you use the boat ramp?" Another asked.

"I thought it would be quicker this way." Fred told him. "It was a long queue."

"And they're all in the water now, while you're stuck mucking about."

Then they were gone; into their boats and off to their favourite spots around the Bay where they knew they would find good amounts of abalone, while Fred was still struggling to get his boat into the water.

Finally, when the boats were floating in deeper water, we waded out and got into the two boats and took off for Point Cook.

We were barely into deeper water when Fred cursed and immediately turned his boat around and headed back to the boat ramp.

"What's wrong now?" Rommy yelled from the other boat.

"I left the top of my bloody suit in the car," Fred yelled back at him.

"You're getting sillier every day."

"It wouldn't have happened if I hadn't got bogged."

"You wouldn't have got bogged if you'd gone down the ramp in the first place."

"Don't rub it in."

"It looks like one of those days…" I mumbled, and Paul just laughed.

Eventually we made it out to the reefs at Point Cook.

Fred Pushing while Rommy Drives; to no avail.

With the car out of the way, it was time to push and drag the boat in.

In as far as they could get it, all they could do was slide the boat down into the water.

Finally, in the water and ready to go, Fred prepares to climb aboard.

And away we go...

We dropped anchor over a long reef that Fred knew well, and within minutes were in the water. It was clear enough to see the bottom two metres below from the boat, and it was also clear enough to see the reef was covered with starfish.

Fred jumped in, and popped up a few minutes later.

"Look at that," he yelled so Paul and I could hear over the noise of the compressor. "Is that a plague, or isn't it?"

"I'm going to move to another spot," Rommy said before taking off further around Point Cook.

I had finished loading the Bolex into its housing and was about to get into the water.

"I could drive along and hook them out with a spike, no worries. I'd fill the boat in five minutes and there'd still be thousands of the bastards down here."

Fred climbed back into the boat and grabbed his bag. He was going to see how many Abs he could get while we were there.

I swam along the reef close to the bottom, filming as I went. There were thousands of starfish clustered over each other and over everything on the reef. I didn't see any fish at all, not even a morwong, one of the most common fish along these reefs. I didn't see any fingerlings or schools of tiny shrimp, nothing at all. The reef was already ruined. As we swam along, we stirred up some of the silt that had been brought in by the storms a few days earlier, and very soon the visibility along the reef was such that it was a waste of time continuing to film. At least we had some footage of how bad the starfish were. Fred came back with hardly any abalone.

"There's nothing left," he said disgustedly.

We returned to the Altona boat ramp and this time Fred backed the trailer down the ramp, which was also muddy, but firm enough to drive on with getting bogged.

Coscinasterias Calamaria attacking mussels

Initially I went down to check exposure, and discovered the reef was in poor condition, A few moments later I went down with the Bolex camera in its housing to shoot some film of the starfish. There wasn't much of a reef left, the starfish had been and gone.

With the channel 9 news team

It took three weeks before the weather cleared up enough for us to film underwater, by which time we thought Channel 9 would have lost interest, but not so. As soon as it started to clear, with a north wind blowing enough to clear our side of the Bay, Stewart Scocroft rang Fred and it was arranged, they would meet us at the Altona boat ramp the next morning.

We were there with two boats; the channel 9 film crew, the camera man and the sound recordist, would go in the boat driven by Dave, Fred's deckhand, and Stewart and I would go in Fred's boat, with the underwater cameras. With everything loaded and ready to go by 9-30 in the morning it looked good even though the wind started to freshen. The news team was waiting at the boat ramp when we arrived. Stewart had his own wetsuit and was already wearing it because he intended to get into the water so he could see for himself how bad the starfish problem was.

Coscinasterias Calamaria is a voracious feeder. They are large, often as big as 30 centimetres across, and don't appear to move much, but this can be deceiving. They can move a lot faster than people expect, making use of thousands of tiny legs under each of its eleven arms. Each of the legs has a tiny sucker on the end and when it sits on top of a shellfish like an abalone or a sea snail, it sucks onto the shell with thousands of tiny suckers and stays there until the animal eventually tires and releases its grip on the rock beneath. Immediately the starfish flips the abalone over so its foot muscle is exposed then sucks it up into its extruded stomach, begins to dissolve the flesh and ingest it.

An abalone, or any other shellfish it attacks cannot escape. The starfish can crawl at least as fast as an abalone so it has no trouble catching one and sitting on top until it stops crawling around and before it can get a tight grip on the rock beneath the starfish flips it over to expose the muscle. Other shellfish like mussels and cockles have not a chance since they can't move. The starfish crawls over them and with its thousands of tiny suckers, exerts a suction pressure that may not seem like much but it can be maintained constantly for more than 24 hours. Eventually the mussel or the cockle weakens and its shell opens a bit. When that happens it's all over. The extruded stomach starts dissolving the flesh inside the shell.

One or two wouldn't be a problem, but when you see the whole seabed carpeted with these starfish, with so many you can't count them, crawling over each other, eating everything on the reefs, they are more than just a pest, they are a disaster that threatens the whole ecology of the sea bed. On the plus side, they also consume dead fish and other biological garbage. The problem is that when they swarm over a reef and eat everything attached to that reef, the tiny creatures that live symbiotically or even as parasites on the various reef inhabitants also die off. This in turn affects the fish that feed on these smaller creatures. Without them the fish abandon the reef or they also die from a lack of food. The food chain is broken and that can have disastrous long-term effects. Once they have denuded a reef the starfish move on to another one. They crawl across the sand without any problems until the find another reef to attack.

Fred was hoping that with channel 9 publicizing the problem in its news broadcast, enough fishermen, amateur as well as professional, would start clamoring for the government to do something about the starfish in the Bay. But exactly what could be done? That was the question no one could answer.

One of the remarkable features of this creature is that it can tear itself in half to reproduce. Each half will grow a new set of legs. This is known as bifurcation. It also reproduces sexually.

Although abalone divers think the population of this starfish has exploded in recent years, there are others who believe the increased numbers are just part of a natural cycle. The truth is that very little is known about Coscinasterias Calamaria, why they are swarming now, where they were before, and whether they will die off and allow the Bay to come back to normal again. No one knows.

The Channel 9 team on board Dave's boat as we head towards Point Cook.

We left the Altona boat ramp at 10.15 am and headed out into a light chop. Stewart was with Fred and myself while the rest of the team with the Arriflex camera and sound equipment accompanied us in the other boat driven by Fred's deck hand. In 1977 TV news was still recoded on 16 mm movie film, taken back to the studios where they processed and edited it in preparation for broadcasting. They didn't have the digital cameras they use today. In fact, video cameras barely existed in 1977. There may have been some available but what they recorded was nowhere near broadcast quality, and TV studios would have nothing to do with them. 16 mm film was still the go and the Arriflex cameras used by the studios were of cinematic quality.

We went straight to Point Cook because the headland would have protected the sea close to shore, and we knew there were plenty of infested reefs there. Stewart gave me a couple of rolls of Ektachrome 16 mm film and I loaded one into the Bolex while we made our way across the Bay.

Although it had been clear, with the water like a still pond earlier, by the time we dropped anchor at Point Cook the wind had freshened and further out in the Bay it was quite choppy, and probably too dirty underwater to see anything. It was overcast as well and that made it dark underwater. I wasn't sure how good the film would turn out.

I went into the water first to check what exposure I would need; visibility was barely two metres and there was still a lot of sand in suspension. It was dark, but fortunately the reefs were only a metre or two under the surface so there would be enough light to film if I opened up the lens to f4.5 or f5.

I came back on board to get the Bolex in its housing.

"We have to start filming now," I told Stewart, "We've only got a couple of hours before it gets too dark and dirty."

"That's fine." Stewart said. He called out to the team in the other boat. "I'm going in to have look."

The cinematographer was holding his camera in a balancing harness and he called back. "I've started shooting. Anytime you're ready…"

Stewart gave a thumbs up signal and then sat on the side of the boat, swung his legs over, and dropped down into the water. I filmed him from under the water as he came in. He swam around the boat and climbed back up onto the ladder at the side of Fred's boat. Half in and half out he started talking about what he had seen. Which was being recorded and filmed from the other boat a couple of metres away. Meanwhile I swam around the bottom and filmed as much of the starfish as I could until the roll was finished and I had to come back on board to change it. By then, Fred was all geared up and he went in to collect some starfish. I followed him underwater and filmed him picking up a starfish to show how it enveloped an abalone to eat it.

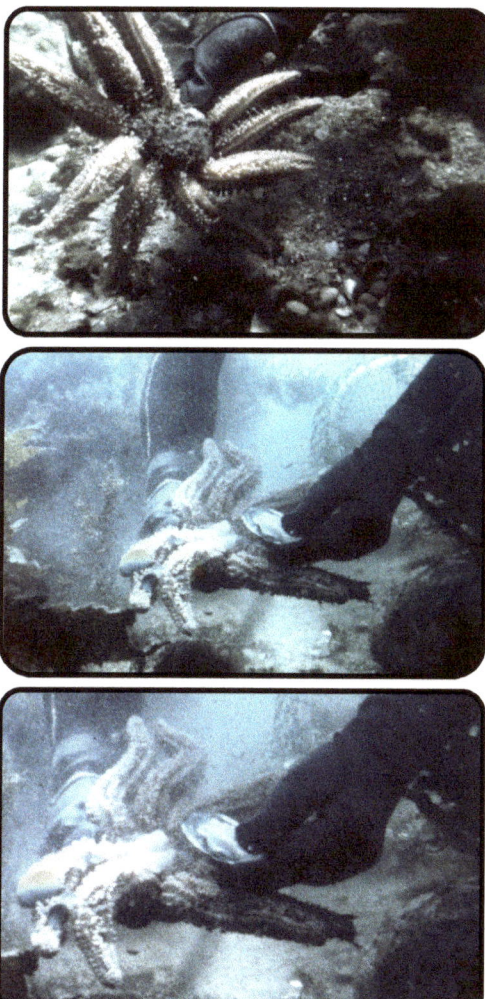

Frames from the 16 mm film shot for channel 9 news. Fred showing how the starfish eats an abalone and how much damage is done.
Below: Coscinasterias starting to attack a reef, crawling over everything in search of food. It won't take long before the entire reef is covered with them, and once they're done, nothing but bare rock and sand will be left.

Above: Coscinasterias attacking Ascidians. Fred bringing up some starfish to show Stewart who was waiting in the boat to interview him.

Ascidians in a bed of mussels. Since they remain fixed to the rocks or the pylons of piers and other structures, they will not survive when Coscinasterias arrives to devour them.

Coscinasterias Calamaria attacking a sea urchin.

— Grab that Moment —

*Fred explaining to Stewart how the starfish consumes an abalone.
Finishing up filming for the day at the Altona boat ramp.*

Back on his boat, Fred showed a handful of half-eaten abalone to Stewart as well as the starfish, while the camera man in the other boat, now alongside us, filmed Stewart interviewing Fred about the starfish and the menace they represented. They shot two sequences. One to be used later in the evening news, and the other to be used in a longer report to be aired on a weekend at the end of the month

Once the filming was done, we returned to the Altona boat ramp where the Arriflex camera was set up on a tripod so they could film Fred and Stewart arriving back at the boat ramp. They also recreated a shot of them leaving, which they hadn't got before, although there was some of the boat traveling out taken from the other boat. Once that was done, they quickly packed up and headed back to the GTV 9 studios to process and edit the film. Before they left, Stewart also gave me some extra film and asked if I would shoot some scenes of Fred collecting abalone, as well as some more of the starfish to be used in the longer report.

"I'll do that. It could be a few days or even a week or two. It all depends on the weather. It's not looking good at the moment."

Already it was a lot windier and the sea choppier than it had been when we left a couple of hours earlier.

"I understand. We plan on airing the longer version in two weeks. But we'll wait until we get the extra footage."

"Fair enough."

Once they'd gone, we also packed up and left.

While we waited for the weather to improve, I wrote an article for ***Skindiving in Australia and New Zealand***, about the channel 9 news team and their report on the Starfish problem. Which was title by the Magazine's editor, *Starfish Increase in Port Phillip Bay*. (*It appeared in Volume 7 #4 in December 1977*)

Monday, April 18th 1977

It was a beautiful morning, but frosty with a temperature of only 10 degrees Celsius. The sun was shining and there was no wind.

We bumped into John Morlock, who specialized in supplying fresh mussels to upmarket restaurants in the city.

He knew I always had underwater cameras with me whenever I went out with Fred, so he said straight up, "It's a waste of time. The water's filthy."

The weather had continued to be lousy from the moment we'd finished the report with the GTV 9 news team.

And he was right. At Fred's favourite spots around Point Cook the visibility was virtually zero. We didn't even get into the water.

— Grab that Moment —

*A reef clustered with Coscinasterias Calamaria. They are attacking mussels which are partially hidden beneath the sea lettuce.
Two starfish attacking two abalone. One tries to escape by crawling away, but the starfish can crawl as fast and will soon catch it.*

The starfish quickly catches up to the abalone and begins to crawl over the top to flip over the abalone to expose the foot upon which it crawls. The abalone will not survive.

Four starfish clustered on Fred's full abalone bag. Fred took them back up to the surface to dispose of them. From the additional film shot for GTV 9.

"We'll go around to Campbell's Cove. It should be clearer there."
That's where we went. The water visibility was a shade under three metres so we went in.

There are not many reefs at Campbell's Cove. The area is mostly sandy with small patches of reef jutting up haphazardly. But they were dead with no seaweed growing anywhere. The rocks were covered with a fine layer of muddy silt deposited by the recent storms and this was stirred up as we swam along. No doubt this would be constantly stirred up as the tide came in and went out. It would take a long time before any of these reefs recovered.

We did find one reef still living and I shot some film of Fred collecting abalone. The second roll I shot of Fred loading the abs into the boat. It was not a good lot, and the sky was once again filling with ominous dark clouds. We headed back to the boat ramp at Altona.

The weather was again shithouse for a couple of weeks, and when it finally cleared on Wednesday the 4th of May, we headed out again. This time we had a good day and managed to collect a good quota of Abalone as well as some film of Fred in action. The film was sent to Stewart at Channel 9, but they didn't go ahead with their longer weekend report.

Fred decided to contact the Melbourne Age newspaper, and they sent a reporter and a photographer to join us on a quick trip into the Bay. This time John Morlock came with us. He and Fred dived and collected within 20 minutes enough Coscinasterias Calamaria to fill three bins (normally used for abalone) which were later dumped on land and left to dry out and die. As a result of the report in Saturday's Age, Channel HSV 7 contacted Fred and arranged to repeat what he'd done for the Age. Again, John Morlock and Fred did the same thing the next day, Sunday. They dived and within no time had filled several bins with the dreaded starfish, which HSV 7 filmed, and broadcast the same night during their evening news.

One result of the article published in the skindiving magazine was that Fred was contacted by Dr Lyn Selwood, a researcher in Echinodermata at La Trobe University. She was interested in the article and told Fred that she had applied for a grant to study *Coscinasterias Calamaria*. The money had yet to come through but once it did, she would certainly be interested in Getting Fred to take her out to the spots where the starfish is most prevalent so she could obtain samples. She also sent him a photocopy of her grant application so he could see she meant business.

Rommy reported to us that around some reefs he dived on for abalone he saw a porcupine fish eating a piece of *C Calamaria*, which was interesting. Porcupine fish are also called puffer fish because when disturbed they fill themselves with sea water and puff up to double their size so the spines all over their body stick out. These fish are poisonous, which is why fishermen throw them back in if they accidentally catch one. They carry a nerve toxin which can paralyze and kill anyone eating them. They also have very few natural enemies in their own environment.

I had seen a lot of starfish crawling up the pylons beneath the old ammunition pier in Altona where they feed on ascidians and mussels. I also saw quite a lot of porcupine fish under that pier as well.

Perhaps *Coscinasterias Calamaria* does have a natural enemy after all.

Coscinasterias Calamari swarming over mussels on the pylons of a pier in Altona.

Dave, Fred's deck hand, and me with our cameras during the film shoot for Channel 9.

An inflatable dinghy

Over a long weekend in winter, probably the Queen's Birthday weekend, George came down from Sydney with his second wife Karin, his eldest son Julius, (from his first marriage to Margaret), and his younger son Benjamin, (from his marriage to Karin), and they came with us to Portarlington for the weekend. George had bought a red inflatable rubber runabout and wanted to see what it was like.

These inflatable dinghies are generally pretty good. Their advantage is that they can be rolled up and stored easily as well as transported by one person. You don't need a trailer for the boat. You simply stow it in the back of a suitable vehicle, obviously one big enough to carry your outboard motor as well. When you get where you want to launch the boat, you unroll or unpack it, pump it up, fix on the outboard motor and away you go. The whole process is pretty quick once you've done it a few times. On this occasion, it was the first time George had assembled his rubber dinghy, and it took a bit longer than he anticipated.

A brief flashback

I first met George Olah at Birdland in St Kilda around 1962. He was playing conga drums with the house band. Since I also played congas, I asked to sit in with the band. After playing a set, I got talking with George and he was impressed with the way I played. He had picked up playing congas when he was in New York. He often went to the Palladium, the night club that featured Tito Puente's big band as well as Tito Rodriguez's orchestra. The Palladium was the home of the Mambo and these two big bands played against each other night after night. Musicians from other bands and other nearby clubs would come and sit in, would also play and compete against each other, and the dancers and other patrons loved it. Timbaleros and congueros also came and sat in and competed against each other as well as against the percussionists featured in both the big house bands. It was a wonderful place to be in the late 1950s.

Since I had learned some things from Albert La Guerre and Antonio Rodriguez, the way I played was somewhat different to the way George played, so we spent a lot of time comparing the differences. And when JoJo Smith from West Side Story appeared and played incredible conga drums, we both immediately got together with him so we could study and learn. We would often play in the backyard of the family home in Benbow street, Yarraville, much to the annoyance or sometimes the delight of the neighbours behind us who often watched us from their side of the back fence.

George and I became great mates and it turned out he was a keen skin-diver as well. He was a strong swimmer, and he loved diving in spots that were considered dangerous by many new divers. We would dive for crayfish at the bommies beside Cape Schanck, or off the heads at Queenscliff. He and Fred also became good mates and Fred actually asked George to be his best man when he married my sister Zara.

George was, by profession, a watchmaker and jeweler. He and his uncle had imported machinery from Italy that stitched gold chains together and they manufactured bracelets and other items for sale in jewelery stores around Australia.

When he sold his share of the business, he moved to Sydney (in the mid-1960s) and set up, initially, a watch repair and jewelery store, which he later relinquished, to set up a more specialized luxury jewelery business in the foyer of a major hotel. He crafted beautiful, expensive, and completely individual works of jewelery art, for sale to discerning tourists who stayed at that hotel. After Monica and I got married, he crafted a magnificent gold ring with an opal in it as a gift for Monica on one of our visits to Sydney.

A Busy boat ramp

Being a long weekend, and with the weather dull but reasonable, there were a lot of people at the boat ramp in Queenscliff, wanting to get into the water. And along came George and us. The boat ramp was a twin ramp, and while Fred backed his boat down one side George dumped his rolled-up rubber dinghy in the middle of the other ramp. He unpacked his car with the marine ply floor and the outboard motor and whatever else he wanted to take with him, and all this he laid down on the ramp beside his now unrolled rubber dinghy. It had to be pumped up and Julius did this with a foot pump.

George holding the back board where the outboard motor is to be attached while Julius starts using the foot pump. Below: slowly the dinghy takes shape.

While George and Julius prepare their boat Fred is launching his on the other boat ramp.

Fred had his boat down the adjacent ramp and into the water while Julius was pumping away. He moored his boat at the end of a short pier while we waited for George to get his rubber boat together.

What George and Julius should have done was to pump up the boat and fix the floor off to one side of the boat ramp. He and Julius should then be able to carry it down and place it in the water, where the motor would then be attached and they could take off. Doing this would have allowed other boat owners to launch their boats fairly rapidly. There were ten or fifteen cars with trailers lined up to launch their boats.

But George took no notice of the others lined up and waiting to launch.

I could see drivers from the cars and boats lined up wondering what was going on, what the delay was. Some of them came down to have a look. George and Julius were pumping up the boat, which was taking a lot longer than they expected.

"What the hell is he doing?" One of them asked.

"He should be doing that over there to the side, not fucking about on the boat ramp."

I could see George was getting pissed off with how long it was taking to inflate his boat. He glared up at the people watching, almost challenging them to say something, but they stood there watching and waiting, and grumbled, but none of them approached. George could look ferocious when he was angry. No one was game to say anything directly to him.

Finally, the dinghy was inflated and sitting at the water's edge. George and Julius placed the floor inside which made the boat as rigid as a regular dinghy. George them picked up the heavy outboard motor, and carried it over to his boat. He installed the outboard motor, and after a much longer time than expected, finally pushed the rubber dinghy out into the water and jumped on board. Julius climbed in as the boat drifted out into the water and away from the boat ramp. I heard a collective sigh of relief from the watching crowd which quickly dispersed back to their vehicles in preparation to launch their own boats.

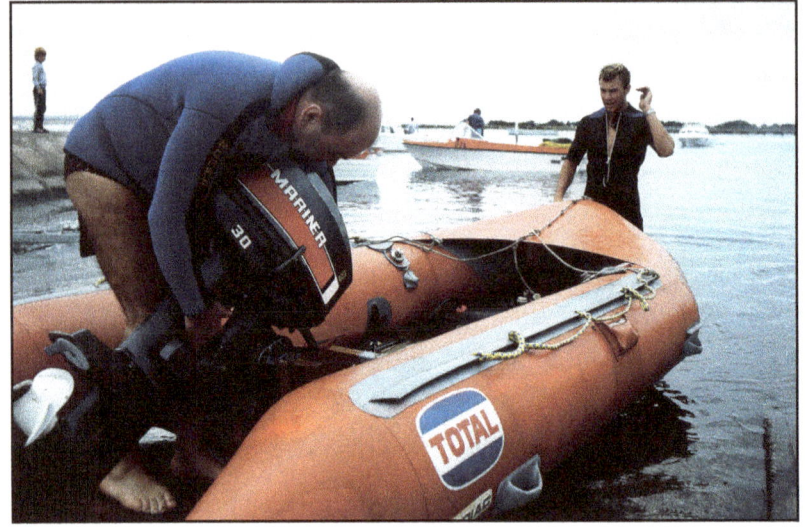

As George attached the outboard, Fred's boat had already been launched and can be seen in the background moving across to a short jetty where Karin and Benjamin and Fred's son David were waiting. They came along for the ride out to Pope's Eye.

Fred and I drove beside them at first, then we went ahead so I could take some pictures as they came out of the boat harbour.

We went to Mud island near the entrance to Port Phillip Bay, and then across to Pope's Eye which sits in a spot that divides the inflow of water from the ocean into the main part of Port Phillip Bay on one side, and into the much smaller bay called Swan Bay. The Queenscliff boat ramp is on the Swan Bay side which is a well-protected area and the mooring place for many yachts and fishing boats. There was hardly anyone out at Pope's Eye on this day because the weather turned bad once we got out into the open. We didn't stay out there for too long before coming back.

There were no seats and anyone in the dinghy had to sit on the sides. Once outside the protected harbour the sea started to get choppy which made for an interesting ride.

The dinghy looked so small once it was well away from the boat harbour. The weather also deteriorated as soon as we got out of the harbour and into the open, becoming grey and very cold.
Below: Julius, George, and Fred, wearing their wetsuits because the water was icy.

— Grab that Moment —

On the day we went out with George and Julius, the weather turned lousy very quickly. It became far too rough to attempt going out through the Heads to dive for crayfish along the reefs on the ocean side, which was something George wanted to do, and too dirty to see much of anything inside the Heads. In effect, after all the mucking about on the boat ramp was a waste of time. George had come down from Sydney for the weekend to visit his uncle and aunt, and to do some dicing with us, but Melbourne's fickle weather betrayed him.

The only thing we managed to do was to confirm that the inflatable dinghy was a good runabout.

Meanwhile, back at the holiday house in Portarlington, Monica was happily ensconced with Mum and Dad where they prepared some lunch for when we came back. Of course, they were hoping we would bring back a few crayfish, but no such luck; The weather had taken a turn for the worse and we came back not long after getting as far as Pope's Eye. It was too rough with the tide coming in to even attempt to go out through the Heads. We would have better luck on other days later in the year.

Monica and Brian, outside the house at Portarlington. By this time, the garden had developed and the place looked more like a home than a holiday house stuck on a hill. Mum and Dad were spending more time there which also helped.

Some beautiful shots of Dad with Brian inside the house. One of my early paintings can be seen on the wall behind them.

On other occasions when the weather was better and we could go out through the Heads we once attempted to dive on Cheviot Beach where Prime Minister Harold Holt disappeared while swimming in the surf. A memorial to him is underwater here and maintained by the navy.

Fred was about to go over the side to have a look after we anchored, when a fast moving navy runabout approached. There were two naval officers on board and they told us somewhat abruptly, "This is prohibited territory. Part of the naval base. You can't dive here." When we protested they told us to "Move along" in a threatening manner. I don't think they would have shot us, but they could have confiscated the boat and arrested us, so we decided to leave. We pulled up anchor and went back through the Heads and ended up diving around Pope's Eye once again.

Pope's Eye

Pope's Eye, sits about seven kilometres inside the Heads and directly in line with the centre of The Rip. It is built of bluestone on a sandy base, but was never completed. It was to be a part of early fortifications set up to detect enemy warships entering Port Phillip Bay. Construction of it began in 1880, but ceased once improved naval guns were established at Queenscliff and Point Lonsdale overlooking the entrance to the harbour. What was left was a wide circle of bluestone rocks with a lagoon in the centre. These photos were taken on another day when we went out to Pope's Eye. We would often go there if we were at Portarlington, and the weather was good.

From a slight distance away, as we approached, you can clearly see how low lying the circle of bluestone rocks are. The coastal town of Portsea can be seen in the background beyond the rock circle. We approached it from the Queenscliff, Point Lonsdale side.

On another occasion when the weather was much nicer, Paul came with Fred and me to Pope's Eye and I climbed the beacon to get a broad view and take photo of the boat beside the small jetty inside the rock circle.

Below: Looking at Pope's Eye from outside on the open sea. There were a few boats there on this fine day. The difference in the water's colour is because it is much shallower inside the rock circle than it is outside.

The view from the top of the beacon at Pope's Eye. The construction was named after a sailor on one of the ships that serviced Port Phillip bay and its settlements and has no religious significance.

Inside Pope's Eye the water is about 3 metres deep, beautifully clear because it is protected from the in and out flow of water through the Heads. It is a safe anchorage for small boats and a popular dive spot, which is why we went there. There's not much there because it is very sandy. There is some seaweed and other stuff on the rocks that are exposed to the open sea outside . Paul is seen here diving with Fred's hookah.

The Chinaman's Hat, looking lost and forlorn out in the middle of nowhere. The birds seen on the roof are Australasian Gannets (takapu) which are members of the booby and gannets family. They are common around the southern Australian coast extending as far away as New Zealand and Norfolk Island. They breed on the islands in Bass Strait as well as along the coastlines of the mainland. Beautiful birds, they are spectacular when dive bombing into the sea for fish.

On another occasion at the Queenscliff boat ramp, getting Fred's boat ready for a trip out to Pope's Eye and other spots nearby. The weather was much warmer and better than the trip we made with George and Julius a few months earlier.

South Channel Island Fort, accessible only by boat is disused naval installation open for visits from tourists during the day. Below: Point Nepean, not accessible to visitors because it is still an active naval base for training. Bottom: The beacon on the edge of the reef that delineates the Point Nepean side of Port Phillip Heads.

— *Grab that Moment* —

The gap between Point Lonsdale and Point Nepean is barely 5 kilometres wide, but the reefs on the Point Lonsdale side extend a fair way across, making the actual gap through which ships have to navigate about 1000 metres wide. This makes it very dangerous for ships entering and leaving Port Phillip Bay. It was even narrower once, but early in the last century, sections of the underlying reef were blasted away to widen and deepen the gap to make more room for larger ships. It is still a dangerous entrance.

When the tide comes in, the water tends to pileup against the reefs on either side of the Heads and flows rapidly into the bay, almost like a shallow waterfall. It takes a number of hours to fill the Bay, because it is a huge landlocked bay, and the water lever across a wide area takes time to rise. When the level reaches the same as the ocean outside the water calms and there is no inflow into the bay. But barely an hour later the tide goes out, and this means that the level outside the bay drops and the piled up water inside the bay now has to flow out that narrow entrance. Once again there is turbulence and very strong currents as the water in the bay rushes out back into the ocean which is why it is known as The Rip. The current flowing in or out can get up to eight knots, and that is one hell of a current.

In the middle of the Rip.
Although there wasn't a heavy swell that day, the condition of the water clearly shows there is a very strong current flowing through the Heads.

A minor digression — a slight forward jump

Although we all loved the house at Port, it was getting too much for Dad to manage. He was already in his late-70s. He had retired at 75 and could not get an age pension because he owned the house at Portarlington which the government considered to be an asset that potentially could earn him enough money to live on, so in their eyes, he wouldn't need a pension. Never mind the fact that he had worked hard for over 50 years and paid his taxes, never mind he had, employed over that time, many people all of whom paid taxes, and that he also paid land tax and state government payroll tax and other imposts, never mind that he didn't actually rent out the house at Portarlington, and earned nothing from it, the fact that he owned it was enough for them not to give him a pension. They gained a lot of money from him and from those who worked for him over his working life, but none of that was considered relevant. It was his assets they looked at and decided he wasn't eligible for a pension.

He was living on his savings and from the money Phillip and I had paid him for buying the dry-cleaning business and property in Williamstown. Once we'd paid off our debt, there was nothing else coming in and whatever savings he and Mum had accumulated rapidly diminished. In desperation, I would think, he divided the house at Portarlington into two by installing a panel to cover the door in the third bedroom which led to the rear section of the house where they had another sitting room and a fourth bedroom and a second bathroom. They added a small kitchen to the sitting room and in effect turned the back portion of the house into a small self-contained apartment. They then rented the front part, two thirds of the house, to families over the summer holidays. In this way they supplemented whatever they had as savings. Mum was able to get a pension and that helped. They could still go there and stay in the apartment at the rear while the main part was rented out.

In effect, that meant none of us could use the house during the peak holiday periods because it was rented out, so we stopped going there, even in the winter when no one else was there. The house was then used by Mum and Dad who went there to make sure everything was up to scratch and to do whatever maintenance was needed. But this became too much as Dad aged and he decided to sell the house. Phillip wanted to buy it, but couldn't get a loan and would have to pay it off over time with Dad, in effect, financing the sale and transfer of title. He couldn't afford to finance it and wouldn't sell it to Phillip, or anyone else in the family for that matter. I offered to buy it as well, but again, couldn't arrange finance since I was paying off the house we'd built at Hoppers Crossing. He sold it to a stranger, which gave him a lump sum to live on, and because after that he no longer had any assets other than the family home, which fortunately isn't considered as part of a means test by the government, he became entitled to a pension. Finally, when he was around 79, approaching 80, they allowed him to have the age pension.

He lived another eleven years before he had a sudden heart attack and died in January 1989 at the supposed age of 91. He was older than that, but there was no record of his birth date, the only record we were ever able to find was his Christening date which was in the church records of the town he was born in; 12th December 1898, Saint Spridon's day. He was named Spiro after his Patron Saint, and that day, his name day, was the day he celebrated his birthday. It was the custom in those smaller country towns in the less accessible parts of Greece, because the infant mortality was high, no child was christened until they had lived at least a year. After a year or more, future survival was more likely so a christening would be performed. Dad would have been at the very least, one year old when he was christened, or perhaps even another 6 months or a year older. There was no way we could ever know exactly.

Two and a half years after Dad died, Mum contracted a severe blood infection after taking a trip to Germany with Zara. She became very ill a few months after returning from the trip and her doctor immediately sent her to a major hospital in Melbourne. The bacteria running rampant in her blood had eaten into one of her heart's valves and she required an emergency heart valve replacement.

It went well. We were allowed to see her in the Intensive Care Unit after the operation and she seemed fine, considering she'd just had open heart surgery. After three days in the ICU she was moved to a regular ward where, unfortunately, she got a Golden Staph infection and it rapidly took over her whole body. Golden Staph was a big problem in older hospitals as it had become immune to every known anti-bacterial treatment.

Mum was not strong enough to fight it. Every time she rallied, we hoped she would recover, but as the infection was impervious to any treatment the hospital staff tried, she got worse. In the end, in desperation, the doctors wanted to try something to poison the infection, but there was a 50 percent chance that the poison would also attack her own organs. We didn't know what to do, and after thinking about it we decided to let the hospital try what they thought would be best for Mum. I think Mum was too far gone for such treatment to work, and that combined with the Golden Staph infection was too much for her. She couldn't and didn't recover, not even a little. Her kidneys and liver started to fail and she faded away…

She died of '*overwhelming sepsis*' according to the hospital medical report. The sense of loss amongst us was at first quite extreme. Dad and Mum had both been there all our lives. They were always there. But now all of a sudden, we were on our own.

Over time, we adapted and adjusted.

Life goes on, and our role as children, although long past, became the role of being parents since we all had young children of our own.

A moment that helped start a career.

At least, that's how I like to think of it…

Sometime towards the end of 1974, Monica and I went to a small restaurant in Lygon street Carlton called *The Keyhole*, which Uncle Eddie had recommended to us.

"There's a young guy there playing conga drums and singing. You might find it interesting."

He knew I'd been playing congas and bongos for years. He even came to see me in the show *Tropicana*, at the Lido, where I performed on stage, along with my sister Zara, and Brazilian dancer and artist, Antonio Rodriguez. He'd probably seen me on the times I occasionally filled in as a percussionist on the Don Lane Show, when Garry Hyde was unavailable. He'd certainly heard me playing them at home (in Benbow Street) long before I went over to Europe and later to Mexico.

After returning home from Mexico, I discovered there was not much music of the kind I liked being played anywhere. It was all rock music with many small groups playing in pubs and the sort of clubs that once played Latin or European and South American or even Jazz music. Everywhere you went, it was just rock music. It was slowly changing though, especially in America where rock bands began incorporating influences from South America and the Caribbean, while simultaneously Latin groups began incorporating blues and rock influences. Santana was the most prominent with a line-up of conga and timbale drummers accompanying his rock group. He adapted a Tito Puente song, Oye Como Va, and made it a worldwide hit. It was his most Latin sounding piece up to that time, but much of what he played was a mixture influenced strongly by Salsa music. He featured his conga drummers a lot and this is one of the things that made him very popular worldwide. Once Armando Peraza and Orestes Vilató became members of his group, it became even more Afro-Cuban/salsa sounding while maintaining its underlying rock and blues influences.

When Uncle Eddie said, "You should go and have a look." I thought; why not?

"The food's pretty good too. Their garlic prawns are fabulous. And on top of that, the Chef and his wife sometimes come out and serenade the guests with Italian opera songs. It's a very popular place."

So, we went there, and the food was as good as he said. The young guy was the son of the owners, and his name was Alex Pertout. Although his family name sounded French, and he had lived in Italy before migrating with his parents to Australia, they were from Chile, so we hit it off right away.

While we ate the garlic prawns, Alex sat down with his one conga drum and played a rough sounding tumbao and sang Guantanamera Guajira to it. I liked the sound of his splaying but it lacked technical skill.

He reminded me of myself when I first started playing 14 years earlier. I had no idea of how to play conga drums. Hardly anyone did back in 1959-60, but I went to nightclubs around the city and sat in with various bands and played as best I could. Sometimes a friend, Danny Green, accompanied me and we alternated with him on congas and me on bongos, and then we'd swap. He was better on bongos than he was on congas. But like most of us at the time, we had no way of knowing how to play properly. By 'properly', I mean how to produce the various sounds the conga and bongo drums are capable of producing. For that you need a teacher, someone who knows how to play. You can't learn these drums by listening to records and trying to imitate the sounds, not unless you know how to produce them in the first place, how to hit the drum heads in certain ways to make the sounds. Once you know that, and have the basics embedded you can then learn by listening to recordings of other experts or master drummers with some understanding of how to get the sounds that you hear. And there were hardly many records of that nature available in the 1960s in Australia. On top of that, you need to know the history of the rhythms involved and how they fit together to gain a proper understanding.

I was fortunate to meet Antonio Rodriguez, and Albert La Guerre, who were good players from Brazil and from Haiti, two very different drumming traditions and cultures. Both of them had worked with the Katherine Dunham folkloric ballet that toured Australia in 1959, or thereabouts, and had stayed here after the ballet left. That ballet focused mainly on Haitian and Brazilian folklore, but also had a small amount of Cuban folklore as well. The drummers who performed accompanying the dancers were from Haiti, Cuba and Brazil. They all learnt each other's ways of playing so they could interchange during performances. In that group, Francisco Aguabella was the lead Cuban drummer, Albert was the lead Haitian drummer. Both were masters of their respective instruments and had enormous knowledge of their culture and history, both secular as well as religious.

Haitian drumming is very different from Cuban and Puerto Rican drumming which is the basis of what is known as Salsa today. Haitian culture and music originated in Dahomey, West Africa where the French had colonized that country and taken slaves to Haiti, whereas the African slaves that gave rise to the music in Cuba mostly came from Nigeria where different languages, religious, and musical cultures existed, which blended with Spanish, became syncretised into what we hear today.

The music, the singing, and the dancing of the Katherine Dunham group absolutely blew me away. I became friends with Albert and Antonio and a couple of others who stayed in Australia when the ballet left, and it was Albert who taught me the basics of a Cuban style of playing. There are many different regional styles and ways of playing, although the end sound is often similar, so there is no one way of playing that you can say is fixed. It continuously evolves as new influences emerge. I later met other Cuban drummers who found themselves in Melbourne for concerts, one in particular who accompanied the George Shearing Quintet on its visit to Australia in the late 1950s: Armando Peraza, one of the greatest bongoceros y congueros to come out of Cuba in the 1940s and 1950s. He knew Albert, and through Albert I met Armando, and of course we talked about and played drums together. He was only here a few days but he was such an inspiration. It would be years before he came back to Australia as a featured performer with Carlos Santana.

Another influence was JoJo Smith from New York who came to Australia with West Side Story in the early 1960s as a dancer. He was a superb conga player and he taught me along with my close friend George Olah, how to play the New York style of conga drumming. After he stayed when the West Side Story Ballet finished its run in the theatres, I ended up doing floor shows with him as his drummer while he danced, or as his accompanying drummer while he soloed on congas as part of his show. Later (1964-65) I went to Europe where I played congas with a Cuban group called Los Matecocos, based in Paris, France, and three years later I went to Mexico where I spent almost a year playing congas and timbales with a couple of groups in Acapulco.

With this background behind me, I felt I needed to give Alex a few hints on how to play, and what kinds of sounds he needed to get from his conga drum, and how what he was playing was part of a greater combination of rhythms and structures that were both secular as well as religious.

We hit it off together and Alex came out to our place in Hoppers Crossing with his friend Peter Gretch, Together, we practiced and studied in the room I'd put aside as an office/music room. They were both eager to learn, and I was happy to have someone to play with in a group situation. Conga drums and associated percussion were not meant to be played alone. The drums all form part of a group in which each drum has a specific role to play; base, counterpoint, time keeping, improvisation based on movement of dancers, or sometimes as it is in a more modern context, improvisation around a theme expressed through melody and singing. Playing in a group is much more fun than alone. It is absolutely essential if one is to understand how the music expressed through the drums evolved.

I'm not sure how Monica put up with the noise, we were pretty loud when playing three or four drums together, but she never complained even though she was pregnant at the time.

The guys came out once a week on a Saturday afternoon to study and practice. We recorded our practice sections so we could listen back to see what had worked and what didn't, which we would then work on to improve. My young brother Paul who was a whiz with electronics, built a 4-channel mixer, so we could overdub what we'd recorded. That way we could experiment with multiple rhythm structures by adding extra tracks to what we'd already recorded. It was a lot of fun.

Even after Brian was born, Alex and Peter would come around once a month and we would practice together. Brian got used to the noise; it was a part of his environment, and when he first started to crawl around, he would crawl over to the bongos sitting on the floor and bang on them. He couldn't reach up to the conga drums because they were much taller than he was.

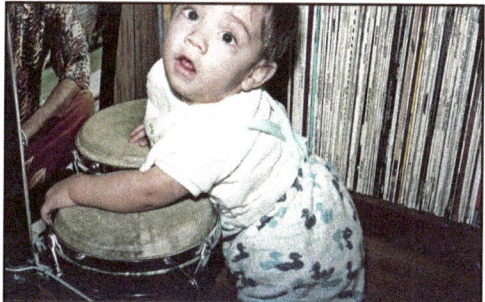

The bongos on the floor were just the right height for him to use as a help in standing. He could lean on them, pull himself up and balance against them.

— John Litchen —

Moments that are never forgotten: Above, Brian holding my knee to stand, and then attempting to bang on the bongos.
Outside on the patio with Monica as he first started to crawl.
Next page: his first attempts at eating solid food, was messy but a lot of fun.

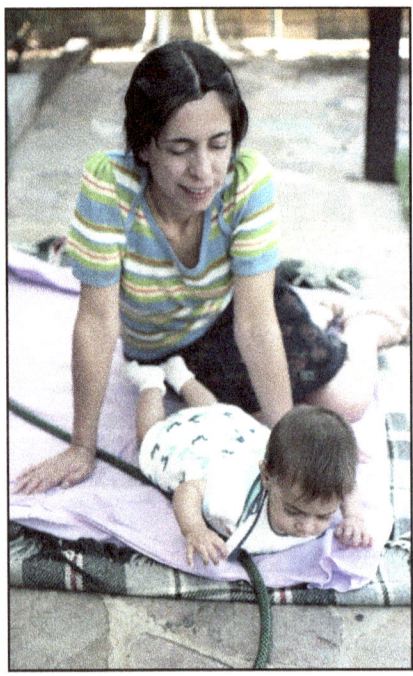 

Grab that Moment

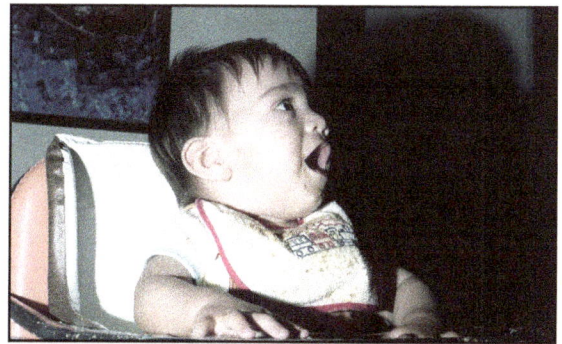

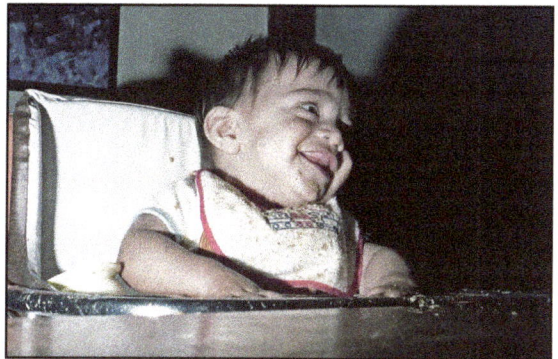

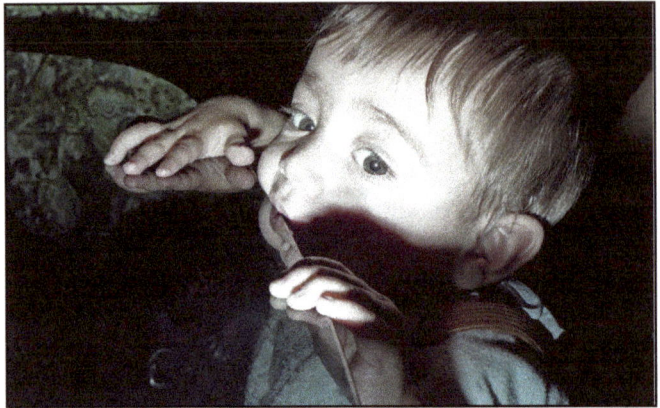
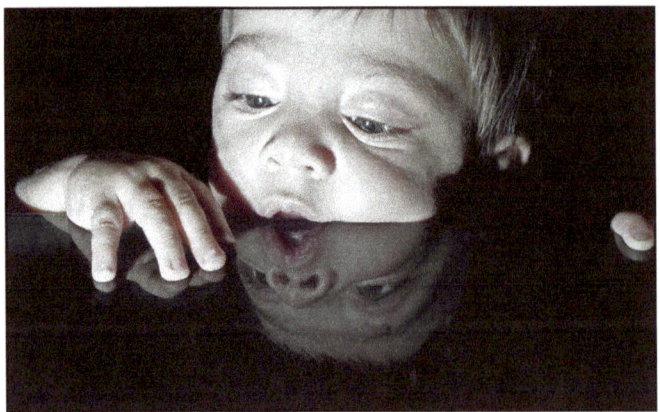

As he started crawling around and became stronger he would stand up against the glass coffee table in the lounge room. It was much higher than my bongos. He was fascinated by his reflection in the glass.
Since I took lots of photos, there were always empty film boxes lying around and Brian spent a good deal of time examining these yellow boxes.

— Grab that Moment —

Father and son, in the backyard at Hoppers Crossing.

Wind and pollen, grass and flies

When we moved to Hoppers Crossing it was a developing suburb about four kilometres from Werribee on the Melbourne side and just beside the Princes Highway. Between Hoppers Crossing and Werribee was open space, grassland, and from there going west across towards the Ballarat Road (the Western Highway) was empty land that was all rye grass, with not a house anywhere until you got to Deer Park on Ballarat Road. Deer Park was the last suburb on the edge of Melbourne's sprawl at that time, and my sister Christine had bought a house there. It was about twenty-five kilometres across to her place via Derrimut Road. That large area of grassland was used to graze cattle and sheep and as a consequence, their droppings not only fertilized the rye grass, but also attracted millions of flies. Hoppers Crossing being rather small at the time when we moved there in 1974, was infested with flies in the summer. You couldn't walk outside without having them swarm all over you. It was not practical to have an outside meal or a barbecue during the day because of the flies. But the other problem was the wind. It blew across that grassland uninterrupted for a long distance and picked up the pollen from the rye grass. With no houses or other buildings to block it, the wind was often very strong, blowing with a ferocity we weren't used to after coming from Yarraville.

Monica would often walk with Brian in his pram along Woodville Park Drive to the supermarket not far down the street where she would do a little shopping. One day, while she was in the supermarket, the strength of the wind increased to the point that when she came out of the supermarket and started to walk back to the house, she was having trouble pushing the pram. With its sun shade up, it acted as a parachute does in trapping air to slow its fall. The wind pushing into the pram was so strong she couldn't walk against it. Brian was getting dust blown into his face, and was crying. Monica simply didn't have the strength to push the pram against the wind. She hadn't noticed it until she came around from behind the supermarket and began walking back along Woodville Park Drive. Then it hit her. She only had about 400 metres to walk, but she could hardly make any headway against the power of the wind. She pushed with all her might and managed to get about halfway before she could push no more.

Fortunately, a neighbour saw her having trouble and he came out and helped her to push the pram back to the house.

When I got home and she told me what had happened, I asked her, "Why didn't you turn around and pull the pram along backwards?"

She looked at me with a blank expression. She obviously didn't understand what I meant.

"The wind would have blown over the top of you and the pram instead of into your face and into the pram. You could have walked back against it easily instead of fighting against the force of it pushing at you."

"Lucky that man across the road saw me and came to help." She said with the implication: *you should have been here to help*, but I was at work.

The wind that day, had also uprooted the trees I had planted in the front garden, because the ground had been previously soaked from several days of heavy rain. I replanted the trees and they survived.

The next day after the incident with the pram, she had red eyes and her face was swollen and lumpy. It turned out she was allergic to Rye grass pollen and the wind had been full of it, having blown across a huge swathe of grass covered land before hitting the houses at Hoppers Crossing. It took days for the swelling to go down. After that, if it was too windy, especially if it was from inland, she wouldn't go out unless it was in the car.

Monica and Brian coming home from the local supermarket. There were no footpaths along Woodville Park Drive and they had to walk along the road. On this particular day there was no wind and she had no problems pushing the pram along and turning into and walking up our driveway.

She was allergic to a lot of things, which were only exacerbated after Brian was born while we were living at Hoppers Crossing. She lost a lot of weight, developed colitis, a horrible affliction. The allergies and the colitis gradually disappeared, but the fear of them returning at any moment made us decide to move. However, it took us four years before we were in a position to be able to move, and those years were often stressful for Monica as she had to undergo a strict diet to control the allergies as well as the colitis.

I think that there was a certain amount of stress involved as well. She was a new mother, at 36 years of age, and everything seemed awkward and difficult. She missed her mother who had returned to Chile, and was perhaps even feeling a little homesick once her mother left. Sleepless nights didn't help much either. Brian never slept throughout an entire night, but always woke up every three or four hours, which meant neither of us got a full night's sleep for quite some time. It didn't bother me that much, but it did affect Monica's health which no doubt led to her condition of colitis.

No matter what she tried she didn't really improve until we moved to Williamstown in 1980, and by that time Brian was four years old.

Looking very slender five months after Brian was born. She had been suffering intermittently with colitis and this caused her to lose weight, not that she was very large to begin with. But for a while she looked exceptionally thin.

Connecting Fragments

Friends for life

Although I know many people, and have, what we normally call, 'lots of friends', the truth is that most of us only ever have one or two or perhaps a few real friends. That is someone with whom you can share things, who will go out of their way to help you if needed without being asked, someone who will always stand by you, who will always put your welfare above their own, and someone for whom you would do the same. How many friends like that does anyone have over their lifetime?

Those 'lots of Friends' we all have are in reality no more than acquaintances of varying degrees. Some you know very well, others hardly at all. Some, you would undoubtedly call friends because you know them fairly well and whose names you would remember, and with whom you have interacted over varying periods of time, but too many others are no more than someone you talk to occasionally or someone who lives in the street and you recognize them enough to say hello to, while may others are simply familiar faces.

Running a business as Phillip and I did, we dealt with literally thousands of people over 30 to 40 years, and we always remembered the names of those we saw frequently. These days people would call them friends and proudly tell everyone how many such 'friends' they have. But they are not friends. They are people whose names you remember because you see them on a regular basis. And if you are in a business where you deal with the public, it is good from the point of view of the customer, that you actually remember their names. I know in my case when I go into a shop that I frequently use, and the staff remember my name, it makes me feel that my being a customer or 'client' is important to them, important enough to remember my name. I'm sure our dry-cleaning customers felt the same whenever Phillip or I spoke to them as if we were old friends and used their name. People always like to be remembered.

In these modern times with social media, young people of today have thousands of friends, but probably none of whom they have ever met personally or have actually had a face-to-face conversation with. It's all about the numbers, of impressing each other with how many they can accumulate. It's electronic, remote, non-existent except in the digital realm of the Internet. But to them it is real, and it is important, because when they lose a friend, or become 'unfriended', they can become quite upset.

In my case, I only had a few real friends. There was Brian Mealey, who I first met when I attended University High School from 1953 until 1957. Although he was in a class one year ahead of me, we hit off immediately. It turned out he had just moved from the other side of town to a house in Williamstown Road just around the corner from my place in Benbow Street. He was often at our place as much as I was at his place. My parents treated him like another member of the family, as did his parents with me. We had quite a few mates who also lived nearby and with whom we went to school, but when they grew older and moved away, we lost contact. Whereas Brian, no matter where he moved to, always maintained contact with me and we always got together for dinners and other events. When he married Maxine, I was his Best Man at the wedding. He remained a part of my family all of his life.

Unfortunately, he died of a massive heart attack, collapsing in the middle of the street in the centre of the city and dying as few days later in hospital without coming out of his unconscious state. Monica and I were in Sydney visiting another friend George, when Mum called to tell me about Brian. I was stunned. It was so unexpected as to be unbelievable. Brian was only 49 when he died, far too young in my view, and I still miss him today 35 years later.

Left: Brian in 1959 after a dive, and above, at my wedding in 1973, the way I'll always remember him.

George Olah, who lived in Sydney, and whom we were visiting when Brian died was a close friend for a number of years while he lived in Melbourne.

I met him when I started playing conga drums at a nightclub called Birdland in St Kilda. We became immediate friends because of the drums, but when I discovered he loved skindiving as did I, we started diving together along with my brother-in-law Fred. We became very good friends. Fred, who was about to become an abalone diver, also became a close friend to George. We went to places like Barwon Heads and Queenscliff where we dived for crayfish, or down the coast on the other side of the Bay towards Cape Schanck where George excelled while diving deep around the massive bommies that housed huge crayfish. He was remarkably strong as a swimmer and diver and would free-dive as deep as 30 metres, holding his breath while enticing a crayfish to crawl into the open bag he held before it. He would do this repeatedly until the bag had half a dozen crayfish in it, before returning to shore. Neither Fred nor I could dive as deep, or hold our breath as long as he could.

We would come back with a bag full of crayfish to cook and eat at home in Benbow Street. George became Fred's best man at his wedding to my sister Zara. When he moved with his family to Sydney, we didn't lose contact, but would often see and visit each other, even though we lived in cities 900 kilometres apart. As time has passed over the last thirty years or so, we don't see as much of each other as we would perhaps like, but I like to think that we are still friends, real friends.

George in 1963, playing conga in the backyard at Benbow Street.

Above: in his backyard at his home in Sydney, September 1973.

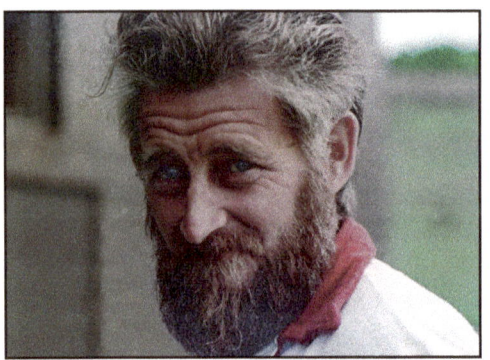

Walter Shaw, Wally, at Portarlington in 1972, and talking to Monica beside our family holiday house.

And then there was Walter Shaw, 'Wally', as we called him, whom I met when I first started to work at the dry-cleaning business in Douglas Parade, Williamstown. Wally worked part time in the nursery next door to us in between shift work at the Mobil Oil refinery in Altona. Wally was a cheerful bloke who loved telling stories and 'dirty' jokes, which he often shared with my brother Phillip, who also worked with me at the dry-cleaning business.

Wally had migrated from England with his wife and first son and was living in Altona. When we first met, he had three boys and had been in Australia for a number of years. Wally was much older than me; at least that's what I thought because he often spoke about his experiences during the Second World War. He had been stationed in Germany immediately after the war while the Allies were helping rebuild some of the damage caused by the war, and could speak reasonably good German.

He was born, I found out later, in 1926, which made him only 14 years older than me, since I was born in 1940. What we had in common —literally the only thing we had in common— was a love of good stories and reading science fiction. He had read many of the same stories as had I and we discussed these continuously whenever we got together. He would lend me books he thought were fabulous and that I had yet to read, and I would do the same for him.

As time went on and we became firm friends we decided that we should write a novel together. This decision came about while I was in Europe, in Germany visiting Fred's parents. I had written a long letter to Wally describing a book I had just finished reading that had impressed me immensely, Rachel Carson's Silent Spring, and from our discussions via letters about this book, evolved the idea of us writing a novel together about a world so polluted that humankind had retreated to live in and under the oceans to escape the pollution and destruction they had brought about on land.

Wally and me, outside the house at Portarlington in 1972, only a few months after my trip to New Guinea.

    We spent many hours writing this giant novel, mostly at my place because for some reason his wife Irene had an intense dislike for me. She didn't like science fiction, and couldn't understand Wally's love for this, and she no doubt thought I was a distraction, taking him away from the family to spend hours writing some silly story.

    What we hadn't considered while writing the novel was that if the land had been polluted and destroyed enough for humankind to retreat to the oceans, the oceans as well would be in no better condition than the land, with acidification of the water, bleaching of coral reefs, and whole ecosystems dying, just as they would have done on land.

    The novel was rejected by everyone we sent it to, and rightly so, because it was awful. We had written it with great enthusiasm, while consuming copious amounts of sherry, or other wines, but what was important about the writing was that it made us closer as friends and we had a fantastic time writing it. Wally later rewrote it taking out excess wordage and tightening up action scenes, and it did the rounds again, but was still rejected, by everyone we sent it to. What we did after that was to break down some of the ideas in the novel and write them as short stories. We also wrote a couple of other shorts which were published in a local magazine called Rats, (similar to the American magazine Mad.). Unfortunately, Rats ceased publishing after half a dozen issues and we never got the last of our stories published even though they had accepted them. What happened to the manuscript of the novel, I have no idea. It disappeared or was tossed out by one of us at some stage, since we had no luck with it. If by some chance it reappears, I would love to read it just to see what we actually wrote all those years ago.

    The fact that Wally spent so much time at our place in Benbow Street as we were writing our stories meant that Mum and Dad accepted him as part of our extended family, Mum especially. She was gregarious and willing to accept anyone at face value. She had a great deal of respect for Wally, for what he had gone though as a young boy in England before and as a young man during the Second World War. Although her circumstances were very different, she too had lived a difficult life as a young girl growing into a teenager in Cobar, NSW, before finally moving to Melbourne. She had been born in Kalgoorlie, Western Australia, in 1915 and was only a young girl when her parents relocated to Cobar in New South Wales where her father managed the copper mines in the nineteen-twenties. She knew how hard life could be.

In 1968 I went to Mexico, to Acapulco where I spent almost a year playing conga drums with a number of groups and after coming back, I was at loose ends for a while. Wally was having problems with his wife Irene who had left him and the boys to run off with the guy who owned the nursery next door to our place in Williamstown. And on Wally's side, his very best friend, also called Fred, who came out to Australia from England at the same time as he did, died of a heart attack leaving a family of five children and his wife Betty. In time, Wally got over Irene walking out on them and formed a close relationship with Betty. Eventually they married and the two families merged into one.

This was about the time I had just met Monica who had moved to Melbourne after a year in Sydney. She was Chilean, and in my eyes, absolutely stunning. Her English wasn't bad, but we often conversed in Spanish which made her feel comfortable, and which helped me maintain that beautiful language that I had learnt in Mexico. She liked Wally and Betty, which was a bonus because it's really great when someone you love also is fond of your friends. It makes everything so much better. Wally also thought Monica was a wonderful person and he was elated that I had found her and that she was my girlfriend.

When we decided to get married in 1973, we asked Wally to be our Best Man at the wedding and he was more than happy to oblige. When we moved to our house in Hoppers Crossing, we were only a short drive away from Altona where Wally and Betty were living, and they often visited us as we did them. When Monica fell pregnant and our son Brian was born, Wally and Betty practically adopted him as a grandson. They absolutely adored him. Wally was a devoted father having had to bring up his three boys by himself after his first wife Irene left, and he'd done a good job too because they were all very caring young men. I had the impression that he regarded me almost as an adopted son, (perhaps because of our 14-year age difference) as well as a friend. Although this never came up in any conversations we had, it's an impression I've gained in retrospect, while thinking about those times, and this has made me realize that he regarded Brian in the same way as he would if his boys had been old enough to have had children of their own at that time. He had gained a couple of grandchildren from Betty's family since some of her children were older than his own boys and had already married. But it was almost as if Brian was his first grandchild. This can be seen in the photos of a trip we did together to Ballarat where we had a picnic beside Lake Wendouree when Brian was about 6 months old.

The moment we got out of the campervan, we were surrounded by swans looking for something to eat. And like everyone else who sees them, we had to feed them with bread scraps. This is not encouraged, but people do it anyway, and the swans certainly know it.

Barely out of the campervan, when one of the swans raised its head and stretched out its neck Monica was 'beside herself'. She let out a squawk that was equal to anything the swans could produce. Betty also was a bit uncertain of how to react to the pushy swans.
Wally and I had no problem feeding them a few scraps.

We had a portable cot which we took with us whenever we went on a trip, which was great because Brian could stand up in it and see what was going on. Whenever he felt tired he could just sit down and have a rest or a nap. The swans didn't bother him.

— Grab that Moment —

We had a fantastic baby seat which simply fitted onto and under any kind of table. We cooked our lunch on a small hibachi. Brian watches with great interest as Wally blows on the flames to get the fire to burn stronger.

I had two other friends whom I only knew for a short time relatively speaking, but both of whom went out of their way to make me welcome; both of whom I will never forget.

Pancho Cataneo, singer and band leader, ex-patriot Cuban who was living in Paris with his wife and family. He was the lead singer and the band-leader of a Cuban *conjunto* called **Los Matecocos**. When I first saw them play, I was 'bowled over' since they were the first real Cuban band I had ever seen live. They were also the most popular Cuban group in Paris (Europe) at that time in 1964. I had a chance to sit in and play congas with them and it was a wonderful experience. Pancho invited me to play with them again. At that time there were big changes happening in music all around the world as Rock and Roll literally exploded onto the scene. Other more traditional groups started to disappear or lost popularity. And in Paris, other Cuban groups, Brazilian groups, and those that played music from other South American countries that had been popular for years suddenly couldn't find any gigs. Everybody wanted the new rock and roll music, and anyone who even vaguely sounded like The Beetles or The Rolling Stones, had more work than they could handle.

Pancho invited me to play with his group at a huge concert because his timbale player had just left. This was a concert put on by Bel Air Records and it featured all of their top bands. **Los Matecocos** was one of their top bands whose records always sold well.

Pancho had me come around to his apartment where he taught me the breaks in all the songs, and lent me some records to listen to so I could study the arrangements of their most popular songs. I had two weeks to familiarize myself with what they played.

Most of it was traditional; son montuno, guaracha, cha cha, mambos and guaguancó, many of which I had heard on records I had studied at home. I was familiar with them and had no trouble playing the breaks. It was the songs that Pancho had written and the new stuff his band had composed that I needed to learn.

After that massive concert, Pancho also did another LP recording for Bel Air Records and he hired me to play congas, while his regular conga player played bongos, and invited Alberto Beltran, who was visiting from Santo Domingo and Cuba, to join us for the recording. Alberto was singer of boleros and merengues, and he played wonderful *Tambora*, the drum used in merengue groups which is a double ended drum played with one stick and one bare hand.

A chance to go to Chad in North Africa came up and Pancho wanted me in the band. I was happy to go, but some of the others didn't want to go to Chad for 6 months because they would miss their families, and also because any money earned there would have to be spent there —no one wanted to exchange money from the Republic of Chad for a useful currency— which meant after 6 months of work they would have nothing to show for it.

When no new gigs were available and the **Los Matecocos** disbanded, I felt very sad. Pancho went to Spain where he could find work as a singer. The others, most of whom were Mexicans (except for Clemente Lozano who played flute; he was Cuban) went back to Mexico.

Pancho had given me the chance to work with a real Cuban *conjunto*, had taken me into his home and his family and treated me as one of them. He looked out for his fellow musicians and singers and always went out of his way to help them. He was a remarkable person. I had such a fantastic time with him and his family and his musicians, I will always be grateful for the opportunity he gave me and for his friendship.

Unfortunately, I have no photos of Pancho other than this one taken from the cover of one of his LP recordings.

Similarly, in Mexico, four years later, (1968) when I first walked along the beach in Acapulco and heard a band playing guaguancó in a restaurant overlooking the beach, I just had to go up and sit in with them and play. Rudy, (Rodolfo Loredo) was playing trumpet in the band. He almost immediately invited me to play with them at a party they were working later than night. They just happened to need a conga player and there I was, the day I arrived in Acapulco and I had a gig the same night. Rudy played piano at the gig. He played piano most nights in a small club at a luxury hotel, while during the day he played trumpet in the restaurant overlooking the beach at La Condessa.

When Rudy found out I was going to be staying in Acapulco for a while he invited me to share his apartment. He had recently divorced and was living alone. He wanted someone to talk to, someone who was interested in the same music as he was and we got on very well. He wouldn't let me pay for anything so I insisted on paying for the young lady who came in a couple of times a week to do the washing and cleaning. It was hardly anything but he was happy with that. I played with his group as an extra (without being paid) almost every night, as well as sitting in with the various bands that played in a number of adjoining restaurants overlooking *Playa Condessa*. This was the place where many famous people, film stars, singers and celebrities came to while away the afternoons when they were in Acapulco. Acapulco had become a jet-setters destination and was extremely popular in the 1960s.

Rudy and I went everywhere together. He treated me as if I was a long-lost brother. He even took me to visit his home town in the north of Mexico, San Miguel de Allende, a beautiful Spanish Colonial town. It was a very long trip in a car that barely worked. It took us a week to get there. Mexico is a very big country, replete with mountains and jungles, and in the north, deserts and rolling plains. Getting anywhere takes considerable effort.

Rudy had played trumpet in a Mariachi band in Guadalajara before he moved to Acapulco to play 'salsa'. That was years before I arrived on the scene. He also had on LP recording under his belt, which had been recorded in Mexico City a couple of years earlier. He was a highly respected musician in Acapulco, and I was very lucky that he took me under his wing and made my stay in Acapulco, and in Mexico so much better that it could possibly have been had I not had the good fortune to meet Rudy the first day I arrived.

And of course, there was Monica, who entered my life in 1971 and who became the most important person ever, my very best friend, my wife, and the mother of my son Brian. Without her, my life would certainly have been different, but I doubt very much if it would have been better.

Acknowledgments.

My thanks to the people listed below for making Paul Stevens and I most welcome while in Sydney for the filming of ***Antifan Strikes back***.

I would also like to thank Carey Handfield for allowing me to use his black and white photos from the filming of the second film and for additional information regarding the production of the film, and Bruce Gillespie for discussions and conversations, via email, which helped unearth memories of that long ago time when we were all young and enthusiastic about everything life had to offer for the future. Those were the days! Long gone, but always remembered with varying degrees of accuracy…

Antifan Strikes Back cast:

Paul J Stevens as Antifan.
Merv Binns, as himself.
Gerald Smith, young fan.
Andrew Brown, Melbourne Zombie.
Gregor Whiley, Sydney Zombie.
Seducers: Kim Lambert, Jane Taubman, Majorie McLeay, Meg Kellaway.
Alien victim, Nick Stathopolous.
Alien, Lewis More.
Committee members: Andrew Taubman, Jack Herman, Shayne McCormack, Peter Tollis, Eric Lindsay, Ken Ozanne, Tony Howe, Karin Lewis, Vera Lonergan, and Carey Lenehan.
John Litchen, Camera, editing, and underwater sequences.
Carey Handfield, producer along with the A 83 Committee.

I don't recall doing any editing for this second Film, although I could have done some of the preliminary editing once the film had been processed (basically joining the rolls of film together in the general sequence of events). Speaking with Carey, my understanding is that he and Don Ashby did the final editing, if not all of the editing, in the week before the film was sent to the USA and the convention in Boston. It was taken to the USA by Robin Johnson, who was in Sydney during the filming but doesn't appear in the film because he was eliminated by Antifan in the first unnamed film five years earlier.

I would also like to thank my lovely wife Monica for putting up with me ignoring her while I spend hours doing stuff on my computer. She has never once complained.

www.ingramcontent.com/pod-product-compliance
Lightning Source LLC
Chambersburg PA
CBHW040326300426
44113CB00020B/2666